Christian Mission
among the Peoples of Asia

D1528679

American Society of Missiology Series, No. 50

Christian Mission among the Peoples of Asia

Jonathan Y. Tan

ORBIS BOOKS

Maryknoll, New York 10545

ORBIS BOOKS
Maryknoll, New York 10545

Founded in 1970, Orbis Books endeavors to publish works that enlighten the mind, nourish the spirit, and challenge the conscience. The publishing arm of the Maryknoll Fathers and Brothers, Orbis seeks to explore the global dimensions of the Christian faith and mission, to invite dialogue with diverse cultures and religious traditions, and to serve the cause of reconciliation and peace. The books published reflect the views of their authors and do not represent the official position of the Maryknoll Society. To learn more about Maryknoll and Orbis Books, please visit our website at www.maryknollsociety.org.

Library of Congress Cataloging-in-Publication Data

Tan, Jonathan Y.
   Christian mission among the peoples of Asia / Jonathan Y. Tan.
      pages cm. — (American Society of Missiology series; No. 50)
   Includes bibliographical references and index.
   ISBN 978-1-62698-104-1 (pbk.)
   1. Missions—Asia. 2. Mission—Theory. I. Title.
BV3151.3.T36 2014
266.0095—dc23

                                                        2014012284

To

my parents

Contents

Preface to the American Society of Missiology Series

The purpose of the ASM (American Society of Missiology) Series is to publish—without regard for disciplinary, national, or denominational boundaries—scholarly works of high quality and wide interest on missiological themes from the entire spectrum of scholarly pursuits relevant to Christian mission, which is always the focus of books in the Series.

By *mission* is meant the effort to effect passage over the boundary between faith in Jesus Christ and its absence. In this understanding of mission, the basic functions of Christian proclamation, dialogue, witness, service, worship, liberation, and nurture are of special concern. And in that context questions arise, including: How does the transition from one cultural context to another influence the shape and interaction between these dynamic functions, especially in regard to the cultural and religious plurality that constitutes the global context of Christian life and mission?

The promotion of scholarly dialogue among missiologists, and among missiologists and scholars in other fields of inquiry, may involve the publication of views that some missiologists cannot accept, and with which members of the Editorial Committee themselves do not agree. Manuscripts published in the Series, accordingly, reflect the opinions of their authors and are not understood to represent the position of the American Society of Missiology or of the Editorial Committee. Selection is guided by such criteria as intrinsic worth, readability, coherence, and accessibility to a range of interested persons and not merely to experts or specialists.

The ASM Series, in collaboration with Orbis Books, seeks to publish scholarly works of high merit and wide interest on numerous aspects of missiology—the scholarly study of mission. Able presentations on new and creative approaches to the practice and understanding of mission will receive close attention.

The ASM Series Committee
JONATHAN J. BONK
WILLIAM R. BURROWS
SCOTT W. SUNQUIST

Abbreviations

ABM	FABC Asian Bishops' Meeting, November 29, 1970
AG	Decree on Missionary Activity, *Ad Gentes*, Vatican II, December 7, 1965
ASIPA	Asian Integral Pastoral Approach toward a New Way of Being Church in Asia
BILA	FABC Bishops' Institutes for Lay Apostolate
BIMA	FABC Bishops' Institutes for Missionary Apostolate
BIRA	FABC Bishops' Institutes for Interreligious Affairs
BISA	FABC Bishops' Institutes for Social Action
BISCOM	FABC Bishops' Institutes for Social Communication
CBCI	Catholic Bishops' Conference of India
CCM	Council of Churches of Malaysia
CDF	Congregation for the Doctrine of the Faith
CFM	Christian Federation of Malaysia
CPCO	Le Conseil des Patriarches Catholiques d'Orient (Council of Catholic Patriarchs of the East)
FABC	Federation of Asian Bishops' Conferences
FABC-OHD	FABC Office of Human Development
FEISA	FABC Faith Encounters in Social Action
GS	Pastoral Constitution on the Church in the Modern World, *Gaudium et Spes*, Vatican II, December 7, 1965
IDPs	internally displaced persons
IOM	International Organization for Migration
MCCBCHS	Malaysian Consultative Council of Buddhism, Christianity, Hinduism, and Sikhism
MEP	La Société des Missions *Étrangères* de Paris (Paris Foreign Missions Society)
NECF	National Evangelical Christian Fellowship
NEP	New Economic Policy (Malaysia)
PAS	Parti Islam Se-Malaysia (Pan Malaysian Islamic Party)
UCAN	Union of Catholic Asian News

Introduction

This book owes its beginnings to a proposition concerning mission that was first articulated by William R. Burrows, the Editor Emeritus of Orbis Books and Research Professor of Missiology at New York Theological Seminary. At the 2001 annual convention of the Catholic Theological Society of America (CTSA), Burrows proposed a shift in understanding from *missio ad gentes* (cf. Matt. 28:19) to *missio inter gentes* in his response to the Indian Jesuit theologian Michael Amaladoss's plenary paper, "Pluralism of Religions and the Proclamation of Jesus Christ in the Context of Asia." According to Burrows, "Christian mission in Asia is already primarily in the hands of Asians, and is better termed *missio **inter** gentes* than *missio **ad** gentes*" (Burrows 2001, 15, emphasis added). To support this new template, he put forward the following five propositions (2001, 15–20).

- First, Asian Christians are in a process that can be imaged best as one of translating the gospel or incarnating Christ in Asia in the gentle, loving, persuasive power of the Spirit.
- Second, many Asian Christians understand the religious traditions of Asia not as demonic or evil, but as vehicles of God's salvific encounter with their followers.
- Third, countering the perception that Christianity is imported from Europe and North America, and not properly "Asian," remains *the* single most critical element of the Christian agenda in Asia. If the accusation that it is a "foreign import" cannot be overcome, Christianity has a doubtful future in Asia.

- Fourth, the *missio inter gentes* model recognizes the task of Christian mission in a pluralistic religious context to be one of proclaiming and making the world ready for God's Kingdom. It views the ultimate reconciliation of the world's contradictions as *eschatological*, one that will bring about a unity not just among *religions* but among *believing persons*. In the context of the religious diversity and plurality of Asia, this model acknowledges that the religious unity of humankind will be an *eschatological* accomplishment—one in which the Spirit is active in other religious ways.

- Fifth, the *missio inter gentes* template proposes a new kind of missional activity that sees other world religions not as Christianity's rivals but as potential allies, *collaborating* and *working together* against the real, *mutual* enemies of all forms of evil, attachment to wealth, power, selfishness, exploitation, as well as the social, cultural, and political structures that support them.

I was inspired by Burrows's trailblazing insight to take the next step of exploring the significance and implications of *missio inter gentes* for Christian mission in contemporary Asia. This resulted in a series of essays (Tan 2004a, 2004b, 2005a, 2005b, 2005c, 2006) in which I sought to make the case that Asia, with its rich diversity and plurality of religions, cultures, and philosophical worldviews, requires a distinctively Asian approach to the task of doing Christian mission that is sensitive to such diversity and pluralism. I then proposed that the missional approach of the Federation of Asian Bishops' Conferences (FABC), as exemplified in its threefold dialogue with the religions, cultures, and the poor of Asia, is best described as *missio inter gentes* rather than *missio ad gentes* because of how the FABC perceives and responds to the challenges of religious pluralism in Asia. At this stage, my attention was directed at linking Burrows's paradigm of *missio inter gentes* with the FABC's mission theology.

Nonetheless, Burrows's groundbreaking *missio inter gentes* model raises intriguing possibilities and challenges. Would it be possible to build on this notion to articulate a new theology of mission that would respond fully to the immense challenges of contemporary postcolonial and plurireligious Asia? With two-thirds of the world's population and their rich and colorful mosaic of cultures, languages, philosophies, and spiritual traditions, Asia continues to defy all attempts at easy categorization. Although the term "Asian" is often used as a convenient label to categorize the diverse range of peoples from the different regions of the continent, in reality this term masks the significant pluralism that differentiates them in terms of languages, ethnicities, cultures, and spiritual traditions under the façade of a monolithic pan-Asian identity that exists more in theory than in reality.

Such diversity and pluralism is evident when one takes a bird's-eye view of Asia geographically across its six principal regions. First, there is North Asia, comprising the sparsely populated Siberian region of the Russian Federation that is aligned politically, socially, and culturally more closely with the European region of the Russian Federation, especially after the resettlement of ethnic Russians in this region in the twentieth century. Second, West Asia, the so-called Near East or Middle East, the cradle of Abrahamic monotheism that birthed Judaism, Christianity, and Islam, is predominantly Muslim with significant pockets of Jewish and Christian presence. Unfortunately, it is also a region that is engulfed in ongoing conflicts and violence along ethnic, religious, and sectarian lines. Third, Central Asia, through which the ancient Silk Road ran, was once marked by a diverse mix of Zoroastrian, Buddhist, and Assyrian Christian presence. Today, it is home to large communities of Muslims living in the various republics that broke away from the former Soviet Union. Fourth, South Asia, comprising the Indian subcontinent, is predominantly Hindu in India and Buddhist in Sri Lanka, with significant Muslim, Christian, Sikh, and Jain minorities. Fifth, Southeast Asia is a world of contrast, with the predominantly Muslim Malay and Indonesian Archipelago, on the one hand, and the predominantly Buddhist Myanmar, Thailand, and Indochina on the other, albeit with significant diversity along ethnic, cultural, and religious lines; it also includes indigenous and migrant communities across the whole region. Finally, East Asia, encompassing China, Japan, and Korea, is heavily influenced by Confucian, Buddhist, and

Daoist traditions, with significant Muslim minority presence in the western region of China that overlaps into Central Asia.

Looking at Asia historically, one would discover the birthplace of ancient civilizations, including the Mohenjo-daro, Harappa, and Dholavira civilizations in the Indus Valley (ca. 3000 BCE), the Yangshao civilization in the Yellow River basin (ca. 5000 BCE) and the Liangzhu civilization in the Yangtze River valley (ca. 3300 BCE). Asia is also the native soil from which the ancient great religions of the world have sprung up. This includes the religious traditions of Hinduism, Buddhism, and Jainism in South Asia, Confucianism and Daoism in East Asia, Zoroastrianism in Central Asia, and the three monotheistic religious traditions of Judaism, Christianity, and Islam in West Asia. These religious traditions are very much alive and influential throughout Asia, nourishing the present spiritual needs of billions of Asians, and are very much intertwined within the sociopolitical and cultural fabric of diverse communities across Asia.

From a sociopolitical perspective, contemporary Asia is a continent of extremes. Asia has the world's oldest extant nation (China), the world's richest countries in West Asia, and three of the world's most populous countries (China, India, and Indonesia). Asia is also a continent facing significant migratory movements of people; these are transforming the sociocultural, religious, and economic landscapes across Asia as they contribute to the breakdown of traditional social order and to an increasing degree of fragmentation and tension, as well as to the loss of stable familial and communal structures.

Asia may be home to some two-thirds of the world's population, but it remains nevertheless the continent with the smallest Christian population despite two millennia of Christian missionary activity, beginning with the Assyrian Christian missionaries who ventured to India and China in the first Christian millennium. According to the Pew Forum on Religion and Public Life's 2011 report, *Global Christianity: A Report on the Size and Distribution of the World's Christian Population*, Christians account for 7 percent of the total population of the Asia-Pacific region, which translates to 13.1 percent of the total World Christian population (2011, 75). *Global Christianity* further identifies the top three Asian countries with a significant Christian percentage of their total population as the Philippines (93.1 percent), Timor-Leste (99.6 percent), and South Korea (29.3 percent), and notes that Christians continue to represent only a small proportion of the residents of China (5 percent) and India (2.6 percent), who collectively make up about one third of the world's population (2011, 75–76). Moreover, it is highly ironic that Christianity is dying out in West Asia, the land of its birth over two millennia ago. In particular, the ancient Eastern Christian churches are gasping for breath, as wars, persecutions, and repeated waves of emigration have led to their decimation in their ancestral lands.

Chapter 1 starts with a bird's-eye view of the history of Christian mission in Asia over the past two millennia, beginning with the Assyrian missionaries moving eastward to China and southward to India, and ending with the beginning of the twentieth century, when many missionaries were optimistic that the Christianization of Asia was within reach. Chapter 2 takes a critical look at two momentous events for Christian mission in the twentieth century: the Edinburgh World Missionary Conference of 1910 for Protestant Christians and the Second Vatican Council (1962–65) for Roman Catholics. This chapter further explores the challenges of postcolonialism, nationalism, fundamentalism, and exclusivism on the task of doing Christian mission in Asia. Chapter 3 analyzes the FABC's mission theology through a five-fold framework of mission embracing the pluralism of Asia, being rooted in a commitment and service to life in Asia, promoting harmony in response to hatred and violence, engaging in a three-fold dialogue with Asian cultures, religions, and the poor, and seeking to usher in the Reign of God in Asia.

Chapters 4 and 5 of this book are centered on my proposal for a new missiological paradigm that I call "mission *among* the peoples in Asia." Going beyond my earlier essays that discussed *missio inter gentes* within the context of the FABC's mission theology, I seek to argue my case in chapter 4 for a model of mission *among* the peoples that is built on four theological propositions. First, this model of mission among the peoples moves away from a sending-receiving church model toward a World Christianity model where there is mutual engagement and collaborative global partnership for Christian mission beyond the North-South or Majority-Minority divide. Second, the *orthodoxy* of the model of mission among the peoples is rooted in the *missio Dei* that seeks to usher in the universality of God's reign in pluralistic Asia, and Christians are called to imitate Jesus, the missional exemplar par excellence of the *missio Dei*. Third, mission among the peoples is inspired by an *orthopathos* that illumines divine empathy and solidarity with the pathos of the suffering and brokenness in the daily life experiences of the Asian peoples. Fourth, mission among the peoples is empowered by an *orthopraxis* that enables the Christian gospel to engage with the religious pluralism of Asia in a spirit of interreligious hospitality.

Chapter 5 seeks to unpack the practical implications of this model of mission among the peoples for the future of Christian mission in Asia by exploring how this understanding of mission could respond to the challenges of Asians on the move across geographical and virtual frontiers. In the case of the former, I focus on the FABC's theology of migration as an example of doing mission among the migrants of Asia. In the case of the latter, I discuss the challenges and implications of doing mission among the youth and millennials of Asia in emergent social media communities across the frontiers of cyberspace.

I thank and express my appreciation for everyone who has assisted me in one way or another in this book project. First, my heartfelt love and gratitude to my parents, especially my mother, who by her own missional witness to family, friends, and neighbors, has exemplified and lived out the *missio Dei* throughout her life. Second, I wish to thank my professors at The Catholic University of America (CUA), especially my *doktorvater* Peter Phan, who introduced me to missiology and David Bosch's *Transforming Mission*, which marked the beginning of my interest in missiology and mission theology, and the late William Cenkner, who taught me the value and importance of dialogue in the *missio Dei*. Although more than ten years have elapsed since I graduated and carved my own path as a scholar of religion and theology, the excellent academic and theological formation that I received at CUA has served me well in my own scholarship and research in general and writing this book in particular.

Bill Burrows has been both a mentor and friend who always encouraged me to take his idea beyond the tentative sketch that he first proposed at the CTSA annual convention in 2001. I am most grateful to Bill for his confidence and trust in my ability to articulate the theological underpinnings for, and extend the ambit of, an important paradigm of mission that was developed by him. The fact that *missio inter gentes* was the theme of the fifth General Assembly and International Conference of the International Association of Catholic Missiologists (IACM) in 2013 is testimony to Bill's farsighted vision of the future direction of missional witness in the third Christian millennium.

Many thanks to two indefatigable Maryknoll missioners: the late Edward Malone, who was the Assistant Secretary-General of the FABC, and James Kroeger at Loyola School of Theology in Manila, for their assistance in obtaining all the FABC documentation and various resources on Asian mission theologies. Chapter 3 could not have been written without their assistance. I am grateful to the interlibrary loan staff of Australian Catholic University (ACU) Libraries for working assiduously to track down and procure various obscure research materials on Asian missiology and mission theology that are critical to the success of this book.

This book also benefited from the valuable critical comments of the participants of several international conferences for their incisive critiques and detailed feedback to various draft versions of selected chapters in this book that I presented as conference papers. I presented an early version of chapter 5 as a plenary paper at the Scalabrini Migration Center's International Conference on Migration, Religious Experience, and Mission with Migrants in Asia in Manila in June 2012. Funding from ACU through the Research Support Team scheme for Asian Theology ("Asian Theology RST") enabled me to present an early draft of chapter 3 at the Australian Catholic Theological Association's annual conference in Melbourne, Australia in July 2012. An International Conference Travel Grant (ICTG) award from ACU funded my travel to and participation in the annual conference of the CTSA in Miami, Florida, in June 2013 to present an abbreviated draft of chapter 4 at the CTSA's Mission and Catholicity Topic Session. The Asian Theology RST also funded my two fabulous teaching assistants in 2013 at ACU, Emma Baynie and Michael Scanlon, which freed up much-needed time for me to focus on writing this book to meet the deadline for submission.

Building on feedback from my CTSA presentation, I delivered a longer draft version of chapter 4 as a plenary address at the Fifth General Assembly and International Conference of the IACM in Nairobi, Kenya, in July 2013. I am grateful for the critical feedback from Sr. Miriam Loretto Okolli and Cardinal Luis Antonio "Chito" Tagle as official respondents to my plenary presentation at IACM 2013. In addition, the detailed critiques and helpful advice from various IACM members, especially Bishop Selvister Ponnumutham, M. D. Thomas, Andrew Recepcion, Frans Dokman, Roy Bertrand, Gerard Goldman, as well as Therese and Jim D'Orsa, have challenged me to revise my ideas and refine my reasoning when they were lacking in clarity or coherence.

A word of thanks to my colleagues at ACU, as well as to wonderful friends and colleagues in Asia, Australia, and the United States, who have been most supportive of my project, including AMA Samy, Michael Amaladoss, Jojo Fung, Jim Kroeger, Steve Bevans, van Thanh Nguyen, Ruben Habito, David Loy, Amos Yong, Grace Kao, Patrick Cheng, Sarah Melcher, Paul Knitter, Dale Irvin, Orlando Espín, Jean-Pierre Ruiz, and Carmen Nanko-Fernández. My writing has been nourished and sustained by their wise counsel, intellectual inspiration, incisive criticisms, invaluable guidance, and detailed advice at every stage of writing. For the successful completion of this book, I am especially indebted to the wonderful team at Orbis Books for their counsel and guidance as they shepherded the book from beginning to completion, beginning with Bill Burrows and Sue Perry, both of whom have since retired and passed the baton to Jim Keane.

I also extend my grateful thanks to my family members, especially my parents in Malaysia, my two younger brothers and their families in Singapore, Ky Ky and Van in the United States, and my family pastor, the Rev. Charles Chin, for their prayers, words of encouragement, and support. Last but not the least, I am grateful for the gift of life from my mother and father. This book is dedicated to them in filial gratitude for instilling in me a deep sense of missional faith and a love for learning.

Chapter 1

Mission in Asia:
Selected Historical Snapshots

This chapter presents an overview of the history of the Christian mission in Asia in four parts. The first reviews the early missionary endeavors of the Assyrian Church of the East in India and China. The second considers the rise of the patronage system of mission as practiced by the Spanish and Portuguese Crowns in their quest to expand their empires throughout Asia. The third evaluates the problems of the patronage model of mission and discusses Rome's efforts to assume direct control of the Asian missions. The final part surveys the rise and historical legacy of the great Protestant missions of Asia from the beginning of the nineteenth century to the early decades of the twentieth century.

Early Beginnings:
The Assyrian Christian Mission to India and China

The Christian mission to Asia traces its initial foundations to the tentative steps taken by the early Assyrian Christian missionaries who crossed the mountains and deserts of what are now Iran, Pakistan, and Afghanistan to reach India and China. Many unresolved questions still surround legends of the apostle Saint Thomas's missionary outreach to India in the mid-first century of the Christian era. In his first volume of *A History of Christianity in Asia*, Samuel Hugh Moffett notes that the received tradition spoke of Thomas landing on the Malabar coast near the ancient port of Muziris around the year 50 or 52, converting many high-caste Indians and founding the seven churches of Craganore, Quilon, Paravur, Kokkamangalam, Niranam, Palayur, and Cayal

(1998, 34). Even if one were to discount the missionary outreach of Thomas as a fanciful legend, evidence nevertheless suggests a thriving center of Christianity along the Malabar coast of India from as early as the fourth century, with the arrival of Thomas of Cana (Knai Thomman) at Cranganore (Kodungalloor), accompanied by Assyrian Christian families and missionaries (Neill 1984, 42–43). The "Saint Thomas Christians," as these early Indian Christians were called, were regarded by their fellow Hindus as having a high social status within the Indian caste system, practicing the sociocultural traditions of high-caste Indians together with their Christian faith.[1]

Long before the first European missionaries would step foot on Chinese soil, the indefatigable Assyrian Christian missionaries made the treacherous journey with the caravans of traders, as well as Buddhist monks and pilgrims, on the ancient Silk Road all the way to Chang'an, the capital of Tang China. There, at the imperial capital of the Tang Dynasty (618–907), the Assyrian missionaries preached the gospel to the Chinese elite, establishing the "Luminous Religion" (*Jingjiao*), the Tang-era Chinese name for Assyrian Christianity in China; this mission lasted from 635 to 1368, when it vanished in the aftermath of the downfall of the Yuan Dynasty (Bays 2012, 4–16). The Assyrian Christian missionaries were able to establish a thriving mission outpost of the Church of the East in Tang China, as recorded in the Assyrian

---

[1]   The Syro-Malabar theologian Kuncheria Pathil gives the following description of the historical practices of the Saint Thomas Christians: "[The Saint Thomas Christians] followed the customs of the nobility such as feeding a newborn with powdered gold mixed with honey, teaching children to write the letters of the alphabet for the first time with rice, ceremonial baths and other purification rituals, the marriage ritual of tying the tali (a gold ornament in the Hindu style, but with the marking of a cross on it) on the bride's neck and giving her *mantrakodi* (bridal veil), as well as upper-caste funerary and death customs and rituals. During this period, the men of the St. Thomas Christian community pierced their ear lobes, wore ornaments and styled their hair akin to the Hindus, but wore a cross on the tuft of hair. The St. Thomas Christians also practiced the rules of untouchability and pollution, with women living in separate quarters where they were specially protected. Churches were constructed according to the model of Hindu temples" (2003, 396).

Stele of Xi'anfu, a marble stele measuring nine feet high by three feet four inches wide. Erected in the year 781 to commemorate the propagation of the Luminous Religion in China, the Assyrian Stele narrated the arrival of a certain Assyrian missionary named Aluoben (Alopen) to the Tang capital of Chang'an (modern-day Xi'an) in the year 635 and the subsequent growth of the Luminous Religion in China.

The contents of the Assyrian Stele were composed in elegant classical Chinese four- and six-character prose by Bishop Adam, also known by his Chinese name, Jing Jing (Ching-Ching) (Tang 2002, 17–32). Samuel Hugh Moffett notes that Bishop Adam was highly regarded for his erudite knowledge of the Chinese language, citing J. Takakusu's discovery of a reference to Adam in a catalogue of late eighth- and early ninth-century Chinese translations of Buddhist sutras. According to this Buddhist record, the Indian Buddhist missionary Prajña, not being well versed in the Chinese language, sought the assistance of Adam from the nearby monastery of Daqin to assist him in translating the Buddhist sutras into Chinese (1998, 301–2).[2]

These Assyrian Christian missionaries to China bequeathed to the world the so-called Jesus Sutras (borrowing Martin Palmer's terminology). Discovered in the Buddhist cave monasteries of Mogao in the ancient frontier oasis town of Dunhuang on the

---

[2]   Moffett goes on to speculate on the missiological and theological implications of this interfaith collaboration between Adam and Prajña: "In the same Buddhist monastery with the Indian missionary there were living and studying at the same time (804) two equally famous figures in the history of Japanese Buddhism. One was the great Kobo Daishi (Kukai), founder of Japan's Shingon ('true word') sect of Tantric Buddhism, who carried back with him to Japan as one of his treasures the sutra on which Prajña and Adam might have been working together. The other scholar from Japan in Chang'an at the time was Dengyo Daishi (Saicho), founder of the Tendai (Lotus) school of Japanese Buddhism, out of which grew such later popular reform movements as Pure Land, Zen, and Nichiren Buddhism. Few have so powerfully influenced the course of Buddhism in Japan. Who can resist the temptation, therefore, to speculate on how much a chance association of these men, through Prajña, with the cooperative Nestorian scholar Adam, might possibly have seeded Christian ideas into the variations of northern Buddhist belief as it developed in Japan?" (1998, 302).

southern branch of the ancient Silk Road, these Chinese Christian sutras represent the earliest attempt to articulate a distinctively Chinese Christianity, using Buddhist and Daoist vocabulary in a manner that was intelligible to the Chinese.

Assyrian Christian missionaries also found favor with the imperial court soon after their first arrival in the year 635, as evidenced by the construction of the Daqin Pagoda within the imperial Daoist complex in Lou Guan Tai in Tang-era China. Martin Palmer (2001) has advanced the thesis that the Daqin Pagoda is an ancient Assyrian Christian pagoda, with the oldest depiction of what is hypothesized to be the Nativity scene in China, dated circa 638. Further archaeological excavations and critical studies of the deteriorating wall paintings remain to be carried out in order to arrive at a conclusive determination of the origins and purposes of the Daqin Pagoda.

The thirteenth and fourteenth centuries witnessed early Franciscan missionary expeditions to Mongol-ruled China, the first of which was led by the indefatigable Franciscan missionary Giovanni da Montecorvino (1247–1328) (Moffett 1998, 456–59; Bays 2012, 12–14). Looking back, we can see that both the Assyrian and the Franciscan Christian missions struggled in the best of times to take root in Chinese soil before finally succumbing to extinction in the aftermath of the collapse of the Yuan Dynasty in 1368. Three major factors account for this sad state of affairs.

First, it appears that Christianity was practiced mainly by the minority tribal inhabitants of China—e.g., Persians, Kerait (Qaraei) and Ongut (Ongud) who inhabited the western and northern fringes of the Chinese hinterland—rather than the mainstream Han Chinese who constituted the overwhelming majority of China's population. For the most part, the majority of the Han Chinese remained wedded to the complex and diverse myriad of Confucian, Daoist, and folk religious precepts and practices that defined the Chinese religious landscape. This made it easy for the Han Chinese to persecute and suppress Christianity as a subversive foreign religion during the many periods of xenophobic hysteria. Second, the Yuan rulers who protected the Christian missions were Mongols, who were hated as foreigners and usurpers by the Han Chinese nationalists. The Yuan emperors' official recognition of the Christian missions, which granted some measure of imperial protection, ultimately became the Christian missions' Achilles' heel in the final xenophobic wave that swept the Mongols out of power and ushered in the ultranationalist Ming Dynasty (1368–1644). Third, the "foreign" status of Chinese Christianity was also aggravated by the fact that the leaders of the fledgling Christian churches were often foreigners, including Assyrian or Franciscan missionary bishops from outside China. There was little local or indigenous leadership to ensure the survival of Christianity in China during the long turbulent periods of xenophobic persecutions. By the emergence of the Ming Dynasty, Christianity had practically disappeared from Chinese soil.

Christian Mission in the Age of European Empire Building

The fifteenth century witnessed the second wave of European Christian mission endeavors in Asia, coinciding with the rise of the European age of geographical exploration and colonial expansion of frontiers to hitherto unexplored lands in Africa, Asia, and the Americas. In the vanguard were the two Catholic nations of Spain and Portugal, emerging rival powers engaged in a protracted struggle for power and hegemony over these newly discovered lands. In the beginning, the papacy upheld the efforts of the Portuguese Crown to conquer and colonize the New World in the name of Christianity. In the papal bull *Dum Diversas* of 1452, Pope Nicholas V authorized the King of Portugal:

> In the name of our apostolic authority, we grant to you the full and entire faculty of invading, conquering, expelling and reigning over all the kingdoms, the duchies ... of the Saracens, of pagans and of all infidels, wherever they may be found; of reducing their inhabitants to perpetual slavery, of appropriating to yourself those kingdoms and all their possessions, for your own use and that of your successors. (Cited in Schineller 1990, 34)

Four years later, Pope Callistus III granted the Portuguese Crown sole rights in trade and missionary activities in the lands of the New World in the papal bull *Inter Cetera* of 1456.

Not surprisingly, the Spanish Crown mounted a strong protest against Portugal's exclusive civil, trade, and missionary privileges in the New World. Both Spain and Portugal brought the matter for arbitration before Pope Alexander VI. By a new papal bull *Inter Cetera* dated May 4, 1493, Alexander defined a North-South demarcation line 100 miles west of the Azores, awarding Spain and Portugal full rights of civil control over the western and eastern zones of this demarcation line, respectively. Spain was still dissatisfied, however, because the Portuguese Crown retained its ecclesiastical control over the newly discovered lands. In a third papal bull, *Eximiae Devotionis Causa*, Spain received full ecclesiastical privileges and jurisdiction over the lands in its sphere of control. Spain and Portugal later accepted a new demarcation line 370 miles west of the Azores, pursuant to the Treaty of Tordesillas of 1494 (Boxer 1969, 20–23). On the one hand, the Treaty of Tordesillas merely arbitrated between the rival claims of the Spanish and Portuguese Crowns over the newly discovered territories in the Americas and Africa. On the other hand, its principal and long-term impact in the history of European colonization of Asia was the introduction of the system of royal patronage of Catholic missions in Asia by the Spanish and Portuguese empires.

The terms *Patronato Real* in Spanish and *Padroado* in Portuguese refer to their respective special ecclesiastical jurisdictions and rights of control over missionary activities by royal patronage in these new lands. Under this system of royal patronage (*ius patronatus*), the Spanish and Portuguese Crowns were responsible for the financial sponsorship of missionary endeavors, held control over the appointment and salaries of colonial bishops and clergy and the supervision of missionary personnel, and also were responsible for protection of the nascent mission centers from hostile indigenous groups in their respective spheres of control (Boxer 1969, 228–48). The papal granting of the privilege of patronage over the Christian missions in the New World to the two expansionist European powers of Spain and Portugal would eventually lead to two unintended consequences.

First, this alliance between Empire and Church sowed the seeds for the subsequent pervasive association of the European-led Christian mission with the worst of European imperialism and hegemony in the many colonial territories. In addition, this alliance also resulted in the blurring of boundaries between colonial expansionism and Christian missionary expansion, such that the missionary task became identified with and defined in terms of European imperial aspirations and colonial expansionism. Seventeenth-century Portuguese commentator Paulo da Trindade explained this relationship:

> The two swords of the civil and the ecclesiastical power were always so close together in the conquest of the East that we seldom find one being used without the other; for the weapons only conquered through the right that the preaching of the Gospel gave them, and the preaching was only of some use when it was accompanied and protected by the weapons. (Cited in Boxer 1969, 228)

Kosuke Koyama was less than sanguine when he quoted the following observation in Brenda and Larkin (1968, 78) that captures succinctly the negative aspects of such an unholy alliance, one not always compatible with the gospel message:

> It was in 1511. The Portuguese fleet, propelled by greed for the monopoly of the Asiatic trade (spice!) and hatred of the infidel Muslim, approached the fortress of Malacca. The captain of the fleet, Alfonso de Albuquerque, spoke to his men to inspire them on the eve of the successful assault on the city. The speech contains a highly interesting theological interpretation of the event: "It is, too, well worthy of belief that as the King of Malacca, who has already once been discomfited and had proof of our strength, with no hope of obtaining any succor from any other quarters—sixteen days having already elapsed since this took place—makes no endeavor to negotiate with

us for the security of his estate, Our Lord is blinding his judgment and hardening his heart, and desires the completion of this affair of Malacca." (Koyama 1999, 33)

Under the banner of empire-church alliances and patronage, Christian missionaries set foot on the Indian subcontinent, Japan, China, the Malay Archipelago, Siam, Vietnam, and the Philippines, though with varying results. On the one hand, in the Philippines, the Spanish Dominicans of the Patronato Real encountered little if any resistance to the might of the Spanish conquistadors. On the other hand, the Portuguese Jesuits of the Padroado encountered cultures and civilizations in India, China, and Japan that were not only more ancient than their own culture but also more resilient to European might.

India

The European Christian mission to India began with the arrival of the Portuguese fleet in India in 1498 under the command of Vasco da Gama (d. 1524). The Portuguese trade mission was soon transformed into one of empire building and control of the trading and sea routes with the capture of Goa in 1510 and Melaka (Malacca) in 1511 by Alfonso de Albuquerque (1453–1515). Concomitant with the rise of the Portuguese empire in Asia (with its headquarters in Goa) was the establishment of the Latin church in India, with its metropolitan see in Goa, by the Padroado missionaries who came with the Portuguese fleet. Of these missionaries, the most well known is undoubtedly the Jesuit missionary Francis Xavier (1506–1552), whose indefatigable efforts led to numerous conversions among the Indians, mostly from the lower castes (Moffett 2005, 3–12). At first, the Portuguese missionary outreach to the high-caste Indians failed miserably. The Indian Syro-Malabar theologian Kuncheria Pathil explained this lack of success as follows:

The 16th-century Portuguese missionary efforts succeeded only among the lower castes of the Hindu society. Following the same approach used in their Latin American mission colonies, the Portuguese missionaries required the newly baptized Indian neophytes to dress, eat, and behave like the Portuguese Christians, including taking Portuguese surnames. High-caste Indians objected to these demands, labelling the neophytes "parangis" (detested foreigners) and treating them as outcasts. (2003, 402)

It fell to the Jesuit missionary Roberto de Nobili (1577–1656) to break this impasse. From the beginning, Nobili had the foresight to realize that Christian missionaries had to reach out and engage with upper-caste Indians if the Christian gospel were to make a significant long-term contribution and have a deep-seated impact in India. Convinced that Christianity failed to make inroads among high-caste Indians because its European trappings alienated their sensibilities, Nobili sought to transform himself by immersing himself in the cultures, customs, traditions, and languages of India, mastering Sanskrit, Tamil, and Telegu. Subsequently, he took the radical step of disassociating himself from his fellow Portuguese, including his fellow Jesuits, when he adopted the lifestyle and dietary habits of a high-caste Brahmin, eating a strictly vegetarian diet, abstaining from alcohol, wearing the sacred thread of the Brahmin, and observing the precepts of ritual purity, including purificatory baths and absolute caste segregation.

Through these strategies, Nobili sought to transcend the stereotypical Indian misconceptions and prejudices about Portuguese missionaries, colonial officials, and traders, all of whom were perceived by the upper castes to be unclean and therefore untouchable because of their consumption of meat and alcohol, as well as their failure to observe caste segregation and other precepts of purity. More significantly, Nobili's transformation into a "Roman Brahmin" won him access to the socioreligious world of the high castes, resulting in many Brahmin converts to Christianity. At the same time, it comes as no surprise that this strategy also alienated him from the lower-caste Indian Christian converts and many of his Jesuit confreres. Eventually, the promising mission to the upper castes was suppressed by the decree of the papal legate, Charles-Thomas Maillard de Tournon, in 1704.

Since then, Indian Christianity, for better or for worse, has come to be identified as a religion of the lower castes and outcastes (Moffett 2005, 20–23; Arokiasamy 1986; Saulière and Rajamanickam 1995; Arun 2007).

Japan

The so-called Christian Century of Japan stretched from the arrival of Francis Xavier (1506–1552) under the patronage of the Portuguese Crown in Japan in 1549 to the Sakoku Edict in 1639, pursuant to which the Tokugawa Shogunate ruthlessly persecuted Japanese Catholics as reprisal for their role in the Shimabara Uprising of 1637–38 (Elison 1973, 1). In contrast to Chinese society, with the emperor and the scholar-gentry governing the land according to Confucian social-ethical precepts, medieval Japanese society was governed not by the Confucian scholar-gentry class but by powerful warlords (or daimyos) with their samurai armies. True power lay with the Shogun, a military dictator who outmaneuvered other daimyos to become the de facto military dictator of Japan. Unlike his Chinese counterpart, the Japanese emperor was reduced to a powerless figurehead. Prior to the seventeenth century, Confucianism, which was first brought from China to Japan during the period of the Tang Dynasty, was reduced to a philosophical discipline for intellectual study by aristocrats and monks (Ross 1994, 86). Diverse schools of Buddhism—ranging from philosophical (Tendai), esoteric (Shingon), Zen (Rinzai, Soto), and devotional Pure Land (Jodoshu, Jodoshinshu) to the various Nichiren Buddhist factions—dominated the religious landscape, coexisting with the indigenous Shinto tradition.

Xavier and his confreres arrived in Japan in the midst of the Sengoku Era, which stretched from the mid-fifteenth century until the beginning of the seventeenth. The Sengoku period was marked by a bitterly divided Japanese feudal society that was being torn apart by constant conflict and strife among warring daimyos and their samurai armies, who together with militant Buddhist monasteries and their monk armies competed for power and control over the land. On discovering that the samurais and daimyos looked with disdain on the plain black garments of the Jesuits, Xavier and his companions exchanged their clerical garb for the fine silk robes of the Japanese nobility (Ross 1994, 26–27; Moffett 2005, 68–72).

As outsiders lacking cultural intelligence, Xavier and his fellow Jesuits depended on Yajiro (or Anjiro), who had fled his homeland and whom Xavier met and befriended in Melaka (Malacca) in 1548. Yajiro became a Christian under Xavier's tutelage in Goa, taking on the Portuguese name Paulo de Santa Fé. Having learned Portuguese, Yajiro in turn became Xavier's first translator in Japan. Although Xavier was aware of the need to inculturate the Christian gospel within the Japanese linguistic and cultural context, he and his colleagues were ill-equipped for this task. Lacking the in-depth linguistic and critical scholarly skills of Matteo Ricci and his Jesuit brethren in China to pursue his own research and study, Xavier opted for a quick fix, putting his trust in Yajiro to find the corresponding terms in the Japanese language to express Christian theological principles. By contrast, Ricci and his colleagues were only able to inculturate the Christian message in the Chinese context after many years of painstaking study of the Chinese language and the Confucian classics.

Unfortunately, Yajiro was a samurai and not a scholar, and therefore he could neither read the classical *kanji* script nor grasp the subtleties of Buddhist philosophical thought. Not surprisingly, Yajiro uncritically chose terms from his Shingon Buddhist background to translate corresponding Christian terms, such as *Dainichi* for God, *jodo* for heaven, *jigoku* for hell, and *tennin* for angels. To his horror and dismay, Xavier soon discovered that the use of these terms only served to confuse the Japanese, who mistook the Jesuits for Buddhist monks from the West preaching another new school of Buddhism. As a result, Xavier and his fellow Jesuits in Japan retreated from any attempt at inculturation. Instead of looking for Japanese equivalents, Xavier chose to transliterate from Latin to Japanese, using *Deusu* from *Deus*, *ekerija* from *ecclesia*, and *artaru* from *altare* (Ross 1994, 28–29, 112; Elison 1973, 28–29; Moffett 2005, 72–73).

Notwithstanding this retreat from the initial attempt to inculturate the gospel in the Japanese context, the fledgling

Jesuit mission gained converts among those daimyos and samurais who felt marginalized in the many internecine feuds of the Sengoku Era and who sought out trade with the Portuguese to raise funds and acquire superior European weaponry to bolster their defenses against their rivals. Within the rigid social hierarchy of feudal Japan, the conversion of a daimyo or samurai often meant that his extended clan, as well as all families and dependents within the territory that he ruled, would embrace his newfound faith. For many of these converts, the Christian faith became tightly intertwined with partisan clan identities and conflicts (Drummond 1971, 91–94), especially in the ongoing civil war among rival Buddhist and Shinto daimyo clans, as the Christian-dominated Shimabara Uprising of 1637–38 so clearly showed (Elison 1973, 1–3; Moffett 2005, 91–92; Boxer 1951, 376–85). The link between faith and clan identity came to define the remnant of the Japanese Christians of the defeated clans who defied the edicts of the Tokugawa Shoguns, choosing to go underground as hidden Christians (*Kakure Kirishitan*) rather than renounce their Christian faith. Some 30,000 of these hidden Christians survived the 250 years of *Sakoku* ("Seclusion"), hiding from the authorities in Nagasaki and its surrounding islands until their discovery by French missionaries in 1865 (Harrington 1993; Turnbull 1998).

At the same time, Xavier confronted a greater challenge. In his many conversations with Buddhist monks, daimyos, and samurais, Xavier found himself being asked a simple yet profound question: If the message that he was preaching was ancient and true, why was it unknown among the Chinese, whom the Japanese looked up to and sought to emulate? Ultimately, Xavier was disappointed that the success and growth of the Japanese mission never matched his hopes and expectations. He came to the realization that he could win over the Japanese for Christ only if he won over the Chinese first. Unfortunately, he never reached China, dying on the island of Sangchuan on December 3, 1552, while waiting in vain for a boat to take him to the Chinese mainland (Elison 1973, 29–30; Moffett 2005, 73).

More significantly, Xavier's attempt at inculturation, coupled with the antagonism that the then-superior of the Jesuit mission in Japan, Francisco Cabral (1529–1609), harbored toward Japanese culture and customs, handicapped the visionary Alessandro Valignano (1539–1606). As the Jesuit "Visitor to the East," Valignano dreamed of establishing truly indigenous Christian movements in East Asia. However, his vision was realized only in China through the efforts of Ricci, Ruggieri, and others, which we will discuss later. The arrival of the Portuguese *fidalgo* and conquistador turned Jesuit missionary Francisco Cabral in 1570 marked a turning point in the Jesuit mission to Japan. Proudly Iberian and critical of all things non-European, Cabral had a low estimation of the Japanese people and their culture and traditions. For example, up to that point in time, the Jesuit missionaries in Japan had routinely dressed themselves in Japanese-style silk finery befitting the status of the Japanese nobility in order to be received by the daimyos and samurais. Perceiving this as a relaxation of Jesuit rules, Cabral mandated the wearing of European-style austere black cotton clergy garb by the Jesuits at all times.

Matters came to a head when Valignano complained bitterly in his letter of October 27, 1580, to the Jesuit Father General concerning Cabral's reluctance to implement his call for Jesuits to learn Japanese upon arrival in Japan. Valignano further took issue with Cabral's condescending attitude toward and poor treatment of the Japanese Jesuit scholastics and indigenous catechists (*dojoku*), even though they were the ones who were directly responsible for evangelizing and catechizing the Japanese at the grassroots level. The clash between Cabral and Valignano resulted in Cabral finding himself increasingly sidelined. Eventually Cabral resigned his office and return to Europe. Nevertheless, his Eurocentric attitude and demeaning perception of all things Japanese, rather than Valignano's more open attitude, remained more influential among many of the remaining Jesuit missionaries in Japan (Ross 1994, 50–65; Moffett 2005, 77–79).

As a result, the Jesuits in Japan never did engage in any meaningful way with the philosophical and religious traditions of medieval Japanese society. Although Cabral did successfully maintain the orientation of Japanese Christianity toward its European roots in the period when he was in charge of the Jesuit mission to Japan, his negative perceptions toward Japanese culture, customs, and way of life arguably was partly responsible for the very public apostasy by the Japanese Jesuit scholastic Fukansai (Fabian Fucan) (1565–1621). By all accounts, Fukansai was a brilliant intellectual and promising Jesuit who aspired to ordination and a leadership role within the Jesuit mission in Japan. Embittered by the entrenched racism and prejudice of European Jesuits against the indigenous Japanese scholastics that resulted in his being bypassed for ordination, he publicly apostatized and published his acerbic anti-Christian polemic, *Ha Daiusu* ("*Deus* Destroyed") in 1620 (Schrimpf 2008, 39, 47; Moffett 2005, 89). Fukansai explained his bitterness toward the Jesuits in the final chapter of *Ha Daiusu*: "Because [the European Jesuits] are arrogant people they don't even consider Japanese to be human beings. . . . Besides, they don't let Japanese become *padres.* You can imagine what feeling it is not being able to realize your heart's desire" (cited in Schrimpf 2008, 47).

In the longer term, the Jesuits' refusal to engage in any meaningful attempt at inculturating the Christian gospel in the Japanese context played a role in shaping the Tokugawa Shoguns' xenophobic perception of Christianity as *jashumon*, "heretical," and therefore antithetical to the Japanese way of life. This meant that Christianity had to be stamped out in the name of national unity. Hideyoshi (d. 1598), the powerful daimyo who was credited with defeating the various warring factions to unify Japan and thus putting an end to the Sengoku period, was very suspicious of missionaries, believing that the European powers were looking to conquer and colonize Japan (Boxer 1951, 166–70; Ross 1994, 76, 115; Moffett 2005, 81). This was not surprising, as the Christian missionaries in Japan were under the patronage of either the Portuguese or Spanish Crowns. Urged on by rival Dutch and English traders, the Tokugawa Shogunate ruthlessly persecuted missionaries from Spain and Portugal, making no distinction between the missionaries and the Iberian empires that they came from, and fearing these missionaries to be spies or a fifth column for a possible invasion of Japan (Ross 1994, 115; Moffett 2005, 86–87; Drummond 1971, 89–90; Boxer 1951, 290).

To protect Japan from European domination and conquest, the Tokugawa Shoguns implemented the policy of *Sakoku* ("Seclusion") that barred all foreigners from Japan on the penalty of death, with the exception of a few Dutch traders who were restricted to the artificial island of Dejima in the port of Nagasaki. In effect, the *Sakoku* policy turned Japan into a closed society from the mid-1630s onward. This self-imposed policy of absolute seclusion lasted until the arrival of Commodore Matthew Perry with four heavily armed US warships in 1853 compelled Japan to open its ports reluctantly to foreign traders and missionaries.

China

The world of Chinese civilization during these centuries was as different from the European civilization as one could imagine, resulting in both challenges and opportunities for Christian missionaries who sought to articulate the message of the Christian gospel in a manner intelligible to the Chinese. In China, these missionaries came face-to-face with an ancient and historic civilization that arose contemporaneously with the Egyptian, Babylonian, and Indus Valley civilizations, well before the birth of Greek civilization, the cradle of European philosophy. Indeed, for thousands of years, the Chinese civilization had prided itself as the "Middle Kingdom" (*Zhongguo*), the center of the inhabited world, "a civilized oasis surrounded by what was thought to be a cultural desert" (J. Ching 1993, 1).

Undergirding Chinese civilization and shaping the worldview of Chinese people was the *ru,* or Confucian tradition. Beginning with its emergence as the officially sanctioned philosophical-religious and sociopolitical system during the Han Dynasty (206 BCE–220 CE), the impact of Confucianism had been felt far beyond the borders of China, shaping the worldviews of diverse East Asian societies over the course of two millennia. Strictly speaking, there is no exact Chinese equivalent of the term "Confucianism." In reality, the term was originally coined by the sixteenth-century Jesuit missionaries to China as a neologism for the venerable, all-encompassing tradition rooted in the socioethical precepts and philosophical norms governing human conduct and social relations in Chinese antiquity that was presumed to be articulated by the historical "Confucius" (Kongzi) (551–479 BCE). The efforts of Matteo Ricci and his Jesuit companions in China to canonize Confucius as the "founder" of Confucianism had more to do with missiological exigencies than being an accurate description of the *ru* tradition in its sociohistorical setting. Unlike the Jesuit missionaries, the Chinese never saw fit to coin a single term to describe the diversity of competing schools within the Chinese weltanschauung that are various referred to as *rujia* (literati family), *rujiao* (literati teachings), *ruxue* (literati learning), or simply as *ru* (literati). Although the *ru* tradition itself *predates* Confucius, the ethical vision of Confucius and his followers has come to define and enrich the *ru* tradition, with Confucius being honored within the Chinese tradition as "Master" (*zi*), "Ancestral Teacher" (*zongshi*)," "First Teacher" (*xianshi*), and "Great Sage" (*zhisheng*). In the absence of other more appropriate terms, the terms "Confucian" and "Confucianism" will be used here as convenient labels for the *ru* tradition accordingly.

As mentioned earlier, Matteo Ricci was convinced that the Christian gospel had to find points of contact with Confucianism in China and assume a Chinese identity in order for it to enter into the lives of the Chinese people. From the outset, Ricci made it his goal to adopt the Chinese way of life as his own. To this end, he embarked on the painstaking task of mastering a very complex and difficult language. After realizing that his original plan of adopting the dress and lifestyle of a Buddhist monk failed to provide him with the necessary means of penetrating the Chinese society, Ricci chose the identity, dress, and language of a Confucian scholar in order to win over the Confucian literati. In an early work written in 1595, *Jiaoyou lun* ("On Friendship"), Ricci sought to reassure the Confucian scholars who were in dialogue with him of his deep appreciation for the social significance of friendship within the Confucian "Five Relations" (*wulun*) framework of ruler-subject, husband-wife, father-son, older-younger siblings, and friends-friends. This is significant because of the five relations, four are hierarchical relations, whereas the fifth is a relationship of *equals*. This paved the way for Ricci to accept and be accepted by the Confucian literati as friends and equals.

Matteo Ricci and his companions also engaged in a profound dialogue with their Confucian hosts in their quest to find a way to present the Christian gospel in a manner that is comprehensible to a Confucian audience. In his seminal 1997 work, *Manufacturing Confucianism: Chinese Traditions and Universal Civilization,* Lionel M. Jensen makes the case that terms such as *Confucius* and *Confucianism,* which have come to define the Chinese tradition and the essence of what it is to be Chinese, first emerged as a Jesuit invention, as mentioned above, that sought to root the Christian gospel in the Chinese world.

First, Jensen explains that the Jesuits invented an indigenous tradition, which they called *xianru* in Chinese, *i veri letterati* in Italian, and *homes letrados* in Portuguese, with "Confucius" or "Kong Fuzi" as its founding patriarch (1997, 80). He argues that "Kong Fuzi" is not how the Chinese would have normally called him, observing that the earliest mention of "Confucius" is found only in the Latin manuscript *Vera et brevis divinarum rerum expositio.* The Latin draft of this early catechism for Chinese converts was originally prepared by Michele Ruggieri (1543–1607) and subsequently translated into Chinese as *Tianzhu shilu* ("Veritable Record of the Heavenly Master"), one of two catechisms that the Jesuits produced for their Chinese converts (Jensen 1997, 70–71).

Second, Jensen argues that the Jesuits invented the superlative title "Kong Fuzi" as a means of elevating Master Kong (Kongzi) above the other *ru* masters of antiquity (Guanzi, Laozi, Zhuangzi, Zengzi, Xunzi, Han Feizi) and the masters of the so-called Neo-Confucian tradition (Zhang Zai, Zhou Dunyi, the Cheng Brothers, and Zhuxi) (Jensen 1997, 86). This was because the Jesuits saw Confucius as one of their own, a "prophet, holy man, and saint," as well as a "spiritual confrere" who "preached an ancient gospel of monotheism now forgotten." Hence, it was incumbent on them to unearth the "true learning" (*zhengxue*) which Confucius supposedly taught but was now forgotten, and which conveniently meshed with their own preaching of the gospel (1997, 33). Ricci's ultimate goal was to contextualize the gospel as *something that flowed from Confucius' teachings* rather than something foreign that was brought by outsiders.

Third, Jensen asserts that the Jesuits' invention of a "Chinese fundamentalist sect that preached a theology of Christian/Confucian syncretism" became the framework by which they were able to represent themselves to the native Chinese literati as one of their own within the native *ru* tradition (1997, 33). In other words, "Confucianism" became the convenient fiction by which the Jesuit missionaries were able to make sense of their position as *insiders* in the Chinese society, realizing that unless they spoke to the Confucian literati as fellow scholars and insiders, they would not be able to gain converts to Christianity from among these Confucian literati. The Jesuits themselves called their approach "accommodation," abandoning the external trappings of their European past in order to accommodate themselves to the natives and become truly Chinese. Through this process of accommodation, the Jesuits went beyond merely drawing a correlation between themselves and the *ru* to becoming *ru* themselves, and therefore reinventing themselves as indigenous Chinese. This strategy of accommodation was effectively a process of sinicization, where the Jesuits accepted the necessity of being Chinese, and the superiority of Chinese ways over European ways, and accommodated themselves to it by diligent study of language, cultural norms, customs, and rites (1997, 39–40). As Jensen rightly points out, this accommodation could not have been accomplished without the indulgence, generosity, magnanimity, and ultimately, embrace and acceptance on the part of the Chinese literati. Jensen goes on to explain: "What is most striking about the accommodationist endeavor is its success in generating a native Chinese identity for the fathers: they conducted themselves in a Chinese manner and were, in turn, recognized as Chinese" (1997, 40). Indeed, Ricci himself acknowledged in his letter of November 1584 to his former schoolmate Giulio Fuligatti, "I have become a Chinaman. In our clothing, in our books, in our manners, and in everything external we have made ourselves Chinese" (1997, 43).

Fourth, Jensen perceives this process of accommodation as leading to Ricci's creative theologizing in his magnum opus, *Tianzhu shiyi* ("True Significance of the Heavenly Master"), the second of two early catechisms that the Jesuits produced for their Chinese converts. In *Tianzhu shiyi*, Ricci argued, among other things, that the "original" *ru* of the "Confucius" of Chinese antiquity enshrined an incipient monotheism and moral-ethical truth that pointed to the preexistent presence of the "true" message of Jesus (Jensen 1997, 56, 61). In addition, Jensen also highlights an often overlooked but significant fact: the Jesuits were responsible for the preeminence of the Four Books (*Sishu*)[3] in the Confucian canon. In order to justify this new interpretation of Confucius as the "founder" of "Confucianism," Ricci and his confreres unilaterally reorganized the traditional Confucian canon, arguing for the precedence of the Four Books, which supposedly comprised the teachings of the "historical" Confucius, over the Five Classics (*Wujing*).[4] Moreover, the Jesuits also *altered* the reading order of the Four Books to support their reinterpretation of the teachings of "Confucius," disregarding the reading order that was first established by the canon's original compiler, the Song-era Neo-Confucian scholar Zhuxi (1130–1200). Instead of following Zhuxi's instructions to start with the *Daxue* (Great Learning), followed by the *Lunyu* (Analects), the *Mengzi* (Book of Mencius), and the *Zhongyong* (Doctrine of the Mean), the Jesuits read the *Lunyu* first (supposedly because it contains the original "teachings" of the "historical" Confucius), followed by the *Daxue*, the *Zhongyong*, and the *Mengzi* (Jensen 1997, 59–60). Jensen correctly asserts that, in doing so, the Jesuits were not only manufacturing a new way of understanding "Confucianism" or the *ru* tradition that is constructed from a selection of texts, but also actively aligning and correlating the Christian scriptures with selected Confucian texts to illustrate the theological compatibility between the Christian gospel and

---

[3] The great Neo-Confucian scholar Zhuxi (1130–1200) formulated the Confucian canon of the Four Books (*Sishu*), namely the Great Learning (*Daxue*), Analects (*Lunyu*), Mencius (*Mengzi*), and the Doctrine of the Mean (*Zhongyong*) as a summation of foundational Confucian precepts.

[4] Originally emerging as a distinctive canon of the state-sanctioned Confucianism during the Han Dynasty (206 BCE–220 CE), the Five Classics (*Wujing*) comprises the Classic of Poetry (*Shijing*), Classic of History (*Shujing*), Book of Rites (*Liji*), Classic of Changes (*Yijing*), and the Spring and Autumn Annals (*Chunqiu*). A sixth Classic, the Classic of Music (*Yuejing*) is no longer extant.

the tradition. Jensen terms this a masterly stroke by the Jesuits to assert that salvation is implicit in Chinese culture and the teachings of "Confucius," thereby making an appeal to ancient Chinese heritage and tradition for the plausibility of the Christian gospel (1997, 61–62).

Vietnam

Confucianism (*Nho-giáo*) was first introduced into Vietnam by the Chinese colonial bureaucracy during the second period of Chinese colonization known as the Hán-Việt (Sino-Vietnamese) Era (43–544 CE). After the suppression of the anti-Chinese uprising of 39–43 CE that was led by the sisters Trung Trắc and Trung Nhị, the Chinese colonial administration instituted a policy of forced sinicization of the Vietnamese people by the imposition of Chinese language and culture as well as Confucian sociopolitical institutions (Taylor 1983, 38–39, 45; Nguyen Ngoc Huy 1998, 92; Woodside 1971, 46). Even after the Vietnamese regained their autonomy in 939 CE in the aftermath of the fall of the Tang Dynasty, Confucianism merely suffered a temporary setback, returning in full force within a few decades as the official ideology of several indigenous Vietnamese dynasties, namely the Lý (1010–1225), Trần (1224–1400), Lê (1428–1788), and Nguyễn (1802–1945) Dynasties. In particular, the Lý Dynasty imported and implemented the Song-era Chinese Confucian statecraft and education as a means of consolidating its grip over its kingdom. For this purpose, the first Confucian "temple of literature" (*văn miếu*) in the imperial capital of Thăng Long (modern-day Hanoi) was dedicated in 1070; the first Vietnamese civil service examination utilizing the Confucian model was instituted in 1075; and the first national university was founded in 1076 (Nguyen Ngoc Huy 1998, 93; Phan 1998, 20–22). As a result, Confucianism penetrated every level of society from the imperial court to the humble village. From the fifteenth century onward, Confucianism became the dominant orthodoxy for maintaining national integration and stability, beginning with the Lê Dynasty and reaching its zenith in the Nguyễn Dynasty, when Gia Long

(1762–1820) and his successors implemented a rigorous policy of Confucianization across all strata of nineteenth-century Vietnamese society (Woodside 1971).

Full-scale Christian missionary activity in Vietnam began with the arrival of a contingent of Jesuits led by Alexandre de Rhodes (1591–1660) in 1624, in the twilight years of the Lê Dynasty. By this time, the weak and decadent Lê ruling house had lost control of the kingdom to two rival warring clans, the Trịnh, which held de facto power in the north (Tonkin) and the Nguyễn, which controlled the south (Cochinchina). De Rhodes's arrival was treated with ambivalence by both feuding clans. The Vietnamese American theologian Peter Phan explains:

> Engaged in an internecine war, the lords of both Tonkin and Cochinchina sought to place their respective countries at an advantage by means of commercial trade with the Portuguese and above all by obtaining Western firearms. They regarded missionaries as useful pawns in their bid for power, allowing them to stay and preach in their lands as long as they could attract foreign trade, and expelling them when their usefulness vanished. (1998, 71)

Phan further points out that de Rhodes found himself hemmed in by the bloody rivalry between the Trịnh and Nguyễn warlords; he did not want to offend either warlord, lest it be construed by the other as disloyalty and provide an excuse to persecute the Vietnamese Christian converts (1998, 71). Ultimately, his efforts came to naught. In Phan's words:

> Ironically, despite all his painstaking caution, the *immediate* cause of de Rhodes's expulsion from both Tonkin and Cochinchina was political and economic. In 1630, it was triggered by the accusation of a former Buddhist monk that de Rhodes and the Christians were involved in a plot with Cao Bang and Cochinchina to overthrow Lord Trinh Trang. In 1645, the apparent cause for banishment was the charge of espionage for Tonkin. (1998, 71)

As for his missionary endeavors in Vietnam, taking a page from Ricci and his confreres in China, de Rhodes tried to master the Vietnamese language and study the social, cultural, and religious traditions of the Vietnamese people. Of the three religions that he encountered in Vietnam—Confucianism, Daoism, and Buddhism—de Rhodes bitterly attacked Daoism and Buddhism, while vacillating between openness and ambivalence toward Confucianism. In his landmark 1998 study on de Rhodes, *Mission and Catechesis: Alexandre de Rhodes and Inculturation in Seventeenth-Century Vietnam*, Peter Phan notes that de Rhodes adopted a more cautious approach to Confucianism than his Jesuit confreres in China. On the one hand, de Rhodes acknowledged the profound and beneficial influence of Confucian moral, social, and political teachings on Vietnamese society. On the other hand, he carefully distinguished between the teachings of Confucius and the cult rendered to him, accepting the former as compatible with Christianity but condemning the latter (1998, 89–92). He also criticized Confucianism for what he perceived to be Confucianism's failure to teach the existence of a supreme creator God, the immortality of the soul, and the existence of an afterlife (1998, 90).

On the issue of the Confucian principle of filial piety (Chinese: *xiao*, Vietnamese: *hiếu*) that formed the cornerstone of Vietnamese culture, de Rhodes conceded the centrality of this principle in the Vietnamese society of his day. To many early Catholic missionaries in Vietnam, the traditional practices of filial piety, which comprised ancestor veneration rituals to deceased family elders such as offering incense and burning paper offerings at the ancestral altars, looked suspiciously like worship of ancestors and were therefore proscribed by Christianity. Rather than simply condemning and prohibiting the traditional practices of filial piety, de Rhodes sought instead to Christianize them by replacing them with overtly Christian practices, such as offering votive masses and prayers for the souls in purgatory and performing works of charity in the name of the dead (Phan 1998, 95–96). Phan cites the example of how de Rhodes persuaded Christian converts to replace the burning of offerings of paper clothes for the dead with the buying of real clothes for the living poor (1998, 96).

Unlike Ricci, de Rhodes was deeply suspicious of the cult of Confucius. While de Rhodes recognized that it was possible to have a civil and political interpretation of the ritual, he argued, given its potential for misinterpretation, for its complete prohibition (Phan 1998, 91). Peter Phan explains this discrepancy between de Rhodes and his confreres in China by pointing out that de Rhodes, not being a scholar of Confucianism, lacked Ricci's in-depth and intimate knowledge of the Confucian classics. Phan thinks that de Rhodes, because he was "deeply in touch with the common people for whom many of the gestures and objects in the Confucian rites, whatever their original symbolism, were susceptible to superstitious interpretation," probably "thought it wise, pastorally, to forbid them altogether" (1998, 92). Phan also recognizes that de Rhodes's absolute prohibition appeared to have offended at least two influential Vietnamese Confucian scholars, deterring them from embracing Christianity (1998, 92).

The politics of this period was not exactly kind to Vietnamese Christians. Both the warring Trịnh and Nguyễn warlords were deeply suspicious of Christians, each side viewing Christians as supporting the other in the ongoing bloody civil war between these two warring clans. The first major persecution erupted in 1698, the culmination of sporadic persecutions in preceding decades. Others followed in the years 1712, 1723, and 1750. Persecutions ceased temporarily in 1787 when the Vicar Apostolic for Cochinchina, Pierre Pigneau de Behaine (1741–1799), brokered a treaty between the French government and the ambitious southern provincial lord, Nguyễn Phúc Ánh (1762–1820). With Pigneau's assistance and French military expertise, Nguyễn Phúc Ánh was able to crush the Tây Son peasant uprising (1770–1802) that wrestled control of much of Vietnam from both the Trịnh and Nguyễn clans. With the final defeat of the Tây Son army in 1802, Nguyễn Phúc Ánh now controlled the whole country from his southern base. He proclaimed himself emperor of a new dynasty of a unified nation, the Nguyễn Dynasty (1802–1945), taking the regnal name Gia Long. As emperor from 1802 to 1820, Gia Long tolerated the foreign missionaries and Vietnamese Christians insofar as he could get arms and favorable trading terms from the French.

Persecution resumed with increased intensity during the reign of his fourth son and successor, Minh Mạng (1820–1841). As a strict Confucian, Minh Mạng feared that Christianity was undermining the Confucian foundation of Vietnamese socio-political life. The final and worst wave of persecution began in 1847 with the ascension of Tự Đúc (1847–1883) to the throne. Cruel, insecure, and intransigent, Tự Đúc distrusted foreign missionaries and Vietnamese Christians, suspecting them of insti-gating and participating in sporadic rebellions against his rule. The ferocity of Tự Đúc's persecutions reached such propor-tions that French emissaries lodged a formal protest at his court in 1856. The decapitation of Bishop José María Díaz in 1857 was the last straw. The French seized upon it as an excuse to invade Vietnam. Tự Đúc's military was no match for the French, who seized control of the southern region (Cochinchina) and advanced toward the imperial capital of Huế. Cornered and defeated, a humiliated Tự Đúc was compelled by the victorious French to sign the Treaties of Saigon (1862) and Huế (1863), which granted among other things, religious freedom to his subjects, as well as freedom of movement within his kingdom to foreign traders and missionaries (Keith 2012, 18–54; Moffett 2005, 612–14).

The Birth of Korean Christianity: Mission by and for Koreans

The Korean situation is unique among Asian cultures in that Christianity was not introduced by foreign missionaries. Instead, Korean Confucian literati who encountered Christianity in China brought the gospel back to Korea in 1784 and established local faith communities (Chung 2001, 3).

A quick review of Korean history is useful to understand the unique situation of Korea. Established by Yi Sŏngkye, who over-threw the Koryŏ Dynasty, and spanning more than five centuries from 1392 until the annexation of Korea by Japan in 1910, the Chosŏn Dynasty has the distinction of being the longest continu-ous Confucian dynasty in the world. Breaking with the domi-nant Buddhist influence over statecraft in the preceding Koryŏ

Dynasty, Yi Sŏngkye and his successors ushered in a renaissance of Confucianism in the Korean peninsula when they instituted reforms that set up a centralized Confucian bureaucracy in the manner of the Chinese system. The *yangban*, the members of the traditional aristocratic ruling class who passed the civil service examinations (*kwagŏ*), were appointed at all levels of the government. The educational curriculum was based on the Neo-Confucianism of Zhuxi, which was taught and implemented at all levels of society (Seth 2006, 121–40; Lee 1984, 162–71).

Nevertheless, over the centuries, the Neo-Confucian ideology of the Chosŏn state retreated from its previous dynamism into rigid formalism, idealized tradition, and ritual archaisms. Korean Confucianism became ultraconservative in orientation, with a slavish adherence to Zhuxi's commentaries on the Confucian tradition. Confucian scholars were reduced to studying Zhuxi's commentaries and reproducing his thought (Chung 2001, 26–28). From the seventeenth century to the nineteenth, progressive *yangban* who were dissatisfied by the obsession with the metaphysical abstractions of Zhuxi's thought and increasingly estranged by the irrelevance of elaborate and formalistic rituals to the practical challenges of daily living banded together in the *Sirhak* ("Practical Learning") movement that sought reform in the Confucian state ideology (Lee 1984, 232–33). The *Sirhak* movement also sowed the seeds for disaffected *yangban* to look for inspiration and ideas in the new learning that was emerging in China in general and in Chinese Christian texts in particular (Chung 2001, 28–29).

In their efforts to block out new ideas from entering and upsetting the Confucian status quo in Korea, the later Chosŏn rulers sealed the kingdom's borders, prohibiting all entry and exit, earning the label of "Hermit Kingdom" for Korea. The only people who were allowed to venture beyond Korea were the *yangban* who constituted the annual delegation that paid tribute to the Chinese emperor. Once inside China, many *yangban* were amazed at the new scientific, philosophical, and religious learning that the Jesuit missionaries had brought to the Chinese court, in contrast to the moribund Neo-Confucian learning that held sway back home in Korea. In particular, their curiosity over

Chinese Christian texts led them to smuggle these texts back to Korea for further study.

By the end of the 1770s, a group of *yangban* scholars who studied these Christian texts on their own were convinced and inspired to become believers. The Confucian scholar Yi Sŭnghun, who traveled as part of the 1783 group of emissaries to Beijing, contacted the missionaries in Beijing and was baptized by the Jesuit missionary Jean de Grammont. When he returned, Sŭnghun converted and baptized his fellow scholar and close friend Yi Pyŏk, followed by others (Chung 2001, 3–6). Another *yangban* convert, Chŏng Yakchong, single-handedly wrote Korea's first indigenous catechism, the *Chugyo yoji* ("Essentials of the Master's Teachings"), in the popular *Hangul* script, ensuring its wide dissemination among the masses who could not read the classical *Hancha* script that was used by the *yangban* (Chung 2001, 11–12; Moffett 2005, 309–13). What is truly amazing is that Chŏng Yakchong was able to write this landmark indigenous Korean catechism without any assistance or guidance by foreign missionaries.

As mentioned, Korean Christianity has the unique distinction of being a Christian movement that was established, not by foreign missionaries, but on their own initiative by indigenous *yangban* who were attracted by the practical ethical orientation of Christianity through the study of Chinese Christian texts that were brought back from China. It was no mean feat that the Korean Christians spread the nascent faith and baptized their own with no outside assistance, as well as celebrated the Eucharist without an ordained priest. Moreover, as previously discussed, they produced and circulated their own catechism without any foreign missionary assistance. When the first foreign missionary to Korea, the Chinese priest Zhou Wenmo, finally crossed the border from China into Korea in 1794, he was amazed to find a thriving lay-led Korean church that had not only survived but thrived for decades without a priest or foreign missionary support (Chung 2001, 6; Moffett 2005, 310).

Over time, however, the Chosŏn rulers and the conservative Korean Confucian elite were threatened by the energetic vitality of Christianity that was slowly but inexorably gaining influence among the *yangban* and common folk alike, and feared that Christianity would undermine the foundations of the Korean Confucian imperial ideology and loosen their grip over the kingdom. Moreover, the Korean Confucian establishment and the Chosŏn kings also perceived the nascent Christian movement as a perversion of the true path of Confucianism. It did not help that Rome's condemnation of ancestor veneration in the Rites Controversy led to Christian *yangban* destroying their ancestral tablets. The Chosŏn rulers and the Confucian elite perceived the Korean Christians' refusal to participate in traditional ancestor veneration rites and rites venerating Confucius, as well as their destruction of ancestral tablets,[5] as acts of treachery that undermined the social order and communal fabric of the Korean society and challenged the heavenly mandate (Chinese: *tianming*) of the Chosŏn kings. Beginning in 1801 and lasting almost to the end of the nineteenth century, the Chosŏn kings ruthlessly persecuted and executed Christians. In particular, the years 1839, 1846, and 1866 witnessed the worst of the waves of persecution. When persecutions finally ceased at the end of the nineteenth century, more than 8,000 Korean Christians had been brutally martyred for their faith. In 1984, Pope John Paul II canonized 103 Korean martyrs who died during this period (Moffett 2005, 311–17).

From Patronage to Propaganda Fide

As time went on, the shortcomings and inadequacies of the *ius patronatus* or patronage system of missionary outreach became apparent. Both the Portuguese and Spanish colonial administrations interfered frequently in the administration of the missions. The Padroado bishops and clergy were often co-opted by the colonial administration to act as civil administrators. Many of the Padroado bishops and clergy often lacked a proper knowledge of native languages and customs. At the same time, there was often

---

[5] In Confucian societies, ancestral tablets, also known as "spirit tablets" (in Chinese, *shenpai*) are wooden tablets that are used to symbolize the presence of the spirit of deceased ancestors. Found on family or household altars, ancestral tablets are the focal point of ancestor veneration rituals in the Confucian tradition.

no effort being made to train indigenous clergy to minister to the local populace. To make matters worse, the local populace was antagonized by the ill-conceived efforts of the Spanish and the Portuguese authorities to suppress the local cultures and traditions in the name of Europeanization.

An example of a botched attempt at Europeanization was the Portuguese Padroado missionaries' ill-advised and clumsy attempt at forcing the ancient Saint Thomas Christians of Malabar, India, to become Latin Catholics. This involved the suppression of the indigenous Malabarese hierarchy and deposition of Mar Joseph Sulaqa as the Syro-Malabar metropolitan of India, as well as the reduction of its primatial see Angamale to the level of a suffragan see of Portuguese Goa, and the forced latinization of the Syro-Malabar liturgy. Convened in 1599 by Aleixo de Menezes, the Padroado archbishop of Goa, the infamous Synod of Diamper suppressed numerous Malabarese customary rights and usages, destroyed priceless ancient Syro-Malabar liturgical and other archival texts on the grounds of their alleged but unproven tainting by Nestorianism, and forcibly latinized the Syro-Malabar church rituals and disciplines (Moffett 2005, 12–19; Thaliath 1958; Nedungatt 2001).

Nonetheless, by the beginning of the sixteenth century, Rome realized belatedly that it had lost control of the missions in the New World to the Portuguese and Spanish Crowns, which often pursued interests that were inimical to the evangelizing mission of the church. Pope Pius V took the first step to redress these problems, forming a commission in 1568 for the evangelization of the East. This commission sought not only to break the Padroado stranglehold in the East but also to establish an indigenous clergy and hierarchy in the mission lands under the direct control of Rome, bypassing Spain and Portugal completely. This commission was renamed *Propaganda Fide* in 1599. Pursuant to the papal bull *Inscrutabili Divinae* dated June 22, 1622, Pope Gregory XV elevated this commission to the status of a Sacred Congregation with the name, the Sacred Congregation for the Propagation of the Faith (Sacra Congregatio de Propaganda Fide).

To fulfill its objectives, Propaganda Fide abandoned the royal patronage (*ius patronatus*) model of foreign missions in favor of sponsoring new mission societies and congregations that were answerable directly to it. Under this new system of foreign missions, which came to be known as *ius commissionis*, Propaganda Fide commissioned new mission societies and congregations for the evangelization of Asia that were under its direct supervision and independent of Portuguese and Spanish control. The most prominent of these new mission societies for Asia was the Paris Foreign Missions Society (La Société des Missions Étrangères de Paris, or MEP), which was established by François Pallu. Over time, Propaganda Fide carved out mission territories around the world and assigned them to various mission societies and congregations. As these mission territories were not canonically named dioceses, religious superiors of the mission societies or congregations that had exclusive charge and responsibility over these territories were appointed as vicars apostolic to administer these territories on behalf of the pope. The theory behind this legal maneuver of *ius commissionis* was that the pope, as leader of the church universal, was merely exercising his jurisdiction in those areas not yet named dioceses. Such a legal device enabled Propaganda Fide to get around Portuguese and Spanish claims to ecclesiastical supervision under the patronage system, and to work around the consequences of the string of Portuguese and Spanish political defeats by emerging Protestant colonial powers such as the Dutch and the British.

In 1658, Pope Alexander VII appointed François Pallu and another MEP missionary, Pierre Lambert de la Motte, as the first two vicars apostolic in Asia. Pallu was assigned to Tonkin, and de la Motte was sent to Cochinchina. The MEP was destined to play a major role in the evangelization of East and Southeast Asia in the nineteenth and early twentieth centuries. Indeed, as foot soldiers for Propaganda Fide, MEP vicars apostolic and missionaries would lead the missionary vanguard in Asia on behalf of Propaganda Fide, thereby setting the stage for the subsequent conflict between the Portuguese and Spanish Crowns clinging on to their papal mandates, on the one hand, and the resurgent Propaganda Fide, on the other hand. We shall explore this conflict in the next section.

In 1659, Propaganda Fide issued an instruction to its newly appointed vicars apostolic, François Pallu and Pierre Lambert de la Motte, titled *Instructio Vicariorum Apostolicorum ad Regna Sina-rum Tonchini et Cocinnae Proficiscentium* ("Instruction to the Vicars Apostolic on Their Departure to the Kingdoms of Tonkin and Cochinchina"). Noteworthy in this instruction was the attempt by Propaganda Fide to distinguish between the substance of the Christian gospel and its European cultural expressions, and its advice against missionary ethnocentricism:

> Do not in any way attempt and do not on any pretext persuade these peoples to change their rites, customs and mores unless these are clearly contrary to religion and good morals. For what could be more absurd than to bring France, Spain, Italy, or any other European country over to China? It is not these countries but faith that you must bring, the faith that does not reject or jeopardize the rites and customs of any people as long as these are not depraved, but rather desires to preserve and promote them. . . . Admire and praise whatever deserves praise. As to things that are not praiseworthy, they should not be extolled, as is done by flatterers. On the contrary, exercise prudence in either not passing judgment on them or in not condemning them rashly and exaggeratedly. As for what is evil, it should be dismissed with a nod of the head of by silence rather than by words, though without missing the opportunity, when people have become disposed to receive the truth, to uproot it without ostentation. (Cited in Phan 1998, 193–94; Latin text in Propaganda Fide 1907, 42)

However, putting this lofty vision into practice was much more difficult than Propaganda Fide had envisaged. For example, in September 1663, Propaganda Fide refused permission for indigenous Vietnamese Christians to celebrate the Tet Festival, the Vietnamese New Year, fearing that it would become an excuse for Vietnamese Catholics to eat meat when Tet fell on a Friday or Saturday or during Lent (1907, 52). In Siam, by a letter dated March 20, 1685, Propaganda Fide forbade the Vicar Apostolic of Siam to allow missionaries to wear the garments of Siamese Buddhist monks or Talapoins (*uti veste talapoi-*

norum) or even garments of the same color (*etiam quoad colorem*) (1907, 537n1). This 1685 decision was reiterated in a directive dated March 23, 1844, prohibiting missionaries from wearing the garb of Buddhist priests (1907, 537). However, Propaganda Fide reluctantly allowed the clergy of Coromondel in India to use white instead of black vestments because the local populace abhorred black garments (1907, 344). It also permitted the Vicar Apostolic of Siam to use vernacular languages in adult baptisms (1907, 414).

Conflict between Padroado and Propaganda Fide

In the early period, Propaganda Fide carefully avoided getting into conflict with the Portuguese and Spanish Crowns by limiting its appointment of vicars apostolic to those regions that were outside the control of Portugal and Spain. In Asia, the Portuguese Crown continued to insist on its prerogative to appoint colonial bishops under its Padroado privilege, claiming that Rome could not unilaterally sidestep its treaty obligations. From Rome's perspective, however, the Portuguese empire was crumbling and the Portuguese Crown was not in a position to maintain its own authority and control in the face of rising Protestant colonial and missionary expansionism.

Nevertheless, Propaganda Fide was soon confronted with the increasing needs of the foreign missions and the pastoral care of indigenous Catholic converts in regions throughout Asia that were controlled by Portugal. In response, it began, cautiously at first, to send vicars apostolic to Portuguese colonial territories (Costa 1997). For example, in Vietnam, the Padroado metropolitan of Macau exercised control over the northern region of Tonkin, and his Padroado counterpart in Goa had jurisdiction over Cochinchina in the south. Alexandre de Rhodes's successful efforts to persuade Propaganda Fide to appoint MEP vicars apostolic to administer these two regions did not sit well with Portugal, causing conflicts between the earlier Padroado missionaries and the subsequent French MEP missionaries (Phan 2011, 134).

Likewise, the arrival of the MEP vicars apostolic in Southeast Asia who were sent by Propaganda Fide were challenged by the Padroado bishops and the Portuguese Crown, which continued to assert control over the Malay Peninsula even though it had lost control of Melaka (Malacca) to the Dutch in 1641. Specifically, the Padroado metropolitan of Goa continued to claim jurisdiction over the defunct Diocese of Melaka, viewing the MEP vicars apostolic as usurpers of his ecclesiastical authority. Matters came to a boiling point when Monsignor Florens, the MEP vicar apostolic of Siam, attempted to claim jurisdiction over the island of Singapore based on the 1827 decree of Pope Leo XII. The Padroado metropolitan of Goa rejected the MEP vicar apostolic's claim on the basis that it violated the Padroado and that he obtained the decree by trickery. In a pastoral letter of 1832 addressed to the clergy and laity of the Malay Peninsula and Singapore, the Padroado metropolitan of Goa forbade anyone from obeying any episcopal authority other than him. Negotiations between Rome and Portugal hit an impasse. Frustrated, Pope Gregory XVI unilaterally appointed vicars apostolic in Padroado territories pursuant to the papal bull *Multa Praeclare* of 1838. In Southeast Asia, Pope Gregory XVI removed the Malay Peninsula and Singapore from the jurisdiction of the Padroado metropolitan of Goa and placed these regions under the MEP Vicar Apostolic of Ava and Pegu (Burma), ignoring the protest from the Archbishop of Goa (Teixeira 1963, 10–16; K. M. Williams 1976, 98–99).

Not surprisingly, the Portuguese refused to surrender their existing missions in Melaka and Singapore. Viewing Pope Gregory XVI's actions as an affront, the Portuguese cut off diplomatic ties with Rome. This sparked the so-called Goan Schism. In India, conflict broke out between the "Padroadists," bishops and priests who were loyal to the Padroado metropolitan of Goa and Portugal, and the "Propagandists," missionaries and indigenous Indian converts in the newer missions in the south who rejected the jurisdiction of Goa in favor of Rome and the oversight of Propaganda Fide. This deadlock between Portugal and Rome was finally resolved by a concordat between Pope Leo XIII and Portugal on June 23, 1886 (Moffett 2005, 432–33). Back in Southeast Asia, the Catholics and clergy living in Melaka and Singapore within the territorial jurisdiction of the old Padroado Diocese of Melaka were transferred to the jurisdiction of the Padroado metropolitan of Macau pursuant to the 1886 concordat (Teixeira 1963, 16; Moffett 2005, 359). Finally, on August 10, 1888, Pope Leo XIII reestablished the Diocese of Melaka as a suffragan see of the Archdiocese of Pondicherry in India and under the direct control of Propaganda Fide. The reestablished diocese encompassed the Malay Peninsula and Singapore. Its bishop was resident in Singapore. Thus, the whole of the Malay Peninsula came under the jurisdiction of Propaganda Fide except the existing Portuguese Padroado parishes in Melaka and Singapore, which continued to be administered by the Padroado metropolitan of Macau pursuant to the 1886 Concordat (K. M. Williams 1976, 99).

Ancestor Veneration and
the Rites Controversy

In the encounter between the Christian gospel and East Asians, nothing was more explosive than the controversy surrounding the ancestor veneration rites traditionally associated with Confucius and his teaching on filial piety (*xiao*). Ancestor veneration rites in China have a long unbroken historical tradition supposedly dating from as far back as the Xia Dynasty (ca. 2090–1600 BCE), although much of the ritual repertoire first emerged during the Shang Dynasty (ca. 1600–1100 BCE), developed during the Zhou Dynasty (1122–256 BCE), and was further refined in the Han Dynasty (Wolf 1974; Wei 1985). These ancestor veneration rites involved a complex interplay of deep-rooted religious, spiritual, and sociological factors across all levels of society. At the domestic level, ancestor veneration rites were performed by living family members in honor of their deceased family members. At the village or city level, the village chieftains or city officials would perform rites in honor of the "God of Walls and Moats" (*chenghuang*), the local patron deity of that village or city. Confucian literati performed ancestor veneration rites in honor of Confucius as the ancestral teacher (*zongshi*) par excellence in Confucian shrines of learning (*wenmiao*). At the highest level, the emperor, as the Son of Heaven (*tianzǐ*), and his court performed the official rites to Heaven (*tian*) for the well-being of the whole nation.

Matteo Ricci and his confreres viewed these rites as purely cultural and civic acts (*ritus mere civilis*), and therefore nonreligious in nature. They perceived these rites as serving merely the social function of preserving good order in the Chinese society by achieving harmony through ritualized performance that simply sought to reaffirm the hierarchical ordering of kinship and generational relations across the different strata of the Chinese society. Controversy erupted when the Dominican missionary Juan Bautista Morales (1597–1664) contended that these rites were superstitious and erroneous. Morales' complaint highlighted the opposing perspectives of the Jesuits, on the one hand, and the Dominicans, Franciscans, and the MEP, on the other hand, over the identification of the normative meaning of the ancestor veneration rites. If the normative meaning of these rites were agnostic and merely ceremonial, as the Jesuits had claimed, then the rites were civil in nature. However, if a religious meaning could be ascribed to the rites, as the Dominicans, Franciscans, and the MEP missionaries insisted, then the rites were superstitious in nature. The Jesuit missionaries had adopted the rationalistic and agnostic approach of the Chinese literati, who, schooled in the Neo-Confucian philosophical thinking that emerged during the Song Dynasty, denied any divinity in the person of Confucius. This paved the way for the Jesuits to regard the ancestor veneration rites in honor of Confucius as purely honorary and ceremonial (Minamiki 1985, 15–76; Ross 1994, 118–54; Moffett 2005, 120–26).

Morales, however, insisted that the folk religiosity surrounding the practice of ancestor veneration rites among the ordinary Chinese was clearly superstitious, and, therefore, the meaning of these rites was anything but nonreligious. After his expulsion in 1637 from China for campaigning against the Chinese Rites, Morales took his fight to Rome in 1643, convincing Pope Innocent X to prohibit the Chinese Rites in 1645. The Jesuits fought back and successfully lobbied the Holy Office to issue a decree in 1656 stating that the Chinese Rites were merely civil and political in nature. Charles Maigrot, the MEP vicar apostolic of Fujian, rejected the 1656 decree and issued his own mandate against the Chinese Rites in his jurisdiction. In the ensuing bitter and highly vitriolic fight between Maigrot and the Jesuits, Maigrot's views eventually prevailed with Pope Clement XI, who issued an absolute prohibition of the Chinese Rites in his papal bull *Ex illa die* of March 19, 1715. Pope Clement XI also required all missionaries who were bound for East Asia to take an oath to comply strictly with this prohibition under the pain of excommunication. This prohibition was reiterated by Pope Benedict XIV in his papal bull *Ex quo singulari* of July 11, 1742. In addition, Benedict XIV went a step further than Clement XI, forbidding all further discussion of this controversy (Minamiki 1985, 25–76; Ross 1994, 178–99; Moffett 2005, 126–39).

Rome's prohibition against the practice of ancestor veneration rites by East Asian converts led to the prolonged persecution of East Asian Catholics in China, Korea, and Vietnam over their refusal to participate in these rituals. In China, the response of the Kangxi Emperor (1661–1722) to Clement XI's 1715 papal bull was critical and angry:

> This manifesto shows how narrow-minded Europeans speak about the high doctrine of China. And still none of the Europeans is versed in Chinese books. Most of what they say . . . makes people laugh. The author of this manifesto is like any other Bonze [Buddhist priest] or Taoist but none has ever gone as far as he. Henceforth, no European missionary will be permitted to spread his Religion in China. Thus we shall avoid further trouble. (Cited in Moffett 2005, 130)

Full-blown anti-Christian persecutions erupted in China after the death of the Kangxi emperor. The Yongzheng emperor (1722–35) issued an edict declaring Christianity to be false teaching and an enemy of the Confucian teachings, and mounted a wave of persecution of Chinese Christians. Successive waves of anti-Christian hysteria resulted in the severe persecutions under his successors. An especially severe wave of persecution took place from 1746 to 1748 under the reign of the Qianlong emperor (1735–96). The Jiaqing emperor (1796–1820) and the Daoguang emperor (1820–50) continued the sporadic but violent persecutions under their respective rules (Moffett 2005, 130–33, 285–89). Christian missionaries enjoyed a partial respite at the end of the First Opium War (1839–42) with the signing of the Treaty of Nanjing in 1842, which paved the way for missionaries to establish missions, churches, and schools, as well as evangelize freely in the five treaty ports of Guangzhou, Xiamen, Fuzhou, Ningbo, and Shanghai, which enjoyed extraterritorial privileges (Latourette 1929, 229). Persecution formally ceased with the signing of the Treaty of Tianjin in 1860 at the conclusion of the Second Opium War (1856–60). Under the Treaty of Tianjin, the Xianfeng emperor was compelled by the European powers and the United States to grant religious liberty to Chinese Christians and permit foreign missionaries unrestricted entry and movement within China (Latourette 1929, 274–81; Moffett 2005, 297–98). Thirty-four of the 120 Catholic Martyrs of China, who were canonized by Pope John Paul II in 2000, died within this period of persecution that stretched from the eighteenth century to the nineteenth (Minamiki 1985, 77–98).

Notwithstanding Pope Benedict XIV's prohibition against any discussion of the Rites Controversy, this issue came to the forefront when the imperial Japanese government required all Japanese students to venerate the war dead and the colonial Japanese authorities in Manchukuo (Japanese-ruled Manchuria) mandated the compulsory participation in civic rites venerating Confucius. Satisfied with the official response from the Japanese authorities that these rituals were strictly civil and patriotic in nature, Rome reversed its prohibition through two instructions from Propaganda Fide titled *Pluries instanterque* (1936) and *Plane compertum est* (1939). In the first instruction, *Pluries instanterque* dated May 26, 1936, Propaganda Fide explained the rationale for reversing the prohibition on Catholics participating in the ancestor veneration rites as follows:

> We are here concerned with those acts which, despite their origin from ethnic primitive religions, are not intrinsically evil but are *per se* different, and which are not

enjoined as signs of religion, but only as civil acts to manifest and foster devotion to one's country, and where every
intent has been removed to put Catholics or non-Catholics under compulsion for the purpose of signifying some
adherence to the religions from which the rites originated.
(Cited in Minamiki 1985, 154–55)

Similarly, in the second Instruction, *Plane compertum est,* dated
December 8, 1939, Propaganda Fide reiterated:

It is abundantly clear that in the regions of the Orient
some ceremonies, although they may have been involved
with pagan rites in ancient times, have—with the changes
in customs and thinking over the course of centuries—
retained merely the civil significance of piety toward
the ancestors or of love of the fatherland or of courtesy
toward one's neighbors. (Cited in Minamiki 1985, 197)

Today, East Asian Catholics worldwide are allowed to participate
in modified forms of ancestor veneration rites that comprise only
the ritual elements that have been secularized over the passage of
time (Minamiki 1985, 183–203).

The Great Protestant Missions of
the Nineteenth Century

Hot on the heels of the Catholic missionaries were the Protestant missionaries, who were inspired to win souls for Jesus
Christ in Asia. William Carey (1761–1834) arrived in India in
1793 under the aegis of the Baptist Missionary Society and eventually settled in Serampore, where he achieved success in evangelizing the Indians. Together with his compatriots Joshua Marsh-
man and William Ward, Carey established Serampore College in
1818 to educate the Indian Christian converts (Moffett 2005,
253–63). Other Protestant missionary societies soon ventured
to Asia in the footsteps of the Baptist Missionary Society. They
included the London Missionary Society, which sent a missionary to India in 1798, followed by the Church Missionary Society,

which established its missionary presence in India in 1807, and the Society for the Propagation of the Gospel, which came to India in 1820.

If William Carey sowed the seeds for a subsequent successful Protestant Christian presence in India, Robert Morrison (1782–1834) did the same for China. Sent to China in 1807 by the London Missionary Society, Morrison struggled against all odds and in the face of persecution to produce the first complete Chinese translation of the Bible (Moffett 2005, 286–91; Bays 2012, 43–50). It took Morrison seven years to gain his first Chinese convert, and his Chinese mission struggled to gain ten Chinese converts in its first twenty-five precarious years of existence (Latourette 1929, 212–13; Moffett 2005, 289). Nevertheless, Morrison was visionary enough to ordain the first Chinese convert, the indefatigable Liang Fa (d. 1855) to be the first Chinese Protestant evangelist who was able to transcend the prohibition against foreign missionaries to preach the gospel directly to the Chinese (Latourette 1929, 223–24; Moffett 2005, 290–93; Bays 2012, 46). Liang Fa is best remembered for his influential work, the apologetical tract *Quanshi liangyan* ("Good Words to Advise the World"), which Moffett notes as "the most complete statement of Protestant doctrine by a Chinese during the first half of the nineteenth century" (Moffett 2005, 291).

Clearly, Morrison's tenacious persistence in the face of adversity paved the way for the rich fruits of subsequent Protestant missions to China. The most successful of the many Protestant missionary outreach projects to the Chinese during this period was the China Inland Mission of J. Hudson Taylor (1832–1905). The China Inland Mission is remembered today for its insistence on denominational independence at the same time as its welcome of interdenominational collaboration, its refusal to seek financial support from established churches or missionary societies, its indefatigable women and indigenous Chinese missionaries, and its willingness to go deep into the Chinese countryside beyond the urban centers that were favored by mainline Protestant missionaries (Moffett 2005, 464–69; Bays 2012, 68–69).

At the same time, the indigenous Chinese reception of the gospel message across linguistic and cultural barriers did not always conform to the expectations of the foreign missionaries, as may be seen in the tragic case of Hong Xiuquan (1814–1864). Hong Xiuquan was a Hakka Chinese from a poor peasant family whose scholarly ambitions were dashed after he repeatedly failed the all-important imperial examinations. Dejected and dispirited, Hong turned to a copy of Liang Fa's *Quanshi liangyan* for consolation. Fired up with messianic zeal from Liang Fa's tract, as well as ecstatic visions that he was Jesus' brother and God's Son, commissioned to overthrow the corrupt Qing dynasty and establish a heavenly kingdom of Great Peace (*Taiping*), Hong set about baptizing himself and rallying a significant number of the Hakka minority in the region to his cause. Eventually, his fledgling movement, Bai Shangdi Hui ("God-worshipping Society"), snowballed into a utopian military insurrection, the millenarist Taiping Uprising of 1851–64.

Hong's views evolved into an idiosyncratic vision of a Christianity that combined biblical exhortations from the Hebrew Bible with a mixture of Christian apocalyptic, Daoist millenarist, and anti-Qing rants. The historian of Chinese Christianity Lian Xi notes that because Hong "had only a brief brush with missionary Christianity" with "the American Baptist missionary, Issacher Roberts for a few months in 1847," he "was quite free to develop a Chinese form of Protestantism that adapted well to local traditions" (Lian 2010, 23–24). His unorthodox ramblings and his quest for an apocalyptic good-versus-evil battle that would establish the heavenly Kingdom of God on earth were quickly disavowed by foreign missionaries as heretical. His nascent movement was ultimately crushed by the Qing rulers with Western military aid (Spence 1996; Bays 2012, 53–56; Moffett 2005, 298–300).

As to the question of whether Hong's Taiping ideology was heretical, Daniel Bays thinks that the formal Taiping articles of faith are rooted in Christianity, pointing out that Hong's early work, including his commentary on the Ten Commandments in the early 1850s, "appears to be standard nineteenth-century Christian fare" (Bays 2012, 54). However, Bays also concedes that many foreign missionaries doubted Hong's orthodoxy because of his "seemingly bizarre display of concern for making the Bible conform to traditional Confucian 'family values'" that led "to his insistence on rewriting the Bible in several instances" as well as his outlandish claim of familial relationship with God as Jesus' brother and God's son (Bays 2012, 54–55).

Samuel Moffett acknowledges that although Hong's pseudo-Christianity may have been distorted, nonetheless "it was thoroughly transcendental and ultra-Chinese, an opening wedge for disturbing knowledge brought from beyond the seas, but spread by the Chinese themselves," which ultimately served as "a catalyst for coming change" (Moffett 2005, 300). In other words, Hong's idealistic yet flawed quest for an indigenous Chinese Christianity would eventually serve to pave the way for the emergence of waves of indigenous Chinese churches and revival movements from the early twentieth century onward, which we will explore in greater detail below.

The greater part of the nineteenth century witnessed a healthy competition for conversions and church growth throughout Asia between the various Protestant missionary societies, on the one hand, and the many Roman Catholic missionary congregations under the sponsorship of Propaganda Fide, on the other. By this time, Spanish and Portuguese control over foreign missions by virtue of *ius patronatus,* or royal patronage, was essentially in its death throes. Its void was filled by the MEP and other new religious congregations that were sponsored by Propaganda Fide, which commissioned these mission congregations and assigned them exclusive territorial rights under the principle of *ius commissionis.* For both Protestants and Catholics, numerical growth and territorial expansion became important, at times overriding objectives of the missionary task. Both the Protestants and the Catholics trumpeted annual statistics of numerical growth and territorial expansion with obvious pride. Although the missionaries might have been divided by theological and ecclesiastical differences, they were nevertheless inspired by the common goal of saving the souls of pagans, heathens, and infidels from the fires of damnation in hell by planting churches (Bosch 1991, 214–19).

For the purposes of evangelization, foreign missionaries typically established mission compounds that had a church or chapel at its center, flanked by hospitals, clinics, and schools, as well as housing for missionaries and new Christian converts. Many of these mission compounds offered food, medical care, and education, all pre-evangelization activities that were geared toward making people more sympathetic to the preaching of the Christian missionaries. Moreover, these mission compounds were often protected by the European colonial powers that controlled the region. On the one hand, it must be acknowledged that there were missionaries who were leery of being co-opted by the European colonial powers to keep the "restive natives" in check, viewing such endeavors by the local colonial authorities as unwanted interference in the task of mission. On the other hand, many missionaries and colonizers collaborated with each other for mutual benefit, as the Indian theologian M. Thomas Thangaraj reminds us: "Missionaries saw the West's colonial expansion as God's own providential way of opening the doors for preaching the gospel in the uttermost parts of the earth," while "colonizers saw missionary work as a way of subduing people in the colonies" (1999, 19). Samuel Hugh Moffett cites a foreign missionary in China as acknowledging that most non-Christian Chinese "regarded the missionary as the vanguard of foreign armies" (2005, 483).

In reality, foreign missionaries often benefited from extraterritorial privileges that the colonial powers negotiated with local rulers. For example, pursuant to the Treaty of Tianjin of 1858, the Qing rulers were obliged to exempt foreign traders and missionaries from local Chinese law. Lian Xi describes the extraterritorial privileges that were given to foreign missionaries in China and Chinese converts to Christianity as follows:

> As a result of the gunboat diplomacy after the Opium War, the prestige and influence of Western missionaries in China increased steadily until, in 1899, Roman Catholic missionaries were accorded official status by the Qing government, with the rank of a bishop corresponding to that of a viceroy or provincial governor and a priest being equal to a prefect. Under the "most-favored nation" clause in the treaties, the same official status applied to Protestant missionaries.

Western evangelists' assistance in lawsuits involving their converts was in much demand. As one missionary puts it, one only had to "get hold of the missionary's card and take it into the Yamen on behalf of a litigant" to win a case. (Lian 2010, 31, citing Broomhall 1901, 309, 311)

Likewise, foreign traders and missionaries received similar benefits in Vietnam under the Treaties of Saigon and Huế as previously discussed in this chapter. More ominously, the unequal treaties with their extraterritorial privileges for traders and missionaries that the Western imperial powers imposed on an enfeebled China in the nineteenth century were viewed by many Chinese as a humiliating affront to national pride. This led to much resentment and outrage, vitriolic xenophobia, and an anti-Christian backlash that exploded tragically in full-blown violence with the Boxer Rebellion from 1899 to 1901, which resulted in thousands of Christian missionaries and indigenous Chinese converts being brutally massacred.

The Boxer Rebellion also marked the end of a period of naiveté for the Chinese converts to Christianity who also shared in the extraterritorial privileges and economic benefits of coming under the protective umbrella of the foreign Christian missions. In particular, the Boxer Rebellion "drove home the point to Chinese Christians that, in the popular mind, their profession of the foreign faith and their membership in churches dominated by Westerners had turned them into disciples of the 'foreign devils' and collaborators in a Western assault on Chinese tradition" (Lian 2010, 32). As a result, the immediate period in the aftermath of the suppression of the Boxer Rebellion witnessed the growth of indigenous Chinese Christian churches. These churches and revival movements were completely independent of foreign missionary control or supervision and beyond Western denominational structures (Lian 2010; Bays 1996; Bays 2012, 121–57).

The first major Chinese indigenous church to emerge in the early twentieth century was the True Jesus Church (*Zhen Yesu Jiaohui*), which was founded in early 1917 by Wei Enbo (1876–1919) in the aftermath of his healing and conversion experience at the hands of a Pentecostal missionary (Bays 1996, 311; Bays

2012, 129–30; Lian 2010, 42–63). Wei and his followers preached an eclectic Chinese Christianity combining sabbatarianism and Oneness Pentecostalism that was xenophobic, nationalist, exclusivist, and millenarist in outlook (Bays 1996, 311; Bays 2012, 130; Lian 2010, 48–49). In particular, Wei was highly critical of the foreign missions, "denouncing the corruption of Western Christianity, and calling for repentance and separation from foreign missions," as well as condemning the ostentatious wealth and power of Western missionaries "in contrast to the egalitarian communalism and simplicity of Jesus' followers at the time of the apostles" (Lian 2010, 47–48; cf. Bays 2012, 130). Moreover, Wei also challenged the vaunted superiority of Western civilization, pointing to the bloody First World War that "'has claimed tens of millions of lives' as 'proof that [the missionaries] have got the [Christian] religion wrong,'" and "Westerners were still 'shameless enough to preach in China'" (cited in Lian 2010, 49–50).

An early twentieth-century indigenous church movement that bore some resemblance to Hong Xiuquan's Taiping movement was the millenarist Pentecostal movement, the Jesus Family (*Yesu Jiating*), that was established by Jing Dianying (1890–1953) (Lian 2010, 64–84; Bays 1996, 311–12; Bays 2012, 131–32). One practice that the Jesus Family had in common with the Taiping movement was the ability of believers to receive divinely inspired visions and apocalyptic prophetic messages in a trance, akin to the spirit possession and similar practices of Buddhist and Daoist millenarist sects like the White Lotus sect and the Boxers (Lian 2010, 70–72, 72–74; Bays 1996, 312; Bays 2012, 132). Lian Xi further notes that the Jesus Family also shared the Taiping movement's utopian dream for a cosmic harmony and peace that was rooted in the "ancient and enduring quest for the 'Great Harmony' (*datong*) in Chinese history" (Lian 2010, 83).

Another prominent example of an indigenous Chinese church movement in the early twentieth century that eschewed contact with foreign Christian missions was the messianic church movement that was established by Ni Tosheng, or "Watchman Nee" (1903–1972), and variously known as Little Flock (*Xiaoqun*), Assembly Hall (*Juhuichu*), or Local Church (*Difang Jiaohui*) (Lian 2010, 155–78; Bays 1996, 311–12; Bays 2012, 132–34).

In the aftermath of the post-1949 Communist crackdown on Christianity, the antidenominational, anticlerical, and decentralized nature of the Local Church movement enabled it to spread throughout the worldwide Chinese diaspora (Bays 2012, 165, 191). Complementing the explosion of indigenous church movements in China was the rise of indigenous Chinese revivalist movements emphasizing their independence from foreign Christian missions and established denominational churches, initiated by itinerant evangelists such as Wang Mingdao (1900–1991) (Lian 2010, 111–18; Bays 1996, 314; Bays 2012, 136) and the indefatigable Song Shangjie or John Sung (1901–1944) (Lian 2010, 137–54; Bays 1996, 315–16; Bays 2012, 137–38). In addition, these church movements and roving evangelists sowed the seeds for the survival of Chinese Christianity during the darkest days of the Japanese occupation of China in the Second World War and the social upheavals of the Cultural Revolution from 1966 to 1976.

Notwithstanding the dark clouds looming over the horizon on the question of the future of foreign missions in Asia, the ostensibly favorable conditions led many foreign missionaries, Protestant and Catholic alike, to believe optimistically that the Christianization of Asia was an attainable goal in the twentieth century. In the next chapter, we will examine both the optimistic Protestant expectations at the 1910 Edinburgh World Mission Conference, with its triumphalistic slogan "the Evangelization of the World in This Generation," as well as similarly optimistic Roman Catholic understandings at the beginning of the Second Vatican Council (1962–65). We will discuss why this optimism was ultimately misplaced and consider the challenges and opportunities facing the task of Christian mission in Asia in the third Christian millennium.

Chapter 2

Mission in Asia in the Face of Religious Pluralism

The year 2010 marked an important milestone in the history of Christian mission. It was the centenary of the 1910 Edinburgh World Missionary Conference. Meeting from June 2 to June 6, "Edinburgh 2010" celebrated this centenary and explored the promises and challenges of doing Christian mission globally in a new century. Edinburgh 2010 was truly global and ecumenical, with representatives from around the world representing the various branches of contemporary World Christianity—Pentecostal, evangelical, mainline Protestant, Roman Catholic, Orthodox, and independent churches. The Common Call that was issued at the end of Edinburgh 2010 invited all Christians to ongoing collaboration and partnership, working together to witness the Christian gospel to the contemporary world:

> We are challenged to welcome one another in our diversity, affirm our membership through baptism in the One Body of Christ, and recognize our need for mutuality, partnership, collaboration and networking in mission, so that the world might believe. (No. 8, in 2010, 2)

One hundred years earlier, on June 14, 1910, delegates representing the mission boards of mainline Protestant churches and mission societies from Europe and North America had gathered at the Assembly Hall of the United Free Church of Scotland in Edinburgh for a momentous event that came to be memorialized as Edinburgh 1910 (Stanley 2009). From the very beginning,

Europeans and North Americans dominated the conference. W. Richey Hogg notes that Edinburgh 1910 reflected "the high tide of Western European optimism and imperialism" that assumed that the imminent Christianization of the world was at hand (Hogg 1980, 146). In his landmark study, *The World Missionary Conference, Edinburgh 1910,* Brian Stanley observes that among the 1,215 official delegates, at most 19 were born outside of Europe or North America: 8 Indians, 4 Japanese, 3 Chinese, 1 Korean, 1 Burmese, 1 Turkish, and possibly, 1 African (2009, 91–92, 97–98).

The fruits of Edinburgh 1910 were undeniable. The International Missionary Council (established in 1921), the World Council of Churches (established in 1948), and the International Congress on World Evangelization (Lausanne 1974) traced their origin and development to Edinburgh 1910. Nevertheless, Edinburgh 1910 is often perceived as the high point of the global expansion of Euro-centric Christianity throughout the world in the early twentieth century. It sparked more than a century of active Protestant missionary expansion, driven by an explosive growth in European and North American mission societies operating within the broader sociopolitical context of European and North American empire building and colonization (Yates 1994, 7–31).

Edinburgh 1910 discussed a range of topics, but one specific issue is just as relevant today as it was in 1910: the theological significance and missiological implications of the relationship between Christianity and other world religions within the broader question of religious pluralism. On this issue, the tenor and direction of Edinburgh 1910 was greatly influenced by the American Methodist missioner John R. Mott, who presided over the conference proceedings and inspired the delegates with his overarching vision of "the Evangelization of the World in This Generation." Mott himself viewed Edinburgh 1910 as "the most notable gathering in the interest of the worldwide expansion of Christianity ever held, not only in missionary annals, but in all Christian annals" (Hopkins 1979, 342). Moreover, Mott harbored the "realistic possibility" of "imminent Christian triumph" over other world religions (Stanley 2009, 15). In a similar vein, Stephen Neill quotes the conference delegates as confidently expecting that "as the lordship of Christ came to be recognized, these other religions would disappear in their present form—the time would come when Shiva and Vishnu would have no more worshippers than Zeus and Apollo would have today" (Neill 1990, 418). Brian Stanley cites the opening address of the Archbishop of Canterbury, Randall Davidson, who confidently asserted that "there be some standing here tonight who shall not taste of death till they see . . . the Kingdom of God come with power" (2009, 1).

Roman Catholics brought a similarly hopeful understanding to the Second Vatican Council. Indeed, the Council Fathers had adopted an overly confident view of missionary success, expecting that church growth would continue unabated. The Filipino Jesuit theologian Felipe Gómez described the Council Fathers' heady optimism concerning the future of the Catholic Church's missionary endeavors as follows:

> On Nov. 6, 1964, in the 116 General Congregation of Vatican II, after Paul VI had presented the "Schema" *On the Missions*, Card. Agagianian, Prefect of *Propaganda Fide* drew a bright view of the situation: "In times of Vatican I," he said, "the Church had 275 mission territories; today, we have 770. In 1870, there was not one autonomous bishop, today we see here 41 archbishops, 126 bishops and 4 cardinals. . . . The popes had assumed the effective protagonism which they intended with the erection of the *Propaganda* in 1622 by Gregory XV. The 20th century had seen the great encyclicals *Maximum illud* (1919), *Rerum Ecclesiae* (1926), *Evangelii praecones* (1951), *Fidei donum* (1957), which channelled the missionary zeal of the secular clergy into Africa; and in the eve of the council, *Princeps pastorum* (1959)." (1986, 29)

Christian Mission Meets the Postcolonial Realities of Asia

Notwithstanding the Edinburgh 1910 delegates' hopeful aspirations, the world's other great religions have not become extinct. On the contrary, they continue to grow and thrive not only in Asia but also in North America and Europe. Similarly, although many Catholic missionaries and missiologies were inspired by the Second Vatican Council's missionary decree *Ad Gentes* to explore new ways of evangelizing in Asia and elsewhere, the realities of new sociopolitical developments in former "mission lands" throughout Asia soon crept in.

To begin with, the cataclysmic events of two world wars and the Shoah undermined the positive confidence of Christian leaders, missiologists, and missionaries, who had expected that missionary endeavors, church growth, scientific progress, and the dominance of European colonial powers would go on unchallenged, as the classic nineteenth-century evangelistic hymn "Onward Christian Soldiers" proclaims triumphalistically. The Indian theologian M. Thomas Thangaraj observes that these world wars not only "demonstrated that humans, while making progress in science, technology, and other fields, are nonetheless very capable of engaging in extreme forms of violence and cruelty," but also deflated the naïveté concerning the untrammeled direction of human progress and development (1999, 17). Consequently, "human progress, though seen as a great ally to the missionary movement at the beginning of the century, was no longer a trusted ally in the task of evangelizing the whole world" (1999, 17). In the eyes of millions of Asians, the two world wars and the Shoah punctured the illusion of superior civilization and higher ethics, as well as might and invincibility, that was carefully crafted by the European colonial authorities. No longer would these Asian masses acquiesce passively to the hegemony of European colonization of their lands in the postcolonial era of world history.

In the initial years after the Second World War, both Protestant and Catholic missionaries and their sponsoring agencies continued their endeavors as though it were business as usual. They failed to realize that the tide had changed and that a new and revolutionary postcolonial fervor was sweeping through Asia. The missiologist Aylward Shorter did not mince his words when he highlighted the shortcomings of

> the old Eurocentric model of mission, in which the Western Church is credited with stability and maturity, and with the right to send missionaries to the "pagan" nations of the non-Western world. Such new Churches are to remain

indefinitely under the tutelage of the Christian West. In this paradigm, missionaries are sent by centralized organizations on behalf of the universal Church. (1994, 155)

In the same vein, one is also reminded of Stephen Neill's devastating critique of the traditional missionary approach:

And the student is again and again amazed at the Westernness of the missions. Almost everywhere it seems to be taken for granted that the missionary period will go on for ever; the duty of the convert is clear—to trust in the superior wisdom of the white man and so to be conveyed without too much trouble in the safe bark of holy Church to the everlasting kingdom in heaven. (1990, 369)

It should be noted, however, that missionaries were able to make a positive impact on the local populace in specific instances. For example, Lamin Sanneh makes the case in his magisterial work, *Translating the Message: The Missionary Impact on Culture* (2009), that missionaries often preserved the local languages that might have otherwise vanished in the fog of globalization and modernity in translations of the Bible. Andrew Walls discusses examples of missionaries training and ordaining indigenous clergy and ministers who were able to stand up for their own communities (2002, 260). However, the popular association of Christianity with colonial imperialism in many parts of the world has overshadowed the good fruits of the Christian missionary enterprise as far as popular perception is concerned. The Indian Jesuit theologian Michael Amaladoss explains the dilemma clearly:

In the former colonies, Church extension is associated in the popular mind with colonialism. They certainly coincided historically and at that time the new Churches were not really built up as authentic local Churches. A certain assertion of autonomy on the part of the local Churches is not without connection to this past. Hence anything foreign is suspected and resented not only by non-Christians, but even by some Christians. (1988, 113)

His Filipino confrere, the Jesuit theologian Felipe Gómez, puts it in blunt terms:

> Vatican II has been accused of blindness to history, for having missed the import of decolonization, not having offered a critique of colonialism, etc. In fact, by 1965 the ancient colonies were practically all independent, only the Portuguese empire ended in 1975. (1986, 53)

From the Protestant perspective, a similar view is echoed by the Sierra Leonean church historian Jehu Hanciles, who contended that the flawed alliance between Christianity and European colonial expansionism meant that "Christianity was bankrupted as a universal ideal by expanding colonial interests and the missionary encounter with the immutable diversity of non-Western societies" (Hanciles 2008, 3; cf. 100–104). Likewise, the Native American theologian George "Tink" Tinker laments the disastrous impact of "euro-western mission practices" on Native Americans (2010).

In other words, the alliance of Christian churches with European colonialism during the heyday of colonial expansionism, especially in the face of hostilities and persecution by native rulers in countries such as Vietnam and China, as discussed in chapter 1, became a problematic liability for foreign Christian missionaries struggling to adapt to the rapidly changing sociopolitical situations throughout Asia. Many Protestant and Catholic missionaries, together with their sponsoring agencies, were slow to grasp the full implications of the rising tide of decolonization, nationalism, and postcolonial fervors that were gathering momentum throughout Asia in the ensuing decades after the end of the Second World War. More ominously, as Gerald Anderson pointed out in his important essay, "A Moratorium on Missionaries?" (1974), these nationalistic and postcolonial currents were influencing many Asians to identify and equate the territorial expansion of Christianity with the territorial expansion of European colonialism. Rightly or wrongly, it could not be denied that in the eyes of many Asians, the missionaries and their proclamation of the Christian gospel were tainted by their association and collaboration with the European colonial powers. Anderson cited with approval the words of the late Paul Verghese, an Indian theologian who later became Paulos Mar Gregorios of the Syrian Orthodox Church in India: "Relief agencies and mission boards control the younger churches through purse strings. Foreign finances, ideas and personnel still dominate the younger churches and stifle their spontaneous growth" (1974, 43).

Within Asian Protestant Christian circles, the Filipino theologian and retired Methodist bishop in the Philippines, Emerito P. Nacpil, shocked many mission agencies and missionaries when he asserted that continued missionary endeavors from the West merely reinforced the continued dependency of the Asian church "upon the strong and the continued dominance of the strong over the weak" (1971, 359). Specifically, Nacpil highlighted the perception among many Filipinos that the foreign missionary was "a symbol of the universality of Western imperialism among the rising generations of the Third World" (1971, 359). As far as Nacpil was concerned, "the most *missionary* service a missionary under the present system can do today in Asia is to go home!" (1971, 360).

The Catholic Church too was not spared the turmoil over missions and missionaries in Asia. The termination of *ius commissionis* in 1966 and the resulting "loss" of territorial exclusivity called into question the raison d'être of many Catholic foreign mission societies that previously operated on a territorial or geographical concept of Christian missions and missionary expansion. At the same time, the impact of decolonization and de-Europeanization in many former mission lands resulted in a prolonged period of debates, disagreements, and doubts among many Catholic missionaries and missiologists on the efficacy of the traditional approaches to doing Christian mission. In view of this, it was not surprising that the 1974 Synod of Catholic Bishops, which met on the theme of "Evangelization in the Modern World," was unable to arrive at a consensus on a definitive understanding of the church's mission as the synod fathers confronted the challenges of doing Christian mission in the modern age (Wilson 1974).

The Christian Minority Presence in
the Sea of Asian Plurireligiosity

For many Asian nations that gained independence from their colonial masters in the aftermath of the Second World War, independence and postcolonial consciousness have led to a discovery of national pride and, with it, a massive revival of traditional Asian religions. Notwithstanding the aspirations of Edinburgh 1910 and Vatican II, the world's great Asian religions have continued to grow and thrive not only in Asia but also in North America and Europe, even challenging the preeminent position of Christianity in many European countries.

More significant, Christians continue to represent only a small proportion of the residents of China and India, who collectively make up about one third of the world's population. There is no shortage of experts predicting an explosive growth of Christianity in China, but there is not a consensus on this issue. On the one hand, the then-president of the National Association of Evangelicals, Donald Argue, spoke enthusiastically of "the single greatest Revival in the history of Christianity" that is taking place in contemporary China (quoted in Lian 2010, 230). David Aikman makes the provocative claim in his book, *Jesus in Beijing: How Christianity Is Transforming China and Changing the Global Balance of Power* that about 20 to 30 percent of the Chinese population would be Christian by the 2030s (2003, 285). Aikman waxes lyrical about a contemporary Christian China collaborating with the United States to "make the world safe for Christian missionary endeavor" and combat the forces of terrorism and "the proliferation of weapons of mass destruction" (2003, 286, 287). Likewise, the former Archbishop of Canterbury Rowan Williams was visibly impressed by the growth in Chinese Christianity on his visit to China in 2006. As he notes in an article that he penned after his visit to China in 2006:

> Numerical expansion in Chinese Christianity in the last couple of decades has occurred at an unprecedented rate. A rate which continues to surprise and alarm some of those observing it. It's surprising partly because of the ambiguous history of Christianity in China, a history

marked both by a high level of cultural and political engagement by the Jesuits in the 17th century, and by a very unashamed alliance with foreign interference and colonial power in the 19th century. In spite of that, China is moving towards having the largest Christian population in the world. A safe guess would be 50–80 million Protestants in China today. (2007, 1)

This line of thinking is also echoed by the *Economist* editors, John Micklethwait and Adrian Wooldridge. In their 2009 bestseller, *God Is Back: How the Global Revival of Faith Is Changing the World*, Micklethwait and Wooldridge sought to make the case, among other things, for China's becoming the world's biggest Christian nation by 2050 (2009, 5).

On the other hand, the research director of the Beijing Center for Chinese Studies, Jean-Paul Wiest, cautions us against making such overoptimistic predictions. Specifically, Wiest points out that China is also in the midst of an impressive Buddhist, Daoist, and Chinese folk religions revival (2007, 531). Yoshiko Ashiwa and David L. Wank share Wiest's sentiments, noting that China has the world's largest Buddhist population, a thriving Daoist community, and an expanding Muslim community that is larger than the total Christian population in China (2009, 1). On the issue of Chinese Muslims, Wiest reminds us that the growing Chinese Muslim population in Gansu and Xinjiang is unlikely to yield up its Islamic faith to become Christians. This is because its Islamic faith is tightly wedded to its non-Han culture and ethnic pride (2007, 531). In a similar vein, Daniel H. Bays, a historian of Chinese Christianity, challenges any romanticized view of the contemporary growth of Chinese Christianity. He takes issue with Aikman's optimistic prognostication, stating that he does "not believe that China is in the process of becoming a 'Christian nation'" (Bays 2012, 204–5). Likewise, Lian Xi disagrees with the simplistic prediction of the ascendancy of Chinese Christianity:

Despite the phenomenal growth of Christianity in twentieth-century China, it has not come to dominate the

religious scene, which is still populated primarily by Buddhist, Daoist, and syncretic folk beliefs. The underground
church has in fact shown a greater tendency to absorb,
and be absorbed by, popular religion than to replace it.
More important, Chinese Christianity is, and will likely
continue to be, primarily a religion of the masses, far from
the center of policy power. (Lian 2010, 242)

Moreover, the Christian minority presence in China and
India is mirrored elsewhere in many parts of Asia. With the
exception of the Philippines and Timor-Leste, the Christian
presence in many parts of Asia is characterized by significant
minority religious communities in the midst of a dominant and
resurgent religious majority: Islam in Pakistan and Malaysia, Hinduism in India, and Buddhism in Sri Lanka. Although the term
"minority" is controversial for its possible pejorative connotations, nonetheless it is popularly used in the demographic sense
to refer to relatively small groups of persons when compared
with the total population in terms of race, ethnicity, gender,
socioeconomic class, culture, religion, and so on. More important, it almost always connotes the imbalance of power relations
between the minority groups vis-à-vis the dominant majority
group, with the latter occupying positions of power and harassing
minority groups to conform to its norms and expectations.

As a religious minority group in many parts of Asia, Asian
Christians experience complex and often tense relational dynamics with their religious majority neighbors. On the one hand,
at the grassroots level one often finds harmonious interreligious
relations as majority and minority religious groups get along in
daily living without any problems, such as Hindus and Christians
making pilgrimages to each other's religious shrines and participating in local communal festivals across religious boundaries
(Raj and Dempsey 2002; Pechilis and Raj 2013). An interesting
example of a popular devotion that transcends ethnic, caste, and
religious boundaries is the devotion to Arokia Matha (Our Lady
of Good Health), better known as Velankanni Matha (Our Lady
of Velankanni) in the town of Velankanni some 350 kilometers
south of Chennai (Madras) in central Tamil Nadu in India. The

feast of Our Lady of Velankanni begins on August 29 and culminates eleven days later on September 8, drawing massive crowds of more than one million Catholic, Hindu, and Muslim pilgrims from across India and the worldwide Indian diaspora, making it third behind Lourdes and Fatima in prominence (Mukherjee 2004, 462–63; see also Meibohm 2002). The throngs of devotees from the Catholic, Hindu, and Muslim communities have created a liminal space for their devotion to Our Lady of Velankanni that transcends sociocultural and religious distinctions. Moreover, centuries of combined Hindu and Catholic devotion to Our Lady of Velankanni have resulted in a hybridization of ritual practices rooted in both Hindu and Catholic traditions, including bathing in the sea, shaving one's head, walking on knees, and rolling in the shrine. These rituals continue to be practiced by devotees across the religious spectrum, notwithstanding clerical disapproval. In addition, Hindu devotees of Our Lady of Velankanni often equate her efficacy as a healer of illness and victor over demonic forces as functional equivalents to similar attributes of the Hindu goddess Mariamman (Bayly 1989, 367–68; see also Meibohm 2002 and Younger 1992).

On the other hand, from the 1970s onward many areas in Asia have witnessed a rise in intercommunal tensions and violence, as religion becomes politicized in response to broader economic problems and their consequential political crises and social dislocations. In many parts of Asia, religious majorities are putting pressure on the Christian minority community in their midst to abandon Christianity as a colonial relic and foreign import in favor of the local religion of the majority. Even religions that claim to uphold the ideals of nonviolence and tolerance, such as Hinduism and Buddhism, have to confront the reality of prejudice, hatred, and sectarian violence by their adherents, both within themselves and against other religious communities. In reality, the popular perceptions of Hindu and Buddhist pacifism and tolerance have been punctured by Hindus in India and Buddhists in Sri Lanka and Myanmar who have become embroiled in sectarian conflicts against ethnic and religious minorities in their midst.

More often than not, interreligious conflicts are often linked inextricably to broader socioeconomic and political issues that are often exacerbated by mass movements of people, voluntary or involuntary, increasing diversity and pluralism throughout the world, and intensifying tensions between the dominant community in the host countries and newcomer minorities. More problematic is the use of terror and violence by a dominant majority community against a vulnerable minority community to force it to conform to the majority's definition of identity and social belonging. With the blurring of boundaries between the majority's legitimate quest for a distinctive sociocultural and religious identity and its hostility toward minorities for being different, the unfortunate result is often greater communal tension and religious strife, as can be seen in Pakistan, India, Sri Lanka, Myanmar, and elsewhere. Moreover, too often religious identities become intertwined in ethnic conflicts, as is the case with Sri Lanka, Myanmar, and throughout the region of West Asia. The World Council of Churches hits the mark on this issue in its groundbreaking document, *Ecumenical Considerations for Dialogue and Relations with People of Other Religions* (2004):

> In some parts of the world, religion is increasingly identified with ethnicity, giving religious overtones to ethnic conflict. In other situations, religious identity becomes so closely related to power that the communities without power, or who are discriminated against, look to their religion as the force of mobilization of their dissent and protest. These conflicts tend to appear as, or are represented to be, conflict between religious communities, polarizing them along communal lines. Religious communities often inherit deep divisions, hatreds and enmities that are, in most cases, passed down through generations of conflict. When communities identify themselves or are identified exclusively by their religion, the situation becomes explosive, even able to tear apart communities that have lived in peace for centuries. (Art. 7)

The World Council of Churches' blunt assessment of sectarian violence against religious minority groups in many parts of Asia is borne out by the violence by Muslims against Ahmadiyya and Christians in Pakistan, Hindus against Muslims and Christians in India, Buddhists against Hindus in Sri Lanka, and Buddhists against Muslims and Christians in Myanmar. The human costs of short-sighted naked power plays that condone or even encourage religious violence in defense of the majority's dominant position is evident as Asian Christians face harassment, find themselves dislocated by persecution and wars, and in the worst situations lose their lives.

A persuasive case can be made that in the current religious climate in Asia, relations between Christianity and Islam are the most strained and bear the most grievous consequences, as can be seen in countries such as Pakistan, Iran, Iraq, Lebanon, and Syria. Indeed, Islam has been on the upsurge, especially in Asia and Africa, making it one of the fastest-growing religions in the world. Unfortunately, this has often resulted in growing antagonism and hardening of attitudes toward Christian minorities living in the midst of Muslim majorities in many parts of Asia and Africa, especially in the post–September 11 world. In Lebanon, relations between the dominant Shi'a majority and the Maronite Catholic minority remain fraught with tension (Sisk 2011, 49–68).

Pakistan is another example of the troubled relations between the Christian minority and Muslim majority. From the time of the military dictatorship of the late General Zia Ul Haq to the present day, Pakistan has witnessed an increase in attacks against the Christian minority as alien outsiders, especially through the misuse of controversial blasphemy laws to intimidate and harass Christians (Jones 2009). It is against this backdrop that the Roman Catholic bishop of Faisalabad, John Joseph, shot himself in the head on May 6, 1998, in protest against the execution of a Christian on spurious blasphemy charges (Walbridge 2002). Unfortunately, Bishop Joseph's death brought no relief to the beleaguered and vulnerable Pakistani Christian minority. The ongoing harassment of Pakistani Christians culminated in the killings of six Christians in Gojra on August 1, 2009, for allegedly desecrating the Qur'an. Christian activists have continued to press for the repeal of blasphemy laws that make it very easy for anyone to single out Christians for harassment (Jones 2009).

India is an example of a country where religion is caught up in a treacherous mix of caste, race, ethnicity, politics, class, and economics. From the very beginning, Indian Christians have wrestled with the challenges of interacting with their Hindu neighbors. Notwithstanding their presence in India of almost two millennia, as explored in chapter 1, Indian Christians continue to make up only a small fraction of the total population of contemporary India. Indian Christianity not only has to coexist with Hinduism, Islam, Jainism, and Sikhism in India, it also has to explore creative means and strategies of witnessing the gospel message in a land that is scarred with religious rivalry. This has become even more urgent since the 1980s, as India has witnessed the rise of the militant Hindutva religious movement that advocates Hindu pride and promotes Hindu nationalism against the constitutionally mandated tolerance of Islam and Christianity in India, on the basis that these minority religious traditions are foreign and alien to the majority Hindu culture of India. Much of the sectarian interreligious violence by the Hindu majority against the Muslim and Christian minorities has been fomented by radical groups within the Hindutva movement such as the Vishwa Hindu Parishad (VHP), Rashtriya Swayamsevak Sangh (RSS), Sang Parivar, and Bajrang Dal. Politically, these radical Hindutva groups are aided and abetted by the Bharatiya Janata Party (BJP), which represents the political face of the Hindutva movement in the corridors of power at state and federal levels (Bhatt 2001).

Against this backdrop of rising Hindu nationalism and fanaticism, Hindu-Christian relations are especially tense and confrontational, as Christians are often accused of targeting the low castes, outcastes, and tribal communities for conversion. Specifically, the radical Hindutva groups stand accused of coercing Indian Christians and Indian Muslims to abandon their faith and embrace Hinduism or be killed (Esteves 2005). More ominously, many Hindutva nationalists have increasingly taken issue with Christian missionary outreach among the Dalits, who hail from the untouchable castes of India, especially in Gujarat and Orissa since the 1990s. The world was shocked by the cold-blooded murder of the Australian evangelical missionary Graham Staines and his two young sons Philip and Timothy, who were burnt alive in their station wagon in 1999. Hindutva agitators also perpetrated violence and mayhem against Dalit Christians in Orissa, blaming them for the assassination of the Hindu fundamentalist Swami Lakshmanananda Saraswati, who was assassinated by Maoist insurgents on August 24, 2008. In addition, Hindu nationalists continue to perceive the endeavors of Indian Christians to articulate an indigenized Indian Christianity as deceptions that mask the "foreign" nature of Christianity under Indian clothing (Ghosh 2013). Seen in this vein, the observations of the Indian theologian T. K. John in 1987 are especially prescient and still hold true today:

> The [Hindu] critics see Christianity as an alien and complex power structure that threatens to eventually undermine India's culture, national integrity and its religions. They feel that a religion that is disappearing from its former stronghold is being dumped, like so many unwanted drugs, on the Third World where it has to be nourished, supported and propagated by foreign money, control and power, instead of drawing its strength from the soil. They conclude that even current efforts at inculturation (which meet with so much inside opposition) are subterfuge measures to win over hesitant or unwilling recruits to the Christian fold. They accuse the Christian missionaries of taking undue advantage of the poverty, the illiteracy and ignorance of the vast majority of the people, and for the proof of this they point to the fact that they have altogether withdrawn their "forces" from the more difficult areas like the caste Hindus, the educated and the economically well-off. (1987, 59)

Sri Lanka continues to be splintered along racial-ethnic and religious fault lines: Sinhalese versus Tamil, Buddhist versus Hindu, and Buddhist versus Christian. The horrors of the long-running internecine strife between the majority Sinhalese and minority Tamil communities have resulted in extremely poisoned relations between these two ethnic communities. It does not help that most Sinhalese are Buddhists, whereas the Tamils are mainly Hindus or Christians, and Sinhalese nationalists have often wrapped their inflammatory political rhetoric in the garments of Buddhist religious pride (Deegalle 2006; Senanayake 2009; Grant 2009). Outright civil war between the Tamils and Sinhalese erupted over "Black July" with anti-Tamil ethnic cleansing riots by the Sinhalese majority that began on July 23, 1983. From 1983 until the military defeat of the Liberation Tigers of Tamil Eelam (LTTE) in 2009, hundreds of thousands died and many more Tamils fled Sri Lanka as refugees. The use of Buddhist religious rhetoric by nationalist political parties such as the Jathika Hela Urumaya (National Sinhala Heritage) Party to legitimize the civil war against the Tamil minority in Sri Lanka has also poisoned peaceful interreligious relations between the Sinhalese and the Tamils (Tambiah 1992; Hayward 2011). Significantly, the Jathika Hela Urumaya was led by Sinhalese Buddhist monks who entered politics in 2004 on a Sinhalese Buddhist nationalist platform, promoting violence and war to drive the Tamil minority out of Sri Lanka (Bartholomeusz 2002).

There have been attempts by the Sinhalese Buddhist majority to initiate interreligious engagements to bring about peace, reconciliation, and healing across racial-ethnic and religious boundaries. For example, the Sinhalese Buddhist activist A. T. Ariyaratne, who founded the Sarvodaya Shramadana Movement to improve the lives of villagers amidst poverty and civil war, has sponsored peace walks and peace conferences to promote reconciliation between the Sinhalese majority and Tamil minority on the basis of shared values that are common to Buddhism, Hinduism, and Christianity (Ariyaratne 1999). However, similar initiatives by the Christian minority have been viewed as "a sinister plan for pan-Christian domination" (Rasiah 2011, 57). Hence, many overt missionary attempts by Christians in Sri Lanka have been viewed as threatening and subversive by the Buddhist Sinhalese majority.

Buddhism has gained a new vitality in East Asia, as new Buddhist movements that first emerged in the early twentieth century blossomed in the decades after the Second World War. For example, the charismatic Daisaku Ikeda (b. 1928) has transformed the

Soka Gakkai Buddhist movement from a small Japanese lay sect of Nichiren Buddhism into a global Buddhist organization with more than 12 million members in over 190 countries worldwide (Seager 2006). Established in 1967 by the Taiwanese Buddhist Dharma Master, the Venerable Hsing Yun (b. 1927), the Fo Guang Shan monastic order is the largest Chinese Mahayana Buddhist organization in the world, with temples, monasteries, schools, and universities in 173 countries across five continents. The Venerable Hsing Yun is one of the main proponents of Humanistic Buddhism, which seeks to integrate Buddhist spirituality with daily ethical living, as well as to work for positive social change in this present world (Chandler 2004). Mention must be made of the well-known international Buddhist relief organization, the Tzu Chi Foundation that was established in 1966 by the Buddhist nun and dharma master, the Venerable Cheng Yen (b. 1937), who is often regarded as the Buddhist counterpart to Mother Teresa (Y. Ching 1995).

The Dilemma and Challenges of Religious Pluralism

This picture of revitalized and flourishing world religions, which is contrary to the expectations of the delegates at Edinburgh 1910 as well as many Christian missionaries and missiologists, clearly shows that religious pluralism will remain an enduring feature of our contemporary world. In reality, religious pluralism is as old as human history. In the course of its two-thousand-year-old history, Christianity has encountered a diversity of peoples, cultures, and religions, beginning with the Jewish and Hellenistic cultures before moving into Roman, Germanic, Celtic, Gallic, and other European cultures from the fourth century onward. In Europe and the Americas, the quandary posed by religious pluralism was resolved by Christianity's becoming the dominant religion and culture. Backed by the full might of imperial power within a church-state alliance, the church in Europe overcame pagan religions and institutions to christianize the Europe of Late Antiquity, leading to the emergence of Christendom in Europe. The missiologist David Bosch (1929–1992)

described this development and its missiological implications succinctly as follows:

> The issue of the attitude Christians and Christian missions
> should adopt to [adherents of] other faiths is, of course, an
> ancient one, with roots in the Old Testament. For many
> centuries, however, this was hardly ever debated. Emperor
> Theodosius' decrees of 380 (which demanded that all citi-
> zens of the Roman Empire be Christians) and 391 (which
> proscribed all non-Christian cults), inexorably paved the
> way for Pope Boniface's bull, *Unam Sanctam* (1302), which
> proclaimed that the Catholic Church was the only institu-
> tion guaranteeing salvation; for the Council of Florence
> (1442), which assigned to the everlasting fire of hell every-
> one not attached to the Catholic Church. (1991, 474)

Bosch explained that the "unshaken, massive, and collective
certitude of the Middle Ages, which existed until the eighteenth
century," perceived the task of Christian mission as that of "conquest and displacement." In other words, "Christianity was understood to be unique, exclusive, superior, definitive, normative and
absolute, the only religion which had the divine right to exist
and extend itself" (Bosch 1991, 475). For him, with the collapse
of Western colonialism, Christianity "lost its hegemony" everywhere and "today has to compete for allegiance on the open
market of religions and ideologies," such that "there are no longer
oceans separating Christians from other religionists" (1991, 475).
On this basis, he contended that "there can be little doubt that
the two largest unsolved problems for the Christian church are its
relationship (1) to *world views which offer this-worldly salvation*, and
(2) to *other faiths*" (1991, 476–77). Clearly, Bosch's nuanced observation on the "two largest unsolved problems" of plurireligious
soteriologies points to the fundamental challenge confronting
missiologists and missioners to rethink the difficult task of doing
Christian mission in the diverse and pluralistic Asian world. As
Bosch succinctly framed it, the issue is deceptively simple, but a
solution is exceedingly elusive: How should contemporary missiologists and missioners understand and respond to the diversity

and pluralism of religions and cultures around the world in general, and Asia in particular? How does Christianity continue to be missional in a plurireligious world?

At the official level of Roman Catholicism, the issue of religious pluralism and its theological ramifications rose to prominence after the Second Vatican Council, catching the attention of Popes Paul VI and John Paul II. In his encyclical *Evangelii nuntiandi*, which was written in response to the 1974 Synod of Catholic Bishops on Evangelization in the Modern World, Paul VI expressed his deep suspicions of religious pluralism, asserting the necessity of Jesus Christ for the salvation of humanity and the inadequacy of the soteriological yearnings of other religions:

> Accordingly, even in the face of the most admirable forms of natural religions, the church judges that it is her special function, by virtue of the religion of Jesus Christ which she proclaims in her evangelization, to bring men into contact with God's plan, with his living presence, with his solicitude. In this way she presents to men the mystery of the divine paternity which extends to the human race; in other words, by virtue of our religion a true and living relationship with God is established which other religions cannot achieve even though they seem, as it were, to have their arms raised up towards heaven. (*Evangelii nuntiandi*, art. 53, in Flannery 1982b, 734–35)

Likewise, John Paul II echoed Paul VI on Christ as the fulfillment of the soteriological yearnings of all religions, when he made the following statement in his apostolic exhortation *Tertio millennio adveniente*:

> Jesus does not . . . merely speak "in the name of God" like the prophets, but he is God himself speaking in his eternal Word made flesh. Here we touch upon *the essential point by which Christianity differs from all the other religions*, by which *the human search for God* has been expressed from earliest times. Christianity has its starting-point in the incarnation of the Word. Here, it is not simply a case of a human

search for God, but of God who comes in person to speak to human beings of himself and to show them the path by which he may be reached. . . . *The Incarnate Word is thus the fulfillment of the yearning present in all the religions of human-kind*: this fulfillment is brought about by God himself and transcends all human expectations. It is the mystery of grace. In Christ, religion is no longer a "blind search for God" but the *response of faith* to God who reveals himself. . . . *Christ is thus the fulfillment of the yearning of all the world's religions and, as such, he is their sole and definitive completion.* (*Tertio millennio adveniente*, art. 6, in John Paul II 1994, 404, emphasis added)

By contrast, Bosch adopted a more open attitude toward religious diversity and pluralism in his book *Transforming Mission* (1991) when he disagreed with Karl Barth's pessimistic understanding of humanity and Barth's negative assessment of religions as useless human creations that are to be rejected because God is known *only* through God's self-revelation in Jesus and his Cross.[1] On this issue, Bosch made it clear that he unequivocally repudiated Karl Barth's "definition of religion as unbelief and his view that mission means going into a void" as unacceptable (1991, 484). Instead, Bosch argued that God is already present in the peoples and their diverse religious traditions:

We go expecting to meet the God who has preceded us and has been preparing people within the context of their own cultures and convictions. . . . God has already removed the barriers; his Spirit is constantly at work in ways that pass human understanding. . . . We do not have him in our pocket, so to speak, and do not just "take him" to the others; he accompanies us and also comes toward us. We are not the "haves," the *beati possidentes*, standing

---

[1] Barth's negative and pessimistic view of humanity meant that humanity is condemned to damnation unless humans embrace the Cross of Jesus. In Barth's theological schema, religions are mere human creations and ultimately false and idolatrous because they lead humanity away from the salvific efficacy of the Cross (1956, 743–97).

over against spiritual "have nots," the *massa damnata*. We are all recipients of the same mercy, sharing in the same mystery. We thus approach every other faith and its adherents reverently, taking off our shoes, as the place we are approaching is holy. (1991, 484)

Although Bosch was writing from a Reformed Protestant Christian perspective, a similar perspective has also been articulated by the Roman Catholic missioner Donal Dorr, who asserts that the traditional image of mission as "sending out" may no longer be useful because "it suggests that mission is a one-way activity, taking little or no account of the prior presence and activity of God in the world—in the great world religions, in the primal religions, and in the secular world" (2000, 189).

Stanley J. Samartha

The idea of God's presence in the diverse religions and faith traditions of other peoples that Bosch sketched out was tentative and cautious. The Indian Protestant theologian and Church of South India presbyter, Stanley J. Samartha (1920–2001), proposed an Indian theology of religious pluralism that would place Christ in the midst of the religious pluralism of India. In doing so, Samartha was motivated by his conviction that the claim of Christian uniqueness and exclusivity was "rude, out of place, and theologically arrogant" in the context of India (1991, 82). In response, Samartha argued for a reexamination of Christian exclusivism with the goal of placing Christ in a multireligious society (1993, 104). Specifically, he was unequivocal in his rejection of the exclusivism of classical Protestant theology, viewing it as promoting an unhealthy rivalry and competitive proselytism among the many religions of Asia. Instead, Samartha wanted to make room for Jesus Christ and the gospel message within the context of Hindu religious pluralism, with its understanding of many religions as many paths toward the ultimate truth (1991, 77). For Samartha, truth is an unbounded apophatic mystery that can neither be defined by creedal formulations nor grasped by the rational mind:

This Mystery, the Truth of the Truth (*Satyasya Satyam*) is the transcendent Center that remains always beyond and greater than apprehensions of it even in the sum total of those apprehensions. It is beyond cognitive knowledge (*tarka*) but is open to vision (*dristi*) and intuition (*anubhava*). It is near yet far, knowable yet unknowable, intimate yet ultimate and, according to one particular Hindu view, cannot even be described as "one." It is "not-two" (*advaita*), indicating thereby that diversity is within the heart of Being itself and therefore may be intrinsic to human nature as well. (1993, 110–11)

More specifically, Samartha proposed a "relational distinctiveness" of Jesus Christ as an alternative to the "normative exclusiveness" of Christ:

It is *relational* because Christ does not remain unrelated to neighbors of other faiths, and *distinctive* because without recognizing the distinctiveness of the great religious traditions as different responses to the Mystery of God, no mutual enrichment is possible. (1991, 77)

Hence, "whether it is in the attempts to redefine the goals of life or in the effort to meet human needs in the dust and heat of the plains, wherever two or three Hindus and Christians are gathered together in his name, there one need not doubt the presence of the living Christ in the midst of them" (1980, 146). In this context of meeting in the "dust and heat of the plains" of Asia, Samartha's delightful metaphor of "helicopter christology" versus "bullock-cart christology" is an apt illustration of what he meant by a Christ that is in touch with, and emerges from, the religious realities of Asia in general, and India in particular. For him, a "helicopter christology" describes a christology "from above" that attempts to land on the religiously pluralistic Asian terrain, raising missiological noise and theological dust, making it difficult for Asians to hear and see the descending divinity. By contrast, a "bullock-cart christology" describes a grassroots christology that has its wheels touching the unpaved roads of Asia and moving forward with a steady pace even as the driver falls asleep, a Christ deeply immersed with, and arising from, the plurireligious reality of Asia (1991, 115–16).

Clearly, Samartha's expansive understanding of religious pluralism that placed the Christian gospel as one of many paths toward the ultimate truth and recognized other saviors such as Krishna, Rama, and the Buddha in addition to Jesus (1991, 125) is designed to appeal to his Indian Hindu interlocutors. Nevertheless, many theologians and missiologists are troubled by Samartha's understanding of religious pluralism and his apparent relativization of traditional Christian soteriology. As far as they are concerned, his apparent abandonment of the soteriological uniqueness of Christ and his gospel when he placed Christianity on par with other religions and Jesus together with the savior figures of the world's religions raised more questions for christology and missiology than answers.

Raimon Panikkar

Samartha's counterpart among Roman Catholic theologians who felt most at home in the midst of religious pluralism was Raimon Panikkar (1918–2010), who lived and did theology in the interstices between the Roman Catholicism of his Spanish mother and the Hinduism of his Indian father. Panikkar was convinced that "no religion, ideology, culture, or tradition can reasonably claim to exhaust the universal range of human experience or even the total manifestation of the Sacred" (1999, 106). Taking this conviction as his starting point, he sought to make the case that "*pluralism*, as distinct from the mere coexistence of a *plurality* of worldviews, becomes today the paramount human and religious imperative" (1999, 106). As far as he was concerned, pluralism is "more than a *de facto* recognition that there are different religious traditions and the acknowledgement that the only way of peaceful coexistence is mutual tolerance," but rather, it "belongs to a *de jure* status of the human condition" (1991, 256–57). He insisted that pluralism "does not mean plurality or a reduction of plurality to unity" (1987, 109). Instead, pluralism "accepts the irreconcilable aspects of religions without being blind to their common aspects"

(1987, 109), because pluralism "belongs to the order of existence and not of essence" (1995, 34). Responding to those of his critics who accused him of being a relativist, Panikkar asserted that pluralism is not identical with relativism:

> Pluralism does not amount to relativism. It does not invalidate the fact that a religion can interpret itself as being of a unique and even superior value, but it will not need to degrade the other religions to be "less unique" and of an inferior order. It will simply say that religions are incomparable since they cannot be compared from a supra-religious point of view. (1991, 273)

On this basis, Panikkar argued against a "single yardstick to measure the merits or demerits of all religions as if this yardstick were recognized by all and were so neutral as to lie outside any religious tradition" (1984, 101). For Panikkar, "truth itself is pluralistic, not plural" (1997, 114; cf. 1991, 273; 1984, 111–12) because "the ideal is not total unity of ultimately one religion or one truth. The real world is one of variety and complexity that does not exclude harmony. Uniformity is not the ideal; monism is wrong. Pluralism penetrates into the very heart of the ultimate reality" (1984, 110). He proposed interreligious dialogue as the answer to the challenges of religious pluralism: "theologies or simply religious reflections can no longer function in isolation from one another and they have to learn from a reciprocally fecundating *dialogical dialogue*. Not a single human problem today can be properly put—let alone solved—if not in a cross-cultural context" (1974, 199).

Jacques Dupuis

Whereas Samartha and Panikkar represented the Protestant and Catholic positions respectively on one end of the theological spectrum with their radical acceptance of religious pluralism as constitutive of human reality, the Belgian Jesuit theologian Jacques Dupuis (1923–2004) was more circumspect and cautious with his theology of "inclusive pluralism" that sought to take the middle road between exclusivism and pluralism. Eschewing Samartha's radical approach, Dupuis's carefully nuanced perspective on religious pluralism was shaped by his close reading of Panikkar (1999) and his own life experiences as a missioner in India, giving him a new perspective that "genuine religion necessarily entails a relationship with the other religions" and leading him to realize that "to be religious is to be interreligious" (1997, 11). This led to his 1997 magnum opus, *Toward a Christian Theology of Religious Pluralism*, as well as his response to his critics in his 1999 essay, "'The Truth Will Set You Free': The Theology of Religious Pluralism Revisited."

In *Toward a Christian Theology of Religious Pluralism*, Dupuis made the case for understanding religious pluralism as going beyond the mere plurality of religions to encompassing a careful discernment of religious pluralism within the divine plan for humanity:

> The question no longer simply consists of asking what role Christianity can assign to the other historical religious traditions but in searching for the root-cause of pluralism itself, for its significance in God's plan for humankind, for the possibility of a mutual convergence of the various traditions in full respect of their differences, and for their mutual enrichment and cross-fertilization. (1997, 11)

Dupuis acknowledged that religious pluralism "is seen as a factor to be reckoned with, rather than welcomed," because it is viewed as one of the causes of "the partial failure of the Christian mission, especially in the vast majority of Asian countries" (1997, 386). He sought to respond to the issue of whether religious pluralism is "merely to be accepted or tolerated as a reality *de facto*," or "on the contrary, be viewed theologically as existing *de jure*" (1997, 386). Taking his starting point from Claude Geffré's influential essays "La singularité du Christianisme à l'âge du pluralisme religieux" (1993) and "Le pluralisme religieux comme question théologique" (1998), as well as Raimon Panikkar's *The Intrareligious Dialogue* (1999), Dupuis presented his case for a wholesale change in our understanding of the implications of religious pluralism. For Dupuis, the model of religious pluralism searches more deeply, in the light of Christian faith, for the meaning in God's design for humankind of the plurality of living faiths and religious traditions with which we are surrounded. Are all the religious traditions of the world destined, in God's plan, to converge? Where, when, and how? (1997, 10)

In his own response to religious pluralism, Dupuis perceived religious pluralism not as a problem to be solved, but rather, as something to be welcomed as part of the Divine Mystery:

Religious pluralism, it is being suggested, has its roots in the depth of the Divine Mystery itself and in the manifold way in which human cultures have responded to the mystery. Far from being a hindrance that must be overcome, or else a fact of life to be tolerated, religious pluralism needs to be welcomed, with thankfulness, as a sign of superabundant riches of the Divine Mystery which overflows to humankind and as an outstanding opportunity for mutual enrichment, "cross-fertilization," and "transformation" between the traditions themselves. (1997, 198)

Dupuis also drew attention to the landmark document of the Pontifical Council for Interreligious Dialogue and the Congregation for the Evangelization of Peoples, *Dialogue and Proclamation: Reflections and Orientations on Interreligious Dialogue and the Proclamation of the Gospel of Jesus Christ* (1991). He explained that this document has an elaborate section on "a Christian approach to religious traditions" (arts. 14–32) and cited what he viewed as a far-reaching paragraph that goes beyond whatever other papal and magisterial documents have enunciated regarding the soteriological efficacy of other religions:

From this mystery of unity it follows that all men and women who are saved, share, though differently, in the same mystery of salvation in Jesus Christ through his Spirit. Christians know this through their faith, while others remain unaware that Jesus Christ is the source of their salvation. The mystery of salvation reaches out to them, in a way known to God, through the invisible action of the Spirit of Christ. Concretely, it will be *in the sincere practice of what is good in their own religious tradition* and by following the dictates of their conscience that the members of other religions respond positively to God's invitation and receive salvation in Jesus Christ, even while they do not recognize or acknowledge him as their Savior. (*Dialogue and Proclamation*, art. 29, in 1997, 127, emphasis added).

Responding to this paragraph, Dupuis was of the opinion that "a door seems to be timidly opened here, for the first time, for the recognition on the part of the Church authority of a 'participated mediation' of religious traditions in the salvation of their members" (1997, 178).

Religious Pluralism at the 1998 Synod of Asian Catholic Bishops

Within the Catholic Church, Dupuis's restrained yet groundbreaking work on religious pluralism was unfairly overshadowed by the cloud of the Congregation for the Doctrine of the Faith (CDF)'s 2001 investigation, which concluded that there are grounds for ambiguities arising from Dupuis's understanding of the relationship between religious pluralism and Jesus Christ, although the CDF did not officially silence him (Burrows 2013). Nonetheless, the missiological implications of his careful theological ruminations on religious pluralism continue to resonate in the Asian context. In particular, the challenges and opportunities posed by religious pluralism for Christian mission in Asia formed the backdrop and context for the Special Assembly of the Synod of Catholic Bishops for Asia ("Asian Synod"). The Asian Synod was first announced in 1995 by Cardinal Jan P. Schotte in response to the call of Pope John Paul II in his apostolic letter *Tertio millennio adveniente* (1994) for, among other things, special synods from different parts of the world to prepare for the coming of the third Christian millennium.

More important, the Asian Synod brought together for the very first time three broad and disparate communities of churches *sui iuris* with their historically unique and ritually distinctive ecclesial traditions, sharing only the adjective "Asian." The first of these three groups were the ancient apostolic churches of West Asia under the aegis of the Council of Catholic Patriarchs of the East (Le Conseil des Patriarches Catholiques d'Orient, or CPCO). The CPCO comprises the communion and patriarchal collegiality of the seven Catholic Patriarchs of West Asia: the Maronite Patriarch of Antioch and all the East for the Maronite Church; the Coptic Catholic Patriarch of Alexandria; the Patriarch of Antioch and all the East, Alexandria, and Jerusalem for the Melkite Greek Catholic Church; the Patriarch of Antioch and all the East for the Syrian Catholic Church; the Patriarch of Babylon for the Chaldean Catholic Church, the Patriarch (*Catholicos*) of Cilicia for the Armenian Catholic Church; and the Latin Patriarch of Jerusalem. The second group consisted of the Syro-Malabar and Syro-Malankara Catholic Churches in India that are heirs to the ancient apostolic "Saint Thomas Christians" of India. The third group encompassed the Roman Catholic episcopal conferences that came into existence throughout Asia in the decades of decolonization and indigenization after the Second World War and who were members of the Federation of Asian Bishops' Conferences (FABC). I explore the FABC and its mission theology in detail in the third chapter of this book.

At the same time, the Asian Synod also enabled bishops across the east-west ecclesial divide and from the four corners of Asia to meet and get to know each other better for the first time in a moment of pan-Asian awakening and awareness (Prior 1998, 657). Never before have Asian bishops from the ancient churches of West Asia that make up the CPCO, as well as the nascent churches of the Central Asian Republics and the local churches of postcolonial East, South, and Southeast Asia that make up the FABC, met and collaborated in a visible sign of ecclesial unity. Although they may come from different social, cultural, and ecclesial backgrounds, the bishops of the CPCO and FABC all share one thing in common: they represent churches that are all minorities in their own milieus, with the exception of the

Philippines and Timor-Leste. Hence, the Asian Synod presented an historic opportunity for the FABC and CPCO to mutually support each other, as well as share and learn from each other's experiences about common concerns, issues, and strategies for being church and witnessing the gospel message in Asia.

The theme of the Asian Synod, "Jesus Christ the Savior, and his mission of love and service in Asia: that they may have life and have it abundantly," reflected the grave concern of the Holy See over the lack of church growth across Asia other than in the Philippines and Timor-Leste. The Asian Synod's introductory document, or *Lineamenta,* provided an overview of the synod's theme and issues for deliberation, as well as invited responses from the Asian bishops to fourteen questions with the aim of provoking reflection on the missionary task and promoting a new evangelization in plurireligious Asia (General Secretariat of the Synod of Bishops 1997; Phan 2002, 13–16). In particular, the *Lineamenta* emphasized that God's salvific design is manifested in Jesus Christ, and therefore "the church in Asia has and wants to proclaim Jesus Christ to her brothers and sisters on the continent so that they may be enriched by the inexhaustible riches of Jesus Christ" (art. 21, in General Secretariat of the Synod of Bishops 1997, 510). It specifically criticized the focus on dialogue instead of proclamation (art. 30, in 1997, 514), insisting:

> The primacy of the proclamation of Jesus Christ in all evangelizing activities has been repeatedly stressed by the council and the magisterium of the church because it is of the essence of the faith and the very continuation of the saving event of Jesus Christ. (Art. 31, in 1997, 514)

In their responses to the *Lineamenta,* many Asian bishops took issue with its negativity toward religious pluralism. For example, while the Catholic Bishops' Conference of India (CBCI) acknowledged that "in union with the Father and the Spirit, Christ is indeed the source and cause of salvation for all peoples," nonetheless they insisted that "this fact does not exclude the possibility of God mysteriously employing other cooperating channels" (art 5.1, in CBCI 1998, 121; Phan 2002, 21). The CBCI also cautioned that the *Lineamenta*'s emphasis on Jesus Christ as the one and only savior should be understood "in a way that takes seriously into account the multicultural and multireligious situations" of the Indian context (art 5.1, in CBCI 1998, 121; Phan 2002, 22). More radically, the CBCI strenuously argued against an exclusivist understanding of salvation and sought to make the case for the soteriological efficacy of other religions.[2]

Echoing their Indian confreres, the Indonesian Catholic bishops were of the opinion that "Jesus does not exclusively belong to Christians, because He is acknowledged and respected by people of other faiths also" (art. 5.3.4, in Indonesian Catholic Bishops 1998, 67). They also agreed with their Indian counterparts' positive attitude toward other religions:

> In pluri-religious societies it is often difficult to directly and explicitly proclaim the central role of Jesus Christ in the economy of salvation. This proclamation must be adapted to concrete life conditions and to the disposition of the hearers. Evangelization ought to start from a "common ground," i.e., belief in the Supreme being as taught by well-respected spiritual leaders and as explicitly stated among the "Five Principles" (Pancasila). (Art. 5.1.5, in Indonesian Catholic Bishops 1998, 64–65)

Going a step further, the Japanese Catholic bishops found a certain "defensiveness" in the *Lineamenta*. They insisted that religious pluralism could instead be a learning experience for

---

[2] Specifically, the CBCI stated, "In the light of the universal salvific will and design of God, so emphatically affirmed in the New Testament witness, the Indian Christological approach seeks to avoid negative and exclusivistic expression. Christ is a Sacrament, a definitive Symbol, of God's salvation for the entire humanity. This is what the salvific uniqueness and universality of Christ means in the Indian context. That, however, does not mean there cannot be other symbols, valid in their own ways, which the Christian sees as related to the definitive Symbol, Jesus Christ. *The implication of all this is that for hundreds of millions of our fellow human beings, salvation is seen as being channeled to them not in spite of but through and in their various socio-cultural and religious traditions. We cannot, then, deny, a priori, a salvific role for these non-Christian religions*" (art. 5.1, in CBCI 1998, 121; Phan 2002, 22, emphasis added)

the church. Moreover, they felt that the *Lineamenta*'s relentless emphasis on the "proclamation of Christ" was counterproductive in the Japanese context. They pointed out the need for collaboration and "creative harmony" in any dialogue between the Christian gospel and other religions in the Japanese context: "In the *Lineamenta* a great deal is made (as in traditional scholastic theology) of 'distinctions' and 'differences.' However, in the tradition of the Far East, it is characteristic to search for creative harmony rather than distinctions" (Japanese Catholic Bishops 1998, 90; Phan 2002, 31).

On the issue of lack of church growth, the Japanese bishops decried the preoccupation with the "number of baptisms" and "a 'success orientation' of 'trying for better results.'" They pointed out that "a vision of evangelization that gives joy and a sense of purpose to a Christian living as one of a minority in the midst of many traditional religions" is needed instead in Japan (Japanese Catholic Bishops 1998, 90; Phan 2002, 31). In addition, the Japanese Catholic Bishops sought support for their argument by appealing to Christianity's experiences with the religious pluralism of the Greco-Roman milieu of its early days and suggesting the necessity of a similar approach for contextualizing the gospel message in the contemporary Japanese milieu:

> Jesus Christ is the Way, the Truth and the Life, but in Asia, before stressing that Jesus Christ is the Truth, we must search much more deeply into how he is the Way and the Life. If we stress too much that "Jesus Christ is the One and Only Savior," we can have no dialogue, common living, or solidarity with other religions. The Church, learning from the *kenosis* of Jesus Christ, should be humble and *open its heart to other religions to deepen its understanding of the Mystery of Christ.* (Japanese Catholic Bishops 1998, 89; Phan 2002, 30, emphasis added)

Hence, the Japanese bishops offered a counterproposal for the evaluation of Christian mission in Asia that acknowledges the "limits felt to the 'Western-type' of missionary activity used up to now," as well as the articulation of an Asian spirituality and inculturation of the Christian gospel in a spirit of dialogue and harmony with other religions (Japanese Catholic Bishops 1998, 91–92).

Likewise, the Sri Lankan Catholic bishops also spoke in favor of the need to situate Jesus and his gospel within the religious pluralism of Sri Lanka.[3] In a similar vein, the Vietnamese Catholic bishops also spoke positively of religious pluralism in the Asian continent and the soteriological efficacy of other religions, insisting that the task of evangelization in Vietnam does not begin on a clean slate, but rather builds on the presence of existing religions whose vitality could help illumine the gospel.[4]

The Asian Synod met in Rome from April 19 to May 14, 1998. According to the Divine Word missioner John Mansford Prior, who has also served as the Vatican-appointed director of the English section of the Asian Synod Press Office, the 191 interventions of the Asian bishops may be categorized as follows:

> Seventy-six percent of the interventions dealt with four Asian topics. At the top of the list comes the mission of the Asian churches to *dialogue with other faith traditions* (43

---

[3] The Sri Lankan Catholic bishops pointed out that Sri Lankan Catholics "live in a multireligious setting in which Jesus Christ is viewed in many different forms: Muslims accept Jesus as a great prophet as he is mentioned in the Koran. Hindus treat him as an avatar, an incarnation of God. Buddhists see him as a social reformer and a great teacher, and for many others he is a great liberator. Generally speaking, there seems to be an awesome respect for Jesus Christ" (Phan 2002, 42–43).

[4] On this issue, the Vietnamese Catholic bishops explain their theological rationale as follows: "The Church in Vietnam believes it must rethink its ways of evangelizing in Asia. The first reason is that this continent is not virgin or fallow soil on which any kind of seed can be sown. Rather, it is a land of very ancient religions and civilizations when compared to Europe. It is a spiritual font of rich and solid ideas about the universe, humanity, and religion. Its peoples are not without knowledge of God. Quite the opposite, they have a certain experience of his presence and invoke him under different names such as 'Sky,' 'Heaven,' 'Brahman,' etc. *Consequently, to 'evangelize,' in this particular case does not mean to present a God, a Christ, as totally unknown, but, in a certain way—to borrow a Buddhist expression—it is to 'make the Light shine more brightly,' present but hidden; it is to help people 'see the Truth illuminated,' which Vatican II recognizes as partially present in other religions, especially those of Asia*" (Phan 2002, 48, emphasis added).

interventions, or 22.5 percent of the total). Second in fre-
quency comes *dialogue with living cultures* by which the
Church becomes truly Asian (41 interventions, or 21.4
percent of the total). At number three comes the *dialogue
of the churches with the poor* (33 interventions, or 17.2 percent). At fourth place, the interventions characterized the
Asian Churches as *churches of the laity* (29 interventions, or
15.2 percent). (Prior 1998, 658)

In the synod proceedings, the vexing issue of religious pluralism in Asia was brought to the forefront by many Asian bishops.
As John Prior observed in his assessment of the bishops' interventions on the synod floor, bishop after bishop spoke eloquently
in support of the FABC's preferred approach of dialogue with
other religions as an Asian Catholic response to the challenges of
religious pluralism. For example, Bishop Paul Nguyen Van Hoa
of Nha Trang, Vietnam, explained that since the majority of the
Asian population belongs to ancient religious and cultural traditions, it was necessary to reflect on interreligious dialogue as
evangelization (Phan 2002, 124; UCAN 1998a). For Cardinal
Peter Seiichi Shirayanagi of Tokyo, religion will touch the lives
of people deeply and answer their deepest longings only when
the dialogues of theological discourse, religious experience, and
life take place (UCAN 1998a). According to Father Alex Ukken,
prior-general of the Carmelites of the Immaculate Virgin Mary,
"The Church will become a powerful moral force in Asia even
as a minority religion, if it enters into interreligious dialogue,
evangelizes cultures, and transforms unjust and inhuman social
and political structures" (UCAN 1998b). Bishop Bunluen Man-
sap of Ubon Ratchathani, Thailand, pointed out the benefits of
Christian-Buddhist interreligious dialogue in Thailand: "I feel
inspired by their simplicity of life, their openness, their humane
relationships, their unassuming ways; these are values I recognize
as values of the Kingdom or the Gospel. . . . Could it be said that
this is the Good News that the Buddhist can offer us?" (Prior
1998, 659; Phan 2002, 121).

The issue of interreligious dialogue took on added urgency
in the context of Christian-Muslim dialogue. As expected, the

Synod Fathers from Islamic countries in Asia were very concerned with the impact of Islam on the Asian Church. Chaldean Archbishop Youssif Thomas of Beirut emphasized the
urgency of genuine interreligious dialogue between Muslims
and Christians to promote peaceful coexistence of Christians
with Muslims and the self-preservation of the Christian minority (UCAN 1998b). In the same vein, Bishop Joseph Coutts
of Hyderabad, Pakistan, brought the synod's attention to the
challenges arising from the increasing militancy and intolerance
of many in Islam toward minority Christian communities in
Islamic countries (UCAN 1998b). Bishop Leo Laba Ladjar OFM
of Jayapura, Indonesia, suggested that the Christian minority in
Indonesia should not only accept their minority status but also
move beyond confrontation to find ways of coexisting peacefully
and harmoniously with the Muslim majority (Prior 1998, 659).

Relating religious pluralism to the task of doing Christian
mission in Asia, many Synod Fathers argued that there must be
authentic witnessing that would embed the gospel in people's
life experiences as the starting point, rather than in the abstract
and intellectual proclamation of doctrines and norms of orthodoxy. Bishop Leo Laba Ladjar of Jayapura, Indonesia, argued
that such an aggressive "superior attitude" has "long humiliated
the Muslim majority" (UCAN 1998c). Archbishop Ignatius
Suharyo Hardjoatmodjo of Semarang, Indonesia, informed the
synod that in doing Christian mission in Asia, "we do not start
with the Church, which is often mistakenly identified with the
great display of institutions, but with what the Spirit is doing
in people, religions and cultures" of Asia (UCAN 1998c).[5]

---

[5] Arguing along similar lines, the Syro-Malabar Bishop Gratian Munda-
ban of Bijnur, India, explained, "In the religious ethos of Asia mere doctrinal, legal and institutional power does not have any appeal. Further, the
image projected by the Church of power, riches, institutional, influential, is
looked upon as a threat" (Prior 1998, 663; Phan 2002, 111). According to
Archbishop Johannes Liku Ada of Ujung Pandang, Indonesia, mission and
evangelization in the Asian context meant the ability to unearth what is
true, good, and beautiful in the Asian religions, "even the Spirit at work in
them" (UCAN 1998c). Such sentiments were also voiced by Bishop Augustine Jun-ichi Nomura of Nagoya, Japan: "In Japan, like the rest of Asia, the
eyes have a more central role than the ears in the process of insight and

In his apostolic exhortation *Ecclesia in Asia* marking the conclusion of the Asian Synod, Pope John Paul II responded to the Asian bishops' concerns by reiterating the uniqueness and universality of Jesus Christ for human salvation (*Ecclesia in Asia* 14, in Phan 2002, 298). The pope asserted that Asians find the fulfillment of their existential quest in Christ: "Contemplating Jesus in his human nature, the peoples of Asia find their deepest questions answered, their hopes fulfilled, their dignity uplifted and their despair conquered" (*Ecclesia in Asia* 14, in Phan 2002, 299). He also insisted, "The question is not whether the Church has something essential to say to the men and women of our time, but how she can say it clearly and convincingly" (*Ecclesia in Asia* 29, in Phan 2002, 313).

At the same time, the Asian Catholic bishops continued to push the case for a rethinking of the relationship between Christianity and other religions at the Asian Synod and beyond. This is not surprising, because John Paul II viewed the challenges of religious pluralism from his own European experiences, witnessing the majority position of European Christianity and the historical dominance of Christendom in Europe being diluted and eroded by the religious pluralism that came to Europe with the arrival of migrants, refugees, and asylum seekers. By contrast, Asian Christians with few exceptions never enjoyed the privileges of being in the majority religious community. On the contrary, most Asian Christians have always struggled as *pusillus grex*, the "little flock" in the sea of Asian plurireligiosity.

Contemporary Asian Theological Responses to Religious Pluralism

From our discussion so far, it is clear that a renewed theology of mission in Asia would have to rethink the relationship between Christianity and the great religious traditions of Asia and critically consider the implications for doing Christian mission in Asia. Without a doubt, Asian Christians cannot escape the reality

conversion. . . . [The Asian peoples] are convinced more by witnessing than by teaching, and . . . they appreciate the contemplative dimension, detachment, humility, simplicity and silence" (UCAN 1998c).

that they are being challenged to reformulate their understanding of the relationship between Christianity and the resurgent world religions amid the *fact* and *reality* that religious pluralism is here to stay in postcolonial Asia. How should Asian Christians respond to the challenges and opportunities of religious pluralism related to the task of doing Christian mission in Asia?

Hwa Yung

In his seminal work titled *Mangoes or Bananas: The Quest for an Authentic Asian Christian Theology* (1997), the Malaysian missiologist and bishop of the Methodist Church in Malaysia from 2004 to 2012, Hwa Yung, asserts that many Asian liberal and evangelical theologians have only superficially engaged with Asian cultures and spiritual worldviews. He views many Asian Christian liberal and evangelical theologies as more akin to bananas rather than mangoes. As he explains, a banana is yellow on the outside (superficially Asian) but white on the inside (Western or European). For him, the mango with its yellow flesh is the quintessential Asian fruit, representing an authentic Asian theology that is deeply rooted in the Asian context and worldview. To break free from being captive to Western theological methods, concerns, and presuppositions, Hwa Yung proposes that an emerging Asian Christian theology ought to be both missiological and contextual in orientation. He outlines the following four criteria for shaping an authentic Asian Christian theology: (1) the ability to address the diverse sociopolitical Asian contexts in which Asian Christians find themselves; (2) the empowerment they bring to the evangelistic and pastoral tasks of the Asian churches; (3) the ability to facilitate the inculturation of the Christian gospel in the Asian milieu, and (4) faithfulness to the Christian tradition.

On the one hand, it is true that Hwa Yung himself does not provide his own constructive Asian theology beyond challenging existing liberal and evangelical Asian theologians for their dependence on Western theological methods. On the other hand, his call to cultivate a "mango" theology and his fourfold criteria for developing an authentic Asian theology are useful starting points for defining the missiological orientation of an Asian Christianity that takes seriously the vitality and deep sapiential insights of Asian religious traditions, while remaining faithful to its foundational roots in the Christian gospel. Moving beyond this starting point, we now turn to the writings of the next two theologians who are working from the Roman Catholic and Pentecostal perspectives, respectively, Peter C. Phan and Amos Yong.

Peter C. Phan

Peter C. Phan does not mince his words when he states that "it is in Asia that the question of religious pluralism is literally a matter of life and death" and "the future of Asian Christianity hangs in [the] balance depending on how religious pluralism is understood and lived out" (Phan 2003, 117). As he puts it bluntly, Asian Christians have to "take their Asianness seriously as the context of their being Christian" (Phan 2000, 218). Although he acknowledges that Asian Christians "must of course proclaim and live the Christian faith, the same faith handed down the ages," nonetheless, they "should do so in the modalities conceived and born from within the Asian context" so that "the Churches *in* Asia become truly *of* Asia" (2000, 219). As far as he is concerned, the Asian church leadership, including missioners, must focus on "how it will respond to the challenges of the Asian social, political, economic and religious contexts and whether and how it will effectively help Christians live their faith in fidelity to the Gospel and the living Christian tradition, here and now, in Asia" (2000, 218). Moreover, Phan further points out in view of the reality that "the report of the demise of Asian religions was premature and vastly exaggerated," and many parts of Asia have witnessed a vigorous revival of Asian religions; therefore, Asian Christians "must come to terms with the fact that they are destined to remain for the foreseeable future a 'small remnant' who must journey with adherents of other religions toward the eschatological Kingdom of God" (2000, 224).

Amos Yong

Working from a Pentecostal perspective, the Chinese American Pentecostal theologian Amos Yong proposes a new way for Christianity to relate to other world religions that is biblically rooted, which he articulated in his plenary paper presented to the American Society of Missiology in June 2006: "The Spirit of Hospitality: Pentecostal Perspectives toward a Performative Theology of Interreligious Encounter." Although Yong's main focus is Asian Pentecostal Christianity's response to the workings of the Holy Spirit outside of institutional Christianity, I would like to submit that his insights have broader implications for all Christians in general, and Asian Christians in particular. Specifically, Yong argues for the retrieval of the forgotten universalism of the Luke-Acts narratives of the outpouring of the Holy Spirit "on all flesh" (Acts 2:17). First, Yong explains that Luke-Acts presents a universal vision of the church and the Reign of God that goes beyond the Jewish self-understanding of a faith centered in Jerusalem. Second, he asserts that given "the interconnections between language and culture, the Pentecost narrative both celebrates the divine affirmation of many tongues, and announces the divine embrace of the many cultures of the world." Third, he argues that the "interrelatedness between language, culture, and religion" leads to the constructive theological argument that "the Pentecost narrative can be understood to hold forth the possibility of the redemption of the diversity of religions." At the same time, he also acknowledges that "languages, cultures, and the religions need to be discerned, and their demonic elements need to be confronted and purified so that if there is any truth, goodness, or beauty in them, such may be redeemed" (Yong 2007, 58–59).

When Asian Christians reflect on the social context of their daily life experiences as Hwa Yung and Peter Phan both suggest, they realize that, with the exception of the Philippines or Timor-Leste, they are not living in a world where Christianity is the dominant force that influences and shapes culture, ethics, politics, and society. Rather, they realize that the other religions define and dominate the social landscape in their homelands, with Christians being the "little flock" amid the overwhelming number of other religious practitioners. Indeed, Asian Christians have the daily experience of being very much at home in the pluralistic religious Asian milieu, having been born into and living within this religious diversity and pluralism. Moreover, many Asian Christians themselves come from a "mixed" religious background, with extended family members following a variety of religious traditions. They live and interact on a daily basis with their family members, relatives, friends, and neighbors from other religious traditions, sharing with them the joys and sufferings as well as blessings and misfortunes of daily living.

Although many European and North American theologians and church leaders wax lyrical about the practice and achievements of interfaith dialogue in Europe and North America, where the other great religions of the world are often viewed as the minority and the exotic "Other" vis-à-vis the dominant Christianity, Asian Christians live permanently amid the practitioners of these great religions. And although theologians and church leaders in Europe and North America may invite representatives of these other religions to meet occasionally for dialogue and conversation, Asian Christians engage in a daily dialogue of life witness with their fellow Asian neighbors who are followers of the great religious traditions of Asia.

At the same time, one must also acknowledge the reality that Asian Christians' interactions with their fellow Asians who are adherents of other religious traditions are not always harmonious and peaceful. Although Asia is often spoken of as the birthplace of the great religions of the world, including Christianity, many of these world religions are experiencing a resurgence of pride and exclusivist chauvinism in many parts of Asia. Thus, Asian Christians also have firsthand experiences of fanatics and fundamentalists who reject the long history of religious diversity and pluralism in Asia, seeking to impose their vision as normative through coercion and violence. As we have read in this chapter, the unwarranted pressure on Indian Christians to renounce Christianity, the simmering Muslim-Christian conflicts in Pakistan and elsewhere, Hindu violence against Christians in India, and restrictions placed on Christians' freedom of association are imprinted in the consciousness of these Asian Christians.

If Asian Christians should take their Asianness seriously for the sake of their faith, as Peter Phan suggests, then Asian Christians need to acknowledge that the Asian context of religious pluralism is not a dilemma to be eradicated, but a distinctive characteristic of being Asian and Christian. Ironically, without diversity and pluralism, there is no room for the Christian gospel in Asia amid the dominance of the great Asian religions. Asian Christians know very well that unless they defend religious diversity and pluralism against exclusivist religious chauvinism, there will be no room at all for Christianity in a continent dominated by the other great religions of the world. In reality, because Asian Christianity will never dominate Asia to the exclusion and extinction of other religions in the manner of medieval Christendom in Europe, it has to become truly immersed and rooted in the Asian milieu for its survival and growth, as Peter Phan rightly notes.

Having reviewed the sociocultural, political, and religious dimensions of contemporary postcolonial Asia, we see that the issue is deceptively simple, but a solution is exceedingly elusive: How should Asian Christians as minority communities respond to and engage with the resurgence and renewed vitality of other religious majorities in postcolonial Asia? In the next chapter, I examine the methodology and theological implications of the mission theology of the FABC, as one example of a distinctively Asian approach to the witness and proclamation of the gospel that is sensitive to such religious diversity and pluralism. I critically study how the Asian Catholic Bishops of the FABC deal with the complexities of religious pluralism and its challenges for Christian mission.

Chapter 3

The Mission Theology
of the Federation
# of Asian Bishops' Conferences

In chapter 2, we saw that the greatest challenge to the task of doing Christian mission in Asia is the question of the religious diversity and pluralism of the Asian milieu and its peoples. In this chapter, I discuss how the Federation of Asian Bishops' Conferences (FABC) has articulated an Asian theology of Christian mission that seeks to respond to the challenges of diversity and pluralism in Asia, with its myriad religions, cultures, and peoples. The FABC has proceeded on the basis that the Asian milieu, with its rich diversity and pluralism of religions, cultures, and philosophical worldviews, requires a distinctively Asian approach to the proclamation of the gospel that is sensitive to such diversity and pluralism. I examine the principal aspects of the FABC's theology of mission and analyze their implications for the task of doing Christian mission in plurireligious Asia.

The Birth of the FABC

The FABC is a transnational body comprising fifteen Asian Catholic bishops' conferences as full members: those of Bangladesh, India, Indonesia, Japan, Kazakhstan, Korea, Laos-Cambodia, Malaysia-Singapore-Brunei, Myanmar, Pakistan, the Philippines, Sri Lanka, Taiwan, Thailand, and Vietnam. The FABC also has ten associate members: Hong Kong, Kyrgyzstan, Macau, Mongolia, Nepal, Siberia, Tajikistan, Turkmenistan, Uzbekistan, and

Timor-Leste. The foundation for the FABC was laid at a historic meeting of 180 Asian Catholic bishops in Manila during the visit of Pope Paul VI to the Philippines in November 1970. Commenting on that groundbreaking event, the Indian theologian Felix Wilfred notes:

> Never before had Asian bishops come together to exchange experiences and to deliberate jointly on common questions and problems facing the continent. The meeting marked the beginning of a new consciousness of the many traditional links that united the various peoples of this region of the globe. (Wilfred 1992, xxiii)

Looking back at the 1970 meeting, we see that the FABC has made a significant impact on the development, orientation, and growth of the spiritual and theological life of the Catholic Church in Asia since its inception (Wilfred 1992; Bevans 1996; Fox 2002; Chia 2003). Wilfred acknowledges that "the FABC has created horizontal communication between the bishops and the bishops' conferences; it has fostered a spirit of collegiality, communion and cooperation among them" (Wilfred 1992, xxix). In a similar vein, the missiologist Stephen Bevans has observed that "the FABC could look back on twenty-five years of activity which had yielded an impressive body of documents that are incredibly rich, amazingly visionary, and truly worth careful reading and study" (Bevans 1996, 2). Since Bevans penned these thoughts in 1996, this "impressive body of documents" has multiplied to fill four volumes (Rosales and Arévalo 1992; Eilers 1997, 2002, and 2007), making a significant contribution to the development and growth of the spiritual and theological life of Asian Catholics.

The FABC convenes once every four years in plenary assembly, the highest body, with the participation of all presidents and delegates of member conferences.[1] In addition to these plenary

---

[1] To date, ten plenary assemblies have been held: FABC I: Evangelization in Modern Day Asia (Taipei, 1974); FABC II: Prayer—The Life of the Church in Asia (Calcutta, 1978); FABC III: The Church—A Community of Faith in Asia (Bangkok, 1982); FABC IV: The Vocation and Mission of the Laity in the Church and in the World of Asia (Tokyo, 1986); FABC V: Jour-

assemblies, the FABC has also sought to make a significant contribution to the development and growth of the spiritual and theological life of Asian Catholics through its various bishops' institutes[2] and programs organized by its offices.[3] More recently, the FABC has sponsored a series of workshops called the Faith Encounters in Social Action (FEISA), which seek to promote interreligious dialogue through social involvement, emphasizing that the Asian church needs to ground its mission and outreach in a threefold dialogue with the Asian peoples within their cultures, religious traditions, as well as poverty and other life struggles.

More noteworthy is the fact that the FABC maintains good working relations with Asian theologians through its Office of Theological Concerns, which comprises bishop theologians who hold leadership positions and lay theologians specifically appointed by bishops' conferences to collaborate with the bishop theologians to produce important studies, position statements, and other documents for use by the wider FABC constituencies. All of these statements and documents have different levels of theological authority, the most authoritative of which would be the Final Statements of the FABC Plenary Assemblies, followed by the documents of the Bishops' Institutes, and other regional or national meetings (Quatra 2000, 23–24). Miguel Marcelo Quatra suggests that the documents of the FABC offices, for example,

---

neying Together toward the Third Millennium (Bandung, 1990); FABC VI: Christian Discipleship in Asia Today: Service to Life (Manila, 1995); FABC VII: A Renewed Church in Asia on a Mission of Love and Service (Samphran, Thailand, 2000); FABC VIII: The Asian Family towards a Culture of Integral Life (Daejeon, South Korea, 2004); FABC IX: Living the Eucharist in Asia (Manila, 2009); and FABC X: FABC at Forty: Responding to the Challenges of Asia (Xuan Loc, Vietnam, 2012).

[2] These bishops' institutes include the Bishops' Institutes on Lay Apostolate (BILA), Missionary Apostolate (BIMA), Interreligious Affairs (BIRA), Social Action (BISA), and Social Communication (BISCOM).

[3] The FABC's many programs are organized by ten specialized offices: FABC Central Secretariat, Office of Human Development, Office of Social Communication, Office of Laity and Family, Office of Education and Faith Formation, Office of Ecumenical and Interreligious Affairs, Office of Evangelization, Office of Clergy, Office of Consecrated Life, and Office of Theological Concerns (formerly the FABC Theological Advisory Commission).

the Office of Theological Concerns (formerly the Theological Advisory Commission) "enjoy an authority that might be called reflected, from the fact that it is an accredited instance of the Federation and of the Bishops' Conferences that chose its members" (Quatra 2000, 24).

In this chapter, all relevant FABC documents will be examined synchronically as an organic whole, on the basis that taken together these documents could give a clearer view of the FABC's approach to the task of Christian mission in Asia. Domenico Colombo explains that although the documents of the various FABC Offices and Bishops' Institutes "do not have the same authority of the Assemblies and are an indirect expression of the FABC," nonetheless "they constitute the mechanism by which the lines of reflection and action offered to the Federation and the Assemblies are in fact drawn up and tried. In reality it is they that blaze the trail and move things forward in various directions" (Colombo 1997, 14; English translation taken from Quatra 2000, 24). Colombo further adds:

> The itinerary of the big Assemblies is interwoven with the activities of the Offices, without which they would remain only an ideal and abstract journey. . . . The texts of the various Institutes correspond to as many paths that wind through the sectors vital for the reflection and praxis of the Church in Asia. They intersect, flow into each other and receive their thrust from the plenary sessions. It is indispensable to know them in order to understand where the FABC is going and how it moves. (Colombo 1997, 18; English translation taken from Quatra 2000, 24)

In its official documents, the FABC has proceeded on the basis that the Asian continent, with its teeming masses and their rich diversity and pluralism of religions, cultures, and philosophical worldviews requires a distinctively Asian approach to doing Christian mission in Asia. This distinctive Asian approach is needed in order to counteract the prejudicial stereotype, however unfair, that Christianity and the church are foreign to the Asian religious landscape, notwithstanding the fact that Jesus was born and died in West Asia. The FABC *Theological Consultation* of 1991 explains the dilemma facing the Asian Catholic Bishops as follows:

> As a social institution the Church is perceived as a foreign body in its colonial origins while other world religions are not. The lingering colonial image survives in its traditional ecclesiastical structures and economic dependence on the west. . . . The Church is even sometimes seen as an obstacle or threat to national integration and to religious and cultural identity. (*Theological Consultation*, art. 13, in Rosales and Arévalo 1992, 337)

I contend that the FABC's mission theology for Asia may be best understood according to the following fivefold missiological framework. First, mission embraces the immense diversity and pluralism of Asia, recognizing that such diversity and pluralism lie at the heart of what it means to be Asian. Second, mission is rooted in a commitment and service to life in pluralistic Asia. Third, in recognition that many parts of contemporary Asia are being torn apart by hatred and violence, mission seeks to promote a vision of harmony among Asians across religious, ethnic-cultural, and socioeconomic classes. Fourth, mission is oriented toward a threefold dialogue with the cultures, religions, and poor of Asia. Fifth, mission seeks to bring about the Reign of God in Asia.

The Challenges of Pluralism in the Asian Milieu

The FABC's theology of Christian mission is rooted in its incarnational ecclesiology, articulated at its inaugural plenary assembly, which met in 1974 on the theme "Evangelization in Modern Day Asia." This assembly spoke of the local church as "the realization and enfleshment of the Body of Christ in a given people, a given place and time" (FABC I, art. 10, in Rosales and Arévalo 1992, 14) that is "incarnate in a people, a church indigenous and inculturated" (FABC I, art. 12, in Rosales and Arévalo 1992, 14). In turn, this incarnational ecclesiology provides the foundation for an incarnational theology of Christian mission that embraces the immense diversity and pluralism of the Asian milieu, recognizing that such diversity and pluralism lie at the heart of what it means to be Asian.

Thus, at the Asian bishops' meeting with Pope Paul VI in Manila (1970), the bishops acknowledged that Asia is "a continent of ancient and diverse cultures, religions, histories and traditions, a region like Joseph's coat of many colors" (ABM, art. 7, in Rosales and Arévalo 1992, 4; see also FABC II, art. 7, in Rosales and Arévalo 1992, 30). Four years later, the First FABC Plenary Assembly that gathered in Taipei in 1974 recognized that the great religious traditions of Asia are

> significant and positive elements in the economy of God's design and salvation. In them we recognize and respect profound spiritual and ethical meanings and values. Over many centuries they have been the treasury of the religious experience of our ancestors, from which our contemporaries do not cease to draw light and strength. They have been (and continue to be) the authentic expression of the noblest longings of their hearts, and the home of their contemplation and prayer. They have helped to give shape to the histories and cultures of our nations. (FABC I, art. 14, in Rosales and Arévalo 1992, 14)

One year after the conclusion of FABC I, the second FABC Bishops' Institute on Social Action (BISA II) articulated, among other things, the following statement on pluralism that would undergird subsequent discussions on pluralism in the various FABC plenary assemblies and FABC bishops' institutes:

> Pluralism is a necessity once we work through the mediation of secular analysis and worldviews. This pluralism should not be a threat to our Christian unity, but on the contrary, a positive and creative sign that our unity is deeper than whatever the concrete technical analysis or viewpoints might show: a genuine value that emphasizes unity in diversity. (BISA II, art. 10, in Rosales and Arévalo 1992, 204)

Indeed, the FABC perceives diversity and pluralism as a source of richness and strength rather than something negative that has to be eradicated:

> Peace and harmony in Asian societies, composed as they are of many cultural, ethnic and linguistic groups, would require recognition of legitimate pluralism and respect for all the groups. Unity, peace and harmony are to be realized in diversity. (BIRA [Bishops' Institutes for Interreligious Affairs] IV/11, art. 15, in Rosales and Arévalo 1992, 321)

As far as the FABC is concerned, diversity and plurality are not to be gotten rid of, but "rejoiced over and promoted" (BIRA IV/11, art. 15, in Rosales and Arévalo 1992, 321). In this regard, the Theological Advisory Commission of the FABC unpacks the FABC's understanding of dialogue in its landmark 1987 document, *Theses on Interreligious Dialogue,* as follows:

> In the course of the last two thousand years the Church has encountered and dialogued with various peoples, cultures and religions, with varying levels of success. Today, however, especially in Asia, in the context of the Great Religions, which are in a process of revival and renewal, the Church is aware of a markedly different situation. We do not ask any longer about the relationship of the Church to other cultures and religions. We are rather searching for the place and role of the Church in a religiously and culturally pluralistic world. (*Theses on Interreligious Dialogue*, art. 0.8, in FABC 1987, 3)

On this basis, the Indian theologian Lorenzo Fernando is able to conclude that from its inception, the FABC has eschewed all forms of religious exclusivism, perceiving religious pluralism as an innate and unique aspect of the Asian socioreligious landscape (Fernando 2000, 864–69).

Significantly, the FABC has built on two important insights on the Holy Spirit that were articulated by the Second Vatican

Council. In the Decree on Missionary Activity, *Ad Gentes*, the Council Fathers noted, "Doubtless, the Holy Spirit was already at work in the world before Christ was glorified" (*AG* 4, in Abbott 1966, 587). This point was expanded in the Pastoral Constitution on the Church in the Modern World, *Gaudium et Spes,* to encompass the Holy Spirit's offering the possibility of salvation for all of humanity:

> For since Christ died for all men, and since the ultimate vocation of man is in fact one, and divine, we ought to believe that the Holy Spirit in a manner known only to God offers to every man the possibility of being associated with this paschal mystery. (*GS* 22, in Abbott 1966, 221–22)

Building on these two important theological insights from Vatican II, the Asian bishops assert that "it is an inescapable truth that God's Spirit is at work in all religious traditions" (BIRA IV/12, art. 7, in Rosales and Arévalo 1992, 326) because

> it has been recognized since the time of the apostolic Church, and stated clearly again by the Second Vatican Council, that the Spirit of Christ is active outside the bounds of the visible Church. God's saving grace is not limited to members of the Church, but is offered to every person. His grace may lead some to accept baptism and enter the Church, but it cannot be presumed that this must always be the case. His ways are mysterious and unfathomable, and no one can dictate the direction of His grace. (BIRA II, art. 12, in Rosales and Arévalo 1992, 115; cf. BIRA IV/1, art. 10, in Rosales and Arévalo 1992, 249).

In other words, building upon *Gaudium et Spes* 22 and *Ad Gentes* 4, the FABC perceives the religious traditions of Asia as "expressions of the presence of God's Word and of the universal action of his Spirit in them" (*Theological Consultation*, art. 43, in Rosales and Arévalo 1992, 344). The Third FABC Plenary Assembly exhorts Asian Christian communities to "listen to the Spirit at work in the many communities of believers who live and experience their own faith, who share and celebrate it in their own social, cultural and religious history," accompanying them "in a common pilgrimage toward the ultimate goal, in relentless quest for the Absolute," and becoming "sensitively attuned to the work of the Spirit in the resounding symphony of Asian communion" (FABC III, art. 8.2, in Rosales and Arévalo 1992, 57).

In particular, the "great religions of Asia with their respective creeds, cults and codes reveal to us diverse ways of responding to God whose Spirit is active in all peoples and cultures" (BIRA IV/7, art. 12, in Rosales and Arévalo 1992, 310). For the FABC, it is "the same spirit, who has been active in the incarnation, life, death and resurrection of Jesus and in the Church, who was active among all peoples before the Incarnation and is active among the nations, religions and peoples of Asia today" (BIRA IV/3, art. 6, in Rosales and Arévalo 1992, 259). On this basis, the FABC speaks of tapping into the movement across Asia "among peoples of various faiths to break down traditional barriers of division and hostility, and their initiative to reach out to neighbors of other faiths in a spirit of love, friendship, harmony and collaboration," and "discern[ing] the hand of God" in "all these aspirations, movements and initiatives" (BIRA IV/11, art. 5, in Rosales and Arévalo 1992, 318–19). As Felix Wilfred observes:

> Any work of mission which does not recognise what God has been doing with a people, with a country and continent and with their history, is simply and purely arrogance vis-à-vis God's own bounteous gifts. . . . Triumphalism and exclusivism of any kind are diametrically opposed to spirituality. They fail to recognise and appreciate the thousand flowers God has let grow, flourish and blossom in the garden of the world; they fail to acknowledge in practice the presence and working of the Spirit in the life and history of peoples. (Wilfred 1990, 590)

In addition, the Final Statement of the 1995 FABC Hindu-Christian Dialogue made it clear that the FABC viewed religious pluralism as constitutive of the Asian reality:

Beyond the extremes of inclusivism and exclusivism, pluralism is accepted in resonance with the constitutive plurality of reality. Religions, as they are manifested in history, are complementary perceptions of the ineffable divine mystery, the God-beyond-God. All religions are visions of the divine mystery. No particular religion can raise the claim of being the norm for all others. We religious believers are co-pilgrims, who share intimate spiritual experiences and reflections with one another with concern and compassion, with genuine openness to truth and the freedom of spiritual seekers (*sadhakas*). In this process we become increasingly sensitive to human suffering and collaborate in promoting justice, peace and ecological wholeness. (BIRA V/3, art. 6, in Eilers 1997, 157–58)

This rejection of any religious exclusivism echoes an earlier statement: "When various religious groups lay absolute claim to truth, aggressive militancy and divisive proselytism follow and, in their wake, bitter religious divisions" (BIRA IV/4, art. 4, in Rosales and Arévalo 1992, 300).

At the same time, the FABC also acknowledges that critics of religious pluralism often raise the specter of unbridled relativism or subjectivism. In *Methodology: Asian Christian Theology, Doing Theology in Asia Today*, the FABC Office of Theological Concerns explains among other things that recognition of religious pluralism does not necessarily lead to an acceptance of subjectivism or relativism:

Pluralism need not always entail a radical subjectivism or relativism, in the sense of claiming that all points of view are equally valid. However, it is also true that the dawn of pluralistic, democratic, modern societies has paved the way to excessive individualism and subjectivism, and a consequent relativizing of all reality. Thus, today there are persons and groups who hold all reality to be relative. For such persons or groups, pluralism means relativism, in the sense that they claim all points of view are equally valid. *Such philosophical or theological positions are to be rejected; and,*

*in fact, all the major Asian religions condemn such relativizing of
reality, especially the relativizing of basic human values.* However, just because certain persons and groups are misled in
their search for truth, and just because they tend to per-
ceive pluralism as relativism, or just because they tend to
relativize all reality, we cannot conclude that all pluralism
leads to relativism. (*Methodology: Asian Christian Theology*,
art. 1.1, in Eilers 2002, 334, emphasis added)

It is clear that the Asian bishops are very much at home with
the diversity and pluralism of the Asian *Sitzen-im-Leben*, eschewing all forms of religious exclusivism, and seeking consistently to
work within the pluralism of the Asian milieu with its diverse
cultures and religions. Not surprisingly, whereas others may
consider the diversity and pluralism of postmodern Europe and
North America as challenges that Christianity has to confront
and overcome, for the Asian bishops, the question rather is how
Asian Christianity can be at home with such diversity and pluralism. This leads us to the next dimension of the FABC's mission
theology: the commitment and service to life in pluralistic Asia.

A Commitment and Service to
Life in Pluralistic Asia

The second aspect of the FABC's theology of Christian mission is its commitment and service to life that arises out of a
holistic view of life together with a traditional sense of reverence
that sees God's Spirit as active in the diverse and pluralistic Asian
milieu. In this regard, one notes that the Final Statement of the
1994 FABC International Theological Colloquium begins simply
with the statement: "Life. Vibrant life pulsating in the fecundity
of Asia" (*Being Church in Asia*, art. 1, in Eilers 1997, 217). Such a
statement aptly describes the panorama of cultural diversity and
religious pluralism in Asia, which comprises a rich and colorful
mosaic of many of the world's ancient religious, philosophical,
and sociocultural traditions. Indeed, this call for service to life
emerges from the theme of the Sixth FABC Plenary Assembly,
which is "Christian Discipleship in Asia Today: Service to Life,"

as well as the first two sections of its Final Statement titled "25 Years of FABC Commitment to Life" and "A Vision of Life amid Asian Realities."[4] The Sixth Plenary Assembly also speaks of the need to "pitch our tents in the midst of all humanity," so as "to immerse ourselves in Asia's cultures of poverty and deprivation, from whose depths the aspirations for love and life are most poignant and compelling," because serving life "demands communion with every woman and man seeking and struggling for life, in the way of Jesus' solidarity with humanity" (FABC VI, art. 14.2, in Eilers 1997, 8). In particular, FABC VI uses the imagery of Jesus' washing the feet of his disciples to underline its call for commitment and service to life.[5]

In a similar vein, the First FABC International Theological Colloquium describes the relationship between theology and service to life as follows in its final statement, *Being Church in Asia*:

> We see the work of theology in Asia as a *service to life*. It has *to reflect systematically on themes that are important to the common journey of life with other peoples in Asia*, to the life of Christians and their churches in Asia, and to the work of the Asian episcopal conferences. To do this service in a way that is pastorally relevant and fruitful to the life, spirituality and mission of the disciple-community, *theol-*

---

[4] In the words of the Sixth FABC Plenary Assembly, "We Asians are searching not simply for the meaning of life but for life itself. We are striving and struggling for life because it is a task and a challenge. But life is a gift too, a mystery, because our efforts to achieve it are far too short of the ultimate value of life. We speak of life as a *becoming*—a growing into, a journeying to life and to the source of life" (FABC VI, art. 9, emphasis in the original, in Eilers 1997, 5). FABC VI unpacks this statement by highlighting "a vision of unity in diversity, a communion of life among diverse peoples" of Asia to undergird the assembly's "vision of holistic life, life that is achieved and entrusted to every person and every community of persons, regardless of gender, creed or culture, class, or color" (FABC VI, art. 10, Eilers 1997, 5).

[5] As the final statement of FABC VI expresses it, "We join Jesus in serving life by washing the feet of our neighbors" (FABC VI, art. 14.3, in Eilers 1997, 9).

ogy has to start from below, from the underside of history, from the perspective of those who struggle for life, love, justice and freedom. The life-long experiences of living the Christian faith by the various churches in their Asian context are the starting points. *Theologizing thus becomes more than faith seeking understanding, but faith fostering life and love, justice and freedom.* It is in this way that theology becomes a dynamic process giving meaning to and facilitating the Asian journey to life. It becomes part of the process of becoming and being Church in Asia. (*Being Church in Asia,* arts. 48–50, in Eilers 1997, 226, emphasis added)

Although it is true that *Being Church in Asia* was discussing the task of theologizing in general in Asia, this call to commitment and service to life is all the more relevant to mission theology in particular in Asia. It is a reminder that a theology of mission ought to be rooted in the daily life experiences of the Asian peoples, rather than in the intellectual arena of the theological academy. More important, the document also points out that mission theology, as theology, is to be articulated not merely *for* the benefit of the Asian peoples, or *about* the Asian peoples, but *together with* Asian peoples and in solidarity with their daily life experiences. As Felix Wilfred explains: "What we are with the people is more important than what we do for them" (1998, 132).

Moreover, the call for missiologists and missioners to make a personal commitment to the Asian peoples and their life experiences entails more than mere sympathy or occasional encounters with their daily lives, especially the poor and marginalized. Rather, it calls for their deep immersion and experiential participation in the lives of these peoples, not as outsiders who drop by sporadically to visit and then leave, but as insiders who remain bound in solidarity and empathy with them. Such a commitment and service to life may be understood from a twofold perspective, namely, an explicit epistemological perspective, which allows one to understand better the Asian peoples and their life experiences, and, more important, an underlying theological perspective, which recognizes the presence and workings of God in the daily lives of the Asian peoples. This underlying theological perspective is deeply rooted in the incarnation, earthly ministry, death, and resurrection of Jesus, revealing God's solidarity with humanity, especially the poor and marginalized, as well as God's participation in the experiences of pain and suffering in their daily lives. Hence, one could say that the experience of daily living is the privileged locus where God is to be found and encountered, because God has made a deliberate choice to be identified with humanity, especially the poor and marginalized.

Accordingly, the FABC is of the view that Jesus Christ is to be encountered in Asia within the specificity of the Asian peoples' life realities, and especially in the midst of the poor and marginalized. As the Fifth Plenary Assembly of the FABC explains, the Christian community "must live in *companionship*, as true *partners* with all Asians as they pray, work, struggle and suffer for a better human life, and as they search for the meaning of human life and progress" (FABC V, art. 6.2, in Rosales and Arévalo 1992, 283). This is because "the human person created in Christ, redeemed by Christ and united by Christ to himself is the way for the Church, the Church must walk along with him/her in human solidarity" (FABC V, art. 6.2, in Rosales and Arévalo 1992, 283). This point was also reiterated by the Seventh FABC Bishops' Institute for Social Action:

> The Lord of History is at work in that world of poverty. Seeing the Lord in the poor, making sense out of his action among them, discerning the direction of his action among them—this we felt deeply within us was the more specific challenge we have to face. (BISA VII, art. 20, in Rosales and Arévalo 1992, 233)

In emphasizing the need for commitment and service to life, the FABC perceives the myriad of rich and deeply profound experiences of life not merely as starting points for mission or pre-evangelization, but also the underlying foundation, framework, and continuous referent for doing Christian mission in the Asian milieu.

The Quest for Harmony
in the Pluralistic Asian Milieu

The overarching vision of harmony in the FABC's theology of mission is rooted in its belief that "there is an Asian approach to reality, a world-view, wherein the whole is the sum-total of the web of relationships and interaction of the various parts with each other, in a word, *harmony*, a word which resonates with all Asian cultures" (*Asian Christian Perspectives on Harmony*, art. 6, in Eilers 1997, 298). Within the many Asian worldviews, harmony is perceived as "the spiritual pursuit of the totality of reality in its infinite diversity and radical unity" that "evolves by respecting the otherness of the other and by acknowledging its significance in relation to the totality" (BIRA V/4, art. 6, in Eilers 1997, 157). Harmony is also predicated upon the commonly held view that since "the ultimate ground of being is unity-in-plurality, the divergent forms of reality [in the Asian milieu] are perceived in the convergent rhythm that harmonizes them" (BIRA V/4, art. 6, in Eilers 1997, 157). Despite "religious, ethnic, linguistic and cultural diversity, one can perceive a unity of values and perceptions" that is epitomized in the spirit of harmony (*Harmony among Believers of Living Faiths*, art. 5, in Eilers 1997, 174). In addition, "Harmony, in the created universe, within the human family, and internalized in the individual person, has for centuries been an ideal to which peoples of the region have striven" (*Harmony among Believers of Living Faiths*, art. 5, in Eilers 1997, 174).

This is reinforced by the FABC's acknowledgment that "the way of harmony does not unfold through aggressive indoctrination, which distorts reality" (BIRA V/3, art. 7, in Eilers 1997, 158). In the Final Statement of its Sixth Plenary Assembly, the FABC speaks of the experience of harmony within an overarching and holistic vision of unity in the Asian milieu:

> We envision a life *with integrity and dignity, a life of compassion* for the multitudes, especially for the poor and needy. It is a life of *solidarity* with every form of life and of *sensitive care* for the earth. . . . At the heart of our vision of life is the Asian *reverential sense of mystery and of the sacred,*

a spirituality that regards life as sacred and discovers the Transcendent and its gifts even in mundane affairs, in tragedy or victory, in brokenness or wholeness. (FABC VI, art. 10, in Eilers 1997, 5; see also the FABC Office of Theological Concerns' statement, "The Spirit at Work in Asia Today," in Eilers 2002, 237–327)

This statement builds on the earlier statement by the Fourth FABC Plenary Assembly: "Asian religious cultures see human beings, society and the whole universe as intimately related and interdependent. Fragmentation and division contradict this vision" (FABC IV, art. 3.1.10, in Rosales and Arévalo 1992, 181).

The FABC recognizes that such an understanding of harmony is also rooted in the foundations of a cosmic harmony and unity that accepts the pluralism and diversity of the Asian religio-cultural traditions as a positive and rich expression of the mystery of the divine plan of creation:

> When we look into our traditional cultures and heritages, we note that they are inspired by a vision of unity. The universe is perceived as an organic whole with the web of relations knitting together each and every part of it. The nature and the human are not viewed as antagonistic to each other, but as chords in a universal symphony. The whole reality is maintained in unity through a universal rhyme (*Rta; Tao*). This unity of reality is reflected in the human person in that his senses, consciousness and spirit are organically interlinked, one flowing into the other. When this unity and harmony are manifested in inter-human relationships of justice, order and righteousness, it is considered *dharmic* (*dharma, dhamma*). (BIRA IV/11, art. 6, in Rosales and Arévalo 1992, 319).

According to the FABC, the paradigm of harmony is well positioned to act as the common underlying foundation for communication amid much diversity and pluralism because it is authentically Christian yet quintessentially Asian. In other words, harmony appears "to constitute in a certain sense the intellectual and affective, religious and artistic, personal and societal soul of both persons and institutions in Asia" (BIRA IV/1, art. 13, in Rosales and Arévalo 1992, 249). In this regard, BIRA V/2 presents the following understanding of harmony that speaks to both Christians and other religious adherents:

> Harmony can be perceived and realized at various levels: Harmony in oneself as personal integration of body and mind; harmony with the Cosmos, not only living in harmony with nature, but sharing nature's gift equitably to promote harmony among peoples; harmony with others, accepting, respecting and appreciating each one's cultural, ethnic and religious identity, building community in freedom and fellowship; harmony in our collaborations as a means of promoting harmony for all in the world; and finally harmony with God or the Absolute or whatever we perceive as the ultimate goal of life. (BIRA V/2, art. 3.2, in Eilers 1997, 151)

At the same time, the simplistic and naïve understanding of harmony as a mere absence of strife is consistently rejected by the FABC: "Harmony is not simply the absence of strife, described as 'live and let live.' The test of true harmony lies in the acceptance of diversity as richness" (BIRA IV/11, art. 15, in Rosales and Arévalo 1992, 321). The FABC goes on to explain:

> Harmony does not consist in leveling off differences in order to arrive at consensus at any cost. Avoiding controversies and bypassing disagreements do not pave the way to harmony. To say that all religions are the same is simplistic and does not promote honest dialogue, but to argue that religions do not meet at all would block any creative interaction. (BIRA V/3, art. 7, in Eilers 1997, 158)

Moving on to Christian perspectives on harmony, the FABC points out that "Christianity teaches a threefold harmony: harmony with God, among humans, and with the whole universe. Union with a personal God is viewed as the source of all genuine harmony" (BIRA V/4, art. 5, in Eilers 1997, 164). From the Christian perspective, harmony is also divinely inspired, because "God is the source and summit of all harmony. He is the foundation and the fulfillment of it" (*Asian Christian Perspectives on Harmony*, art. 5.1.1.4, in Eilers 1997, 288). In this respect, harmony as a theological notion also draws its inspiration and strength from the harmonious unity of the Trinity: "The marvelous mystery of unity and communion of the Trinity is a model as well as a powerful challenge in our efforts to create harmony in all areas of life" (BIRA IV/11, art. 7, in Rosales and Arévalo 1992, 319). The trinitarian dimension of harmony was further elaborated by the FABC Office of Theological Concerns in the following manner: "The harmony of the universe finds its origin in the one Creator God, and human harmony should flow from the communion of Father and Son in the Spirit, and ought to be continually nourished by the 'circumincession' (*perichoresis*) in divine life" (*Asian Christian Perspectives on Harmony*, art. 4.11.3, in Eilers 1997, 285). Such trinitarian and cosmic perspectives of harmony give rise to an understanding of harmony that "acknowledges the sacredness of nature and invites us to live in harmony with nature and to foster its growth" (BIRA IV/12, art. 33, in Rosales and Arévalo 1992, 330). This notion of harmony is inspired by a universal concern that is "geared ultimately to the well-being and peace of the universe and humankind" (BIRA IV/11, art. 21, in Rosales and Arévalo 1992, 322).

Mission as Dialogue with the Threefold Reality of Asian Religions, Cultures, and Poverty

From its earliest days, the FABC has chosen the quintessential Asian trait of dialogue as a "manifestation of lived Christianity" (Fernandes 1991, 548) to undergird its mission theology in response to the multicultural, multiethnic, and plurireligious challenges of the Asian milieu, as well as the proximity of Asian Christians to their coreligionists. The Asian bishops recognize that the task of doing Christian mission in Asia has to take place within a threefold dialogue with Asian cultures, religions, and poverty in a spirit of goodwill. Thus, the Final Statement of the First FABC Plenary Assembly maintains that at the heart of the task of mission of the Asian local church lies the dialogical encounter between the local church and the Asian milieu with its threefold reality of Asian religions, cultures, and poverty:

> A church in continuous, humble and loving dialogue with the living traditions, the cultures, the great religions—in brief, with all the life-realities of the people in whose midst it has sunk its roots deeply and whose history and life it gladly makes its own seeks to share in whatever truly belongs to that people: its meanings and its values, its aspirations, its thoughts and its language, its songs and its artistry. Even its frailties and failings it assumes, so that they too may be healed. (FABC I, art. 12, in Rosales and Arévalo 1992, 14)

The First FABC Plenary Assembly further clarifies that this "dialogue of life" requires "working, not for them merely (in a paternalistic sense), but *with* them, to learn from them" their "real needs and aspirations" and to "strive for their fulfillment" (FABC I, art. 20, in Rosales and Arévalo 1992, 15, emphasis in the original).

Looking back at the First FABC Plenary Assembly, Michael Amaladoss comments that the Asian bishops saw mission as a dialogue with "the threefold realities of Asia," that is, "its rich cultures, its ancient and great religions, and the poor" (Amaladoss 1991, 362). Amaladoss also suggests that the Asian bishops accepted Asian religions as "significant and positive elements in the economy of God's design of salvation" because they have "*a living experience of other religions*" (Amaladoss 1991, 362, emphasis added). In turn, this commitment and service to life in the pluralistic Asian milieu demands an appropriate missiological approach that would enable Asian Christians to affirm and build on the realities that promote and empower life in the Asian milieu while purifying and transforming the realities that cause suffering, oppression, and death.

Implicit in such a theology of mission is the acknowledgment and acceptance of a fundamental ontological, soteriological, and existential relationship between the Christian gospel and the Asian peoples with their rich religious and cultural traditions, as well as their daily socioeconomic challenges. More specifically for the FABC, interreligious dialogue "is based on the firm belief that the Holy Spirit is operative in other religions as well" (BIRA IV/2, art. 8.5, in Rosales and Arévalo 1992, 253). In addition, such a deep and profound theology of mission enables the Asian church to move away from "an institution planted in Asia" toward "an evangelizing community of Asia" (*Theological Consultation*, art. 15, in Rosales and Arévalo 1992, 338). Clearly, the FABC has great hopes for the local church to be deeply inculturated in the Asian soil so that it becomes not simply a church in Asia but truly an Asian church (BIRA IV/12, art. 50, in Rosales and Arévalo 1992, 333).

Indeed, it is the overarching vision of the FABC that "the Church is called to be a community of dialogue. This dialogical model is in fact a new way of being Church" (BIRA IV/12, art. 48, in Rosales and Arévalo 1992, 332). The FABC perceives that the Asian church "is never centered on itself but on the coming true of God's dream for the world. It seeks not to exclude others but to be truly catholic in its concerns, in its appreciation of the gifts of others, and in its readiness to work with others for a world at once more human and more divine" (BIRA IV/12, art. 49, in Rosales and Arévalo 1992, 333). Building on the incipient insights of the First FABC Plenary Assembly, the Asian bishops have subsequently accepted interreligious dialogue as a constitutive element of being church in Asia: "Interreligious dialogue flows from the nature of the Church, a community in pilgrimage journeying with peoples of other faiths towards the Kingdom that is to come" (BIRA IV/4, art. 2, in Rosales and Arévalo 1992, 300).

For the FABC, dialogue is "an integral part of evangelization" (BIMA [Bishops' Institutes for Missionary Apostolate] II, art. 14, in Rosales and Arévalo 1992, 100) that is "intrinsic to the very life of the Church," (BIRA I, art. 9, in Rosales and Arévalo 1992, 111). In addition, article 19 of the 1979 International Congress on Mission also made it clear that dialogue is an "essential mode of all evangelization" (Rosales and Arévalo 1992, 131).[6]

---

[6] Article 4b of the Third Consensus Paper that was presented at this FABC International Congress on Mission speaks of dialogue as bringing

In particular, "religious dialogue is not just a substitute for or a mere preliminary to the proclamation of Christ, but should be the ideal form of evangelization, where in humility and mutual support we seek together with our brothers and sisters that fullness of Christ which is God's plan for the whole of creation, in its entirely [*sic*] and its great and wonderful diversity" (BIMA I, art. 10, in Rosales and Arévalo 1992, 94). In the context of the diverse religions of Asia, dialogue is also perceived by the FABC as leading to "*receptive pluralism*": "That is, the many ways of responding to the promptings of the Holy Spirit must be continually in conversation with one another. A relationship of dynamic tension may open the way for mutual information, inspiration, support and correction" (BIRA IV/3, art. 16, in Rosales and Arévalo 1992, 261).

On the one hand, this call for dialogue does not mean that the FABC has abandoned the task of proclaiming the Christian gospel in Asia. In its groundbreaking document, *Theses on Interreligious Dialogue* (1987), the FABC Theological Advisory Commission sought to explain the relationship between dialogue and proclamation in the task of Christian mission in Asia. Of the seven theses enunciated in the document, thesis 6 asserts:

> Dialogue and proclamation are integral but dialectical and complementary dimensions of the Church's mission of evangelization. Authentic dialogue includes a witness to one's total Christian faith, which is open to a similar witness of the other religious believers. Proclamation is a call to Christian discipleship and mission. As a service to the mystery of the Spirit who freely calls to conversion, and of the person who freely responds to the call, proclamation is dialogical. (*Theses on Interreligious Dialogue*, thesis 6, in FABC 1987, 15)

"to the local churches in Asia which are in danger of being ghettos an openness to and integration into the mainstream of their cultures. Christians grow in genuine love for their neighbors of other faiths, and the latter learn to love their Christian neighbors" (International Congress on Mission Consensus Paper III, art. 4b, in Rosales and Arévalo 1992, 142).

As the *Theses on Interreligious Dialogue* unpacks this statement, it warns against any facile reduction of one to the other:

> The relation between dialogue and proclamation is a complex one. In making an effort to understand this relationship, we must avoid from the beginning any attempt to reduce one to the other. Some would tend to say that dialogue itself is the only authentic form of proclamation since the Church is only one among the many ways to salvation; others would tend to say that dialogue is only a step, though with an identity of its own, in the total process that culminates in proclamation. While the former approach robs proclamation of any specific meaning, the latter instrumentalizes dialogue. (*Theses on Interreligious Dialogue*, art. 6.2, in FABC 1987, 15)

The document then stresses that proclamation should be understood not in the abstract, but within the context of, and integrated into, the threefold dialogue:

> The Asian bishops have understood evangelization as the building up of the local church through a threefold dialogue with the cultures, the religions and the poor of Asia. Inculturation, interreligious dialogue and liberation are the three dimensions of evangelization. Proclamation is not a fourth dimension added to these three, but is the aspect of witness that is an integral element of all the three dimensions of evangelization. (*Theses on Interreligious Dialogue*, art. 6.4, in FABC 1987, 16)

On the other hand, the FABC does not exclude the explicit verbal proclamation of the Christian gospel as mission, but it recognizes that context plays a very important role in determining which is the best approach to mission. In this regard, the Fifth FABC Plenary Assembly explains that dialogue *does not preclude* the need for the proclamation of the Christian gospel. FABC V points out that there could be a moment when "we shall not be timid when God opens the door for us to *proclaim* explicitly the

Lord Jesus Christ as the Savior and the answer to the fundamental questions of human existence" (FABC V, art. 4.3, in Rosales and Arévalo 1992, 282). However, FABC V also states that a distinctively Asian approach of proclamation that is sensitive to the Asian weltanschauung is needed:

> Mission may find its greatest urgency in Asia; it also finds in our continent a distinctive mode. We affirm, together with others, that "the proclamation of Jesus Christ is the center and primary element of evangelization." (*Statement of the FABC All-Asia Conference on Evangelization*, Suwon, South Korea, August 24–31, 1988)

> But the proclamation of Jesus Christ in Asia means, first of all, the witness of Christians and of Christian communities to the values of the Kingdom of God, *a proclamation through Christ-like deeds*. For Christians in Asia, to proclaim Christ means above all to live like him, in the midst of our neighbors of other faiths and persuasions, and to do his deeds by the power of his grace. Proclamation through dialogue and deeds—this is the first call to the Churches in Asia. (FABC V, art. 4.1, in Rosales and Arévalo 1992, 281–82)

Based on the foregoing, the Fifth FABC Plenary Assembly equates the threefold dialogue with the Christian mission imperative. More specifically, FABC V explains that the task of doing Christian mission is all about

> being with the people, responding to their needs, with sensitiveness to the presence of God in cultures and other religious traditions, and witnessing to the values of God's Kingdom through presence, solidarity, sharing and word. Mission will mean a dialogue with Asia's poor, with its local cultures, and with other religious traditions. (FABC V, art. 3.1.2, in Rosales and Arévalo 1992, 280)

In addition, this identification of proclamation with the "witness of life" builds on the earlier statement made by the Third

Bishops' Institute for Missionary Apostolate meeting in Changhua in 1982:

> It is true that in many places [in Asia] Christ cannot yet be proclaimed openly by words. But He can, and should be, proclaimed through other ways, namely: through the witness of life of the Christian community and family, and their striving to know and live more fully the faith they possess; through their desire to live in peace and harmony with those who do not share our faith; through the appreciation by Christians of the human and religious values possessed by their non-Christian neighbors, and through these same Christians' willingness to collaborate in those activities which promote the human community. (BIMA III, art. 10, in Rosales and Arévalo 1992, 105)

Moreover, through a threefold dialogue with Asian cultures, religions, as well as with the poor and marginalized, not only could the FABC's missional endeavors enrich the Asian socioreligious realities; in turn the FABC's mission theology could be enriched by the Asian socioreligious realities. BISA I hits the mark when it points out that dialogue and missional outreach ought to "be truly Asian, employing the procedures for arriving at consensus for action which our people have themselves elaborated, rather than alien techniques which may work well enough in other cultures, but not in our own" (BISA I, art. 9, in Rosales and Arévalo 1992, 200). On this basis, Michael Amaladoss is able to say that evangelization in Asia as a threefold dialogue with the realities of Asia "means that we do not import readymade structures of 'salvation' from somewhere, but we let the people of Asia dialogue with the Good News in a creative and relevant way" (Amaladoss 2000, 340).

In addition, the FABC perceives its call for a threefold dialogue to be linked to its broader quest for harmony in response to the challenges of violence and conflict in pluralistic Asia. The Fifth FABC Plenary Assembly elaborates on the relationship between harmony and dialogue and the "proclamation through dialogue and deeds" within its theology of mission as follows:

Mission in Asia will also seek through *dialogue* to serve the cause of unity of the peoples of Asia marked by such a diversity of beliefs, cultures and socio-political structures. In an Asia marked by diversity and torn by conflicts, the Church must in a special way be a sacrament—a visible sign and instrument of unity and harmony. (FABC V, art. 4.2, in Rosales and Arévalo 1992, 282)

Indeed, this call for the church to be a sacrament of unity and harmony is especially prophetic and poignant today, in view of the occurrence of religious strife in many parts of Asia, as discussed in chapter 2. In this regard, proclamation without dialogue runs the risk of aggressive proselytism with its highly negative connotations, thereby playing right into the hands of religious fundamentalists and zealots who are looking for excuses to crack down on Asian Christians, as discussed in chapter 2 of this book. Hence, the Asian church will have "to discern, in dialogue with Asian peoples and Asian realities, what deeds the Lord wills to be done so that all humankind may be gathered together in harmony as his family" (FABC V, art. 6.3, in Rosales and Arévalo 1992, 283).

As for the relationship between dialogue, proclamation, and conversion, the FABC has pointed out that "dialogue and proclamation are complementary. Sincere and authentic dialogue does not have for its objective the conversion of the other. For conversion depends solely on God's internal call and the person's free decision" (BIRA III, art. 4, in Rosales and Arévalo 1992, 120). Elsewhere, the FABC has reiterated that "dialogue aimed at 'converting' the other to one's own religious faith and tradition is dishonest and unethical; it is not the way of harmony" (BIRA V/3, art. 7, in Eilers 1997, 158). In this vein, the late Angelo Fernandes, Archbishop Emeritus of Delhi, insisted in his keynote address at BIRA IV/12 in February 1991 that Asians of other faiths were not to be regarded as "objects of Christian mission," but as "partners in the Asian community, where there must be mutual witness" (Fernandes 1991, 548). Archbishop Fernandes explained that the dialogue between the Asian church and the Asian peoples should be seen as a "manifestation of lived

Christianity" with its own integrity that leads toward the Reign of God (1991, 548). One of the inherent dangers of proclamation is that it often comes across as being overly discursive and defensive; that is, there is an abundance of words in proclamation that aims to prove or emphasize particular truth claims in debates with other religious adherents. By contrast, Felix Wilfred has pointed out that in the Asian mind-set "truth does not impose itself, but rather *attracts* everyone and everything to itself by its beauty, splendour and fascination" (Wilfred 1988, 427).

Building Up the Reign of God in Asia

The FABC's regnocentric approach to the task of Christian mission is "rooted in the conviction of faith that God's plan of salvation for humanity is one and reaches out to all peoples: it is the Kingdom of God through which he seeks to reconcile all things with himself in Jesus Christ" (*Theses on Interreligious Dialogue*, art. 2.3, in FABC 1987, 7). As the document *Theses on Interreligious Dialogue* puts it:

> The focus of the Church's mission of evangelization is building up the Kingdom of God and building up the Church to be at the service of the Kingdom. The Kingdom of God is therefore wider than the Church. The Church is the sacrament of the Kingdom, visibilizing it, ordained to it, promoting it, but not equating itself with it. (*Theses on Interreligious Dialogue*, art. 6.3, FABC 1987, 16)

One year later, this statement in the *Theses on Interreligious Dialogue* was subsequently affirmed at the 1988 FABC All-Asia Conference on Evangelization, which explains that the "ultimate goal of all evangelization is the ushering in and establishment of God's Kingdom, namely God's rule in the hearts and minds of our people" (BIMA IV, art. 5, in Rosales and Arévalo 1992, 292). The FABC clarifies the relationship between the church and the Reign of God as follows:

The Reign of God is the very reason for the being of the Church. The Church exists in and for the Kingdom. The Kingdom, God's gift and initiative, is already begun and is continually being realized, and made present through the Spirit. Where God is accepted, when the Gospel values are lived, where man is respected . . . there is the Kingdom. *It is far wider than the Church's boundaries.* This already present reality is oriented toward the final manifestation and full perfection of the Reign of God. (BIRA IV/2, art. 8.1, in Rosales and Arévalo 1992, 252, emphasis added)

Similarly, article 30 of the *1991 Theological Consultation* insists:

The Reign of God is a universal reality, extending far beyond the boundaries of the Church. It is the reality of salvation in Jesus Christ, in which Christians and others share together. It is the fundamental "mystery of unity" which unites us more deeply than differences in religious allegiance are able to keep us apart. Seen in this manner, a "regnocentric" approach to mission theology does not in any way threaten the Christo-centric perspective of our faith. On the contrary, "regno-centrism" calls for "christo-centrism," and vice-versa, for it is in Jesus Christ and through the Christ-event that God has established his Kingdom upon the earth and in human history. (Rosales and Arévalo 1992, 342)

Hence, Lorenzo Fernando observes that for the Asian bishops of the FABC, the "Kingdom of God is neither identified with the Church nor restricted to particular religions but is within and beyond all religions. It is the Kingdom that becomes the meeting point of all religions" (2000, 867).

Thus, the FABC's regnocentric theology of mission is based on the Asian bishops' positive approach to the diversity and pluralism of the Asian world, acknowledging that the grace and presence of God permeate all of creation in a mysterious manner (FABC I, art. 15, in Rosales and Arévalo 1992, 14; BIRA III, art.

2, in Rosales and Arévalo 1992, 119). The FABC sees the Asian church as "constantly [moving] forward in mission, as it accompanies all humankind in its pilgrimage to the Kingdom of the Father" (FABC III, art. 15, in Rosales and Arévalo 1992, 60). In addition, the 1991 FABC *Theological Consultation* concludes: "If the Church is the sacrament of the Kingdom, the reason is that she is the sacrament of Jesus Christ himself who is the mystery of salvation, to whom she is called to bear witness and whom she is called to announce. To be at the service of the Kingdom means for the Church to announce Jesus Christ" (*Theological Consultation*, art. 33, in Rosales and Arévalo 1992, 342).

In arriving at this conclusion, the FABC is convinced that the divine plan of salvation is wider than the church and that the "Church does not monopolize God's action in the universe," as the *Theses on Interreligious Dialogue* makes clear:

> The one divine plan of salvation for all peoples embraces the whole universe. The mission of the Church has to be understood within the context of this plan. *The Church does not monopolize God's action in the universe.* While it is aware of a special mission from God in the world, it *has to be attentive to God's action in the world*, as manifested also in the other religions. This twofold awareness constitutes the two poles of the Church's evangelizing action in relation to other religions. While proclamation is the expression of its awareness of being in mission, *dialogue is the expression of its awareness of God's presence and action outside its boundaries. . . .* Proclamation is the affirmation of and witness to God's action in oneself. Dialogue is the openness and attention to the mystery of God's action in the other believer. *It is a perspective of faith that we cannot speak of the one without the other.* (*Theses on Interreligious Dialogue*, art. 6.5, in FABC 1987, 16, emphasis added)

As the FABC Theological Advisory Commission sees it, the call to conversion and discipleship points primarily toward God and only secondarily toward the Church:

The pilgrim Church witnesses not to itself but to the mystery; and calls to conversion and discipleship refer primarily to the relationship between God who calls and the person who responds. Only secondarily do they refer to the Church-community. The identity of the Church does not lie in being the exclusive "ark of salvation" but in *being in mission to transform the world from within as leaven*, without being fully aware of the forms that such transformation may lead to. (*Theses on Interreligious Dialogue*, art. 6.12, in FABC 1987, 18, emphasis added)

Moreover, a regnocentric theology in Asia also challenges the Asian church to work "with the Christians of other Churches, together with our sisters and brothers of other faiths and with all people of goodwill, to make the Kingdom of God more visibly present in Asia" (FABC V, art. 2.3.9, in Rosales and Arévalo 1992, 279). Elsewhere in the same statement, the Fifth Plenary Assembly of the FABC asserts that mission in Asia seeks "to proclaim the Good News of the Kingdom of God: to promote the values of the Kingdom such as justice, peace, love, compassion, equality and brotherhood in these Asian realities" (FABC V, art. 1.7, in Rosales and Arévalo 1992, 275).

The inclusivity of the Reign of God holds great appeal to the FABC, which "acknowledge[s] the Kingdom at work in sociopolitical situations and in cultural and religious traditions of Asia" (*Theological Consultation*, art. 39, in Rosales and Arévalo 1992, 344). As Felix Wilfred explains, the inclusive nature of the Reign of God is able to encompass those people who are inspired by Jesus Christ and his Good News, but choose for various reasons to remain Hindus, Buddhists, Daoists, or Muslims, and who are otherwise excluded from the dialectical setup of present ecclesial structures:

We have in Asia the phenomenon of a lot of men and women who are gripped by Jesus, his life and teachings. They are his devotees while they continue to be Hindus, Buddhists, Taoists. What is particularly remarkable is that they can be Hindus, or Buddhists, etc., and devotees of Christ without being syncretistic. Syncretism, they feel, is something which is attributed to them from the outside, while from within, at the level of their consciousness, they experience unity and harmony, and are not assailed by those contradictions and conflicts which may appear to those who look at them from without. (Wilfred 1988, 429)

Toward "Active Integral Evangelization"

At the beginning of the third Christian millennium, some thirty years after the Asian Catholic bishops gathered for the first time in Manila to greet Pope Paul VI on his historic visit to Asia, the Seventh Plenary Assembly of the FABC was convened with the theme "A Renewed Church in Asia on a Mission of Love and Service." At this assembly, the FABC coined a new term, "active integral evangelization" (Eilers 2002, 3), to describe a distinctively Asian approach to Christian mission that integrates commitment and service to life, life witness, dialogue, and bringing about the Reign of God in the pluralistic Asian world:

> For thirty years, as we have tried to reformulate our Christian identity in Asia, we have addressed different issues, one after another: evangelization, inculturation, dialogue, the Asian-ness of the Church, justice, the option for the poor, etc. Today, after three decades, we no longer speak of such distinct issues. We are addressing present needs that are massive and increasingly complex. *These issues are not separate topics to be discussed, but aspects of an integrated approach to our Mission of Love and Service. We need to feel and act "integrally." As we face the needs of the 21st century, we do so with Asian hearts, in solidarity with the poor and the marginalized, in union with all our Christian brothers and sisters, and by joining hands with all men and women of Asia of many different faiths. Inculturation, dialogue, justice and the option for the poor are aspects of whatever we do.* (Eilers 2002, 8, emphasis added)

At this pivotal plenary assembly, FABC VII reiterates what it previously stated at FABC VI: it is committed to the "emergence of the Asianness of the Church in Asia" that is "an embodiment of the Asian vision and values of life, especially interiority, harmony, a holistic and inclusive approach to every area of life" (Eilers 2002, 8). In addition, FABC VII is convinced that this "Asianness of the Church in Asia" is "a special gift the world is awaiting" (Eilers 2002, 9). As it explains, "The whole world is in need of a holistic paradigm for meeting the challenges of life" and "together with all Asians, the Church, a tiny minority in this vast continent, has a singular contribution to make, and this contribution is the task of the whole Church in Asia" (Eilers 2002, 9). In addition, the FABC reiterates that the "most effective means of evangelization and service in the name of Christ has always been and continues to be the *witness of life*" (Eilers 2002, 12, emphasis added). It is only through such witnessing that the "Asian people will recognize the Gospel that we announce when they see in our life the transparency of the message of Jesus and the inspiring and healing figure of men and women immersed in God" (Eilers 2002, 12–13). This witness of life which flows from active integral evangelization is needed more than ever in response to the challenges posed by religious fundamentalists and exclusivists in many parts of Asia that were discussed earlier in chapter 2.

The FABC's mission theology does not begin from above or from the center, but from below and from the periphery, moving toward the center. For the FABC, the task of Christian mission is not a one-way street; it is not a unidirectional proclamation of abstract creedal principles and doctrinal truths in competitive debates with the creedal principles and truths of other religions. In articulating its approach to the task of doing Christian mission, the FABC begins not with abstract and universalistic theological concepts and categories, but with the daily life experiences and challenges arising from the ongoing encounter with the diverse and pluralistic Asian realities and contexts today.

From the discussion in this chapter, it is clear that the bishops of the FABC are interested not in an Asian Christian presence that is over and against Asian religions and cultures, but rather a presence that is relational and dialogical. While the Asian Catholic bishops accept the necessity of the task of mission in the Asian milieu, they also realize that this does *not* mean that they are called to conquer the postcolonial Asian world in the name of a triumphant Christ or build a triumphant Christendom on Asian soil. As far as the FABC is concerned, the Asian peoples are not objects of mission, to be converted and brought into the church, although Christians do not hesitate to extend such an invitation if the context warrants it.

More significant, the bishops of the FABC acknowledge and rejoice in the religious pluralism that lies at the heart of what it means to be Asian and Christian, perceiving the church's mission in Asia as inspired by God's prior activity in the world through the missions of the Father and the Spirit. As far as the FABC is concerned, the deep soteriological underpinnings of Asian religions and philosophies that have inspired multitudes of Asians are not evil, but are divinely inspired. More specifically, the FABC is unequivocal in asserting that the wisdom of Asian philosophies and the soteriological elements of Asian religions are inspired by the Spirit working outside the boundaries of the institutional church. The FABC also views one aspect of the Christian mission in Asia as embracing and encouraging other Asian religions to collaborate with Christianity toward the goal of ushering in the Reign of God in Asia.

The principal means of the FABC's mission theology is the quintessential Asian trait of dialogue, a two-way encounter of the Christian gospel with the threefold reality of Asian cultures, religions, and the poor. Here, it is the case that not only the Asian socioreligious realities may be enriched by Christianity, but also that Christianity may be enriched by the Asian socioreligious realities. For the FABC, both life witness and dialogue are the two sides of the coin that define the relationship between the Christian gospel and other religious traditions in the pluralistic Asian landscape, enabling Asian Christians to share the Good News with their fellow Asians. Undoubtedly, the FABC regards dialogue as necessary to redress the damage that has been perpetrated by centuries of European imperialism and colonial domination. In particular, dialogue has the potential to bring about opportunities for two or more parties, with their different worldviews, to enter into each other's horizons in order to foster improved relations between them. It must also be pointed out that although the sapiential "Asian" vision of the FABC does not neglect the importance of proclamation, it also values friendship and trust, relationality and relationship-building, as well as dialogue and solidarity as constitutive elements of the task of Christian mission in Asia.

The FABC's preferred mode of mission as a threefold dialogue with Asian peoples in the fullness of their myriad cultures, religions, and poverty in promoting the Reign of God in Asia points to a missional outreach that is geared, not merely to the Asian peoples, but also in solidarity and collaboration with the Asian peoples. In this regard, the FABC has reiterated repeatedly that the task of Christian mission, although necessary, is to be done not for its own sake, or even for the sake of church growth, but to bring about the Reign of God *among* the peoples of Asia. As far as the FABC is concerned, mission is regnocentric rather than ecclesiocentric, seeking to integrate "inculturation, dialogue, justice and the option for the poor" (FABC VII, Eilers 2002, 8) in the task of doing Christian mission in Asia.

Hence, the FABC has chosen to focus on prophetically critiquing, transforming, and healing the brokenness in Asian realities in the name of bringing about the Reign of God in Asia. For the FABC, Asian Christians are called to collaborate with the *missio Dei* when they seek to bring about the Reign of God in Asia through their life witness and threefold dialogue with the Asian peoples and their cultures, religions, and marginalizing life challenges. More important, because the church is at the service of the Reign of God, Asian Christians are called to contribute to Asian cultures, religions, and redressing socioeconomic challenges, even if these cultures, religions, and societies do not become institutionally Christian.

To conclude, the FABC's mission theology entails a commitment to work in harmony with the life realities of the Asian *Sitzen-im-Leben*. In this regard, the Asian Catholic Bishops have pointed out that Asian Christians are called to mission by giving of themselves and bringing the life and hope of the Good News of Jesus Christ to a world beset with challenges and problems. To be truly Asian and at home in the Asian milieu, Asian Christians are challenged to embrace the religious pluralism of postcolonial Asia, while prophetically challenging and purifying its oppressive and life-denying elements in the name of the Christian gospel. In the case of the latter, the FABC perceives the task of Christian mission as working for the redemption of humanity in Asia not by pouring oil on the fires of religious conflict and violence and engaging in competitive proselytism against the practitioners of other religions. In a continent that is being torn apart by violence and conflicts in the name of exclusivist religious fanaticism, Asian Christians are challenged to break the impasse by going beyond the superficiality of quantitative church growth in favor of a qualitatively prophetic approach that seeks to critique, transform, and heal the brokenness in Asian realities.

In the final analysis, the FABC accepts that the Asian church will always be a "little flock" in the sea of diverse Asian religions and cultures in pluralistic Asia for the future. In the context of the immense pluralistic Asian *weltanschauung*, Asian Christians as a religious minority are able to witness to the redemptive power of the Christian gospel by the example of their daily living in companionship, empathy, and solidarity with their neighbors across religious boundaries, working, struggling, and suffering as fellow humans on a common quest for the meaning of life. Seen in this light, inculturation, interreligious dialogue, and human liberation are not mere pre-evangelistic activities, but rather integral dimensions of the FABC's mission theology of "active integral evangelization."

Chapter 4

Toward a Theology of
Mission among the Peoples in Asia

In the preceding three chapters, we evaluated the successes and shortcomings of two millennia of Christian mission in Asia. In this chapter, I propose a new approach to doing Christian mission in Asia that takes seriously the challenges and opportunities that are afforded by the contemporary Asian context. Asian Christians realize that the clarion calls for a new wave of evangelization that are emanating from Europe or the Americas, whether Protestant or Catholic, have to be carefully nuanced and tempered. They are aware that the call for a new wave of evangelization originated from places where the dominant position of Christianity as the religious majority has come under siege from rising secularism, relativism, and the rapid influx of religious minorities as the result of globalization and transnational migration. In their own context, they also acknowledge that they ignore at their peril the plurality of ancient religions and spiritual traditions that define the Asian milieu. Indeed, religious pluralism is an inescapable part of the Asian landscape, not to be confronted and overcome, but accepted and celebrated as a definitive aspect of the Asian world.

Notwithstanding the rise of modernity, globalization, and emergent interlocking transnational networks, religion continues to be deeply embedded and influential at all levels of society across Asia. As discussed in chapter 2, Asian Christians are often confronted with the reality that they are, with few exceptions, minority communities, surrounded by majorities who are often very suspicious of them, accusing them of being a fifth column threat to traditional "Asian" values. Unfortunately, Asian Christians, as religious minorities, often experience fear, insecurity, vulnerability, and backlash from their religious majority neighbors for being different from the mainstream. Specifically, Asian Christians have to contend with prejudice, bigotry, chauvinism, and intolerance at the very least, or outright harassment and persecution in the worst-case scenario. The historical situation described in chapter 1, that of Western colonial powers protecting Christian missionaries and native Christians from harassment or persecution by hostile natives, is no longer the case today in postcolonial Asia.

Hence, Asian Christians are fully cognizant of the fact that they have to search for new ways of doing Christian mission in Asia, to enable Christianity to take its rightful place in Asia among the other great religions of Asia. On the one hand, it is true that in pluralistic societies, religious leaders are often challenged to be the source of reconciliation, healing, and peace between their own communities and other communities within their societies, overcoming intolerance and extremism with acceptance and solidarity. It goes without saying that the religious leaders of the majority communities have to do their part to change their rhetoric and official policies and stop scapegoating minorities for underlying political and economic problems. Otherwise, minority communities have every reason to be suspicious of the majority. On the other hand, minority communities, Asian Christians included, have to step up to the plate, too, and engage with skeptical and suspicious majority communities, demonstrating their willingness to seek reconciliation, healing, and peace building between all communities.

Mission among the Peoples: Four Propositions

One common thread of the preceding three chapters of this book is the reality that Christian mission in the culturally diverse and religiously pluralistic Asian milieu is challenged by the complex interplay of the forces of postcolonialism, globalization, transnationalism, migration, economic disparities, and political totalitarianism, as well as rising religious exclusivism and nationalist chauvinism. How should Asian Christians witness the

Christian gospel to their families, friends, and neighbors in such a highly complex reality? In this chapter, I would like to lay out a new missiological template that I call mission *among* the peoples. Within the Asian milieu, this understanding of mission among the peoples builds on the missional quests of Matteo Ricci and Roberto de Nobili, who became Chinese and Indian, respectively, to witness among fellow Chinese and Indians. It is also inspired by the mission among the peoples of the Korean Confucian *yangban* who spread the gospel among their fellow Koreans independently of foreign missionaries, the missional outreach of indigenous Chinese Christian churches and evangelists, as well as the FABC's "active integral evangelization" that emphasizes *life witness* of the gospel among fellow Asians. More important, I intend to make the case that this model of mission among the peoples is built on the biblical and theological underpinnings as outlined in the following four propositions:

Proposition 1: The model of mission among the peoples moves away from a sending-receiving church model toward a World Christianity model where there is mutual engagement and collaborative global partnership for Christian mission beyond the North-South or Majority-Minority divide.

Proposition 2: The *orthodoxy* of the model of mission among the peoples is rooted in the *missio Dei* that seeks to usher in the universality of God's reign in pluralistic Asia, and Christians are called to imitate Jesus, the missional exemplar par excellence of the *missio Dei*.

Proposition 3: Mission among the peoples is inspired by an *orthopathos* that illumines divine empathy and solidarity with the pathos of the suffering and brokenness in the daily life experiences of the Asian peoples.

Proposition 4: Mission among the peoples is empowered by an *orthopraxis* that enables the Christian gospel to engage with the religious pluralism of Asia in a spirit of interreligious hospitality.

Proposition 1

The model of mission among the peoples moves away from a sending-receiving church model toward a World Christianity model where there is mutual engagement and collaborative global partnership for Christian mission beyond the North-South or Majority-Minority divide.

Writing from a Protestant perspective, the missiologist Andrew Walls points out that the "center of gravity of the Christian world" has shifted away from Europe and North America to Africa, Asia, Latin America, and the Pacific (2002, 85). "Christianity began the twentieth century as a Western religion, and indeed, *the* Western religion; it ended the century as a non-Western religion, on track to become progressively more so" (2002, 64). Jehu Hanciles concurs with Walls as he argues the case for the shifting of the heartlands of Christianity from Europe and North America to Africa, Latin America, and Asia in his book *Beyond Christendom: Globalization, African Migration, and the Transformation of the West* (2008, 3). Likewise, the US church historian Philip Jenkins makes the case for the future of Christianity in the Global South or the Majority World in his provocative work, *The Next Christendom: The Coming of Global Christianity* (2007). Specifically, Jenkins asserts that as the result of significant demographic shifts, the future of Christianity lies not in the Global North or Minority World of Europe and North America, but in the Global South or Majority World encompassing Africa, Asia, and Latin America, where he notes that two-thirds of all Protestant Christians live today (2007, 45). He also notes that the Christianity of the Majority World is vibrant, thriving, and growing rapidly, in contrast to the Christianity of Europe and North America (Jenkins 2006).

From the Roman Catholic perspective, this is what the missiologist Aylward Shorter speaks of as a "new mission paradigm" in his seminal work, *Evangelization and Culture* (1994):

> The new mission paradigm offers the model of a *koinonia* Church, in which local Churches are responsible for mission-sending and reaching out to help one another in a variety of needs. . . . *Missionary vocations are recognized wherever they occur, without reference to any standard ecclesial maturity.* In the new paradigm there are no geographically, or even demographically, defined mission territories. *Mis-*

sion takes place wherever a Christian crosses a human frontier to supply a felt need, in accordance with the priorities of the local Church, and this includes Europe and North America. . . . In the new paradigm, missionary activity is multidirectional and there is a *growing interdependence or partnership among local Churches. . . .* The paradigm envisages an egalitarian world communion of mutually respected local Churches, serving and enriching one another. . . . The recently founded local Churches of the non-Western world are already sending missionaries and founding missionary societies. Non-Western Christians already outnumber those of the West. (1994, 69–70, emphasis added)

The observations of rapid church growth in the majority world that are discussed in the preceding paragraphs all point to the important fact that much of this growth is largely the result of the hard work of indigenous missioners and church leaders. This development has important implications. The classical missiological framework of the traditional sending churches in Europe and North America and emerging receiving churches in Asia, Africa, and Latin America is no longer relevant in view of these developments that mark the rise and growth of World Christianity.

Using China as an example, self-initiated Chinese efforts have led to an impressive growth of Chinese Christians, with the majority of converts belonging to newly emerging independent house churches that are primarily Pentecostal or Charismatic in orientation (Bays 2012, 183–207; Lian 2010; Rubinstein 1996). In chapter 1 of this book, we saw how the rise of self-initiated Chinese endeavors began with Hong Xiuquan's homegrown but potent synthesis of Christian apocalypticism and Daoist millenarianism in the mid-nineteenth century. This led to the emergence of indigenous Chinese church movements and revivalist preachers, demonstrating the viability and vibrancy of an indigenous Chinese Christianity that was independent of European missionary control. In turn, they paved the way for the growth in independent house churches (in Chinese, *jiating jiaohui*, literally "family churches") in Communist China from the latter half of the twentieth century onward.

Clearly, Christianity's fate in China is no longer tied to European or North American churches and the endeavors of their mission societies. It is slowly becoming an indigenous Chinese religion in the same manner as Chinese Buddhism, which evolved from a foreign religion to become a Chinese religion. Just as Buddhism became the popular religion of the masses in the countryside, so too Christianity is going down the same path and taking root in the countryside. Daniel Bays points out that the revival and expansion of Christianity in China from the 1980s onward "was substantially a rural phenomenon for both Catholics and Protestants" (Bays 2012, 193). In his groundbreaking study of indigenous popular Chinese Christianity, *Redeemed by Fire: The Rise of Popular Christianity in Modern China* (2010), Lian Xi also explores how the independent and sectarian Protestantism that was brought to China by European missionaries took root and was transformed into a popular religion that is both Chinese and Christian (2010, 238–47).

The same is true of indigenous Chinese Catholicism. Based on his fieldwork among rural Chinese Catholics in the 1990s (Madsen 1998), the sociologist Richard Madsen concludes that Chinese Catholicism is best understood as rural Chinese folk religion. In a groundbreaking essay, "Beyond Orthodoxy: Catholicism as Chinese Folk Religion," Madsen asserts:

> Catholicism in China, especially in the rural areas where the vast majority of Catholics live, is as much folk religion as world religion. I would not advocate abandoning a top-down view of Chinese Catholicism as part of a world religion and a universal Church. I will argue, however, that this view should be complemented by one that sees Chinese Catholicism as a localized folk religion. Such folk-Catholicism should not simply be seen as an impure form of a genuine Catholic faith, but *an authentic form of belief and practice to be understood on its own terms.* (2001, 234, emphasis added)

Madsen goes on to draw important parallels between rural folk Catholicism and rural folk Buddhism, pointing out how rural folk

Catholicism has been able "to blend more fully into the fabric of village and family culture" (2001, 246). For example, he notes that Chinese Catholics "honored their ancestors not by offering sacrifices of food on the ancestors' graves, but by praying fervently to them on the Feasts of All Souls and All Saints, by having priests say Masses for the Dead, and by offering Catholic prayers in front of their graves at the Qing Ming Festival" (2001, 246–47).

In other words, it is no longer possible to accept uncritically the hierarchy, paternalism, and dependence of the traditional hierarchical missionary structure, which sees the "mature" churches of Europe and North America as offering missionary leadership and sending foreign missionaries to the exotic mission lands of Asia, Africa, and Latin America (Neill 1990, 362, 380–448; Anderson 1974; Nacpil 1971). In this regard, the late Camerounian Jesuit theologian Engelbert Mveng (1930–1995) wrote of Christianity being enriched and transformed by African cultures and traditions, and of Africans having something to offer in dialogue with European Christians (1985). In a similar vein, Jehu Hanciles makes the case that African migrants are changing the face of Christianity in Europe and North America, with significant implications for the emergence of a global and transnational Christianity that is anchored by the energetic vitality and spiritual fervor of these African migrants (2008).

Likewise, the Kenyan theologian John Mbiti succinctly expresses the challenges of this shift in understanding when he points out that the dichotomy between the "older" churches of Europe and the "younger" churches of the Majority World is untenable in this present time. Mbiti observes that this one-sided or one-way flow from the Minority World to the Majority needs to change to a mutual or two-way flow that challenges the theologians in the "older" churches of Europe to learn from their counterparts in the Majority World. Specifically, he emphasizes the necessity for collaboration, reciprocity, and mutuality between the churches of the Majority World and the Minority World when he writes:

There cannot be theological conversation or dialogue between North and South, East and West, until we can embrace each other's concerns and stretch to each other's horizons. Theologians from the southern continents believe that they know about most of the constantly changing concerns of older Christendom. They would also like their counterparts from the older Christendom to come to know about their concerns of human survival. (Mbiti 1976, 17)

Hence, the model of mission among the peoples responds to the challenges and opportunities posed by the growth and vitality of indigenous Christianity in postcolonial Asia by eschewing the artificial dichotomy or division of labor between "mission sending" and "mission receiving" nations. Instead of paternalism and dependence, it seeks to redefine the relationship among the churches of Asia with the churches in the rest of the world to be one of equal partners in mission. It endeavors to foster and promote mutuality and collaboration among the various churches without regard to geographical locations or supposed maturity levels. Moreover, it makes it clear that a new mission theology for today's global and interconnected world is rooted in *koinonia*, interdependence, and solidarity, whereby all nations are both senders and recipients at the same time, engaging in mutual collaboration to promote the liberative and life-giving Good News of Jesus Christ.

Proposition 2

The orthodoxy *of the model of mission among the peoples is rooted in the* missio Dei *that seeks to usher in the universality of God's reign in pluralistic Asia, and Christians are called to imitate Jesus, the missional exemplar par excellence of the* missio Dei.

In the introduction to *Transforming Mission: Paradigm Shifts in Theology of Mission*, David J. Bosch observed:

Until the sixteenth century, the term *mission* was "used exclusively with reference to the doctrine of the Trinity, that is, of the sending of the Son by the Father and of the Holy Spirit by the Father and the Son." The Jesuits were the first to use it in terms of the spread of the Christian faith among people (including Protestants) who were not members of the Catholic Church. (1991, 1, citing Ohm 1962, 37–39)

Bosch went on to explain that the term *mission* in the above sense

was intimately associated with the colonial expansion of the Western world into what has more recently become known as the Third World (or, sometimes, the Two-Thirds World). The term "mission" presupposes a sender, a person or persons sent by the sender, those to whom one is sent, and an assignment. The entire terminology thus presumes that the one who sends has the *authority* to do so. Often it was argued that the real sender was God who had indisputable authority to decree that people be sent to execute his will. In practice, however, the authority was understood to be vested in the church or in a mission society. (1991, 1)

The missiologist and contextual theologian Stephen Bevans reminds us that mission, first and foremost, is about God's mission, or *missio Dei*, or, as he puts it, mission "in the first place, is primarily the work of God in the world" (2013, 160). The theological paradigm of mission as *missio Dei* first emerged in the early twentieth century, as David Bosch discussed in *Transforming Mission* (1991, 389–91). According to Bosch, the "decisive shift toward understanding mission as God's mission" or *missio Dei* marked a profound move away from earlier understandings of mission as "saving individuals from eternal damnation," "introducing people from the East and the South to the blessings and privileges of the Christian West," or "the expansion of the church" (Bosch 1991, 389–90).

In particular, Bosch identified the 1952 meeting of the International Missionary Conference in Willingen, Germany, as the important milestone that marked the emergence of a new understanding of mission as "being derived from the very nature of God" and rooted "in the context of the doctrine of the Trinity, not of ecclesiology or soteriology" (1991, 390). He unpacked the missiological significance of the 1952 Willingen meeting as follows:

> The classical doctrine on the *missio Dei* as God the Father sending the Son, and God the Father and the Son sending the Spirit was expanded to include yet another "movement": Father, Son and Holy Spirit sending the church into the world. As far as missionary thinking was concerned, this linking with the doctrine of the Trinity constituted an important innovation. Willingen's image of mission was mission participating in the sending of God. *Our mission has no life of its own: only in the hands of the sending God can it truly be called mission, not least since the missionary initiative comes from God alone.* (1991, 390, citing Aagaard 1974, 420, emphasis added)

Bosch went on to explain that *missio Dei* should be understood "not primarily an activity of the church, but an attribute of God" (1991, 391). He cited Jürgen Moltmann with approval: "It is not the church that has a mission of salvation to fulfil in the world; it is the mission of the Son and the Spirit through the Father that includes the church" (1991, 391, citing Moltmann 1977, 64). He further clarified:

> Mission is thereby seen as a movement from God to the world; the church is viewed as an instrument for that mission. . . . There is church because there is mission, not vice versa. . . . To participate in mission is to participate in the movement of God's love toward people, since God is a fountain of sending love. (Bosch 1991, 391)

In this vein, Peter Phan is emphatic that because the church's mission is not its own but flows from the trinitarian *missio Dei*, therefore, "The church must obey the divine command and follow God's modus operandi in the world through God's Son and Spirit" (2010, 166). In particular, Phan concludes that as Christians, we are not missioners on our own accord, "determining for ourselves and on our own authority the goal, method, location, and time of our own mission," but rather "we are sent by the Spirit, by the Son, and ultimately by the Father" (2010, 165, 166).

In *Constants in Context: A Theology of Mission for Today*, Stephen Bevans and Roger Schroeder propose a theology of mission that is shaped by three interrelated models of mission as participation in the mission of the Triune God (*missio Dei*), liberating service for the reign of God, and proclamation of Jesus Christ as universal savior (2004, 281–84). In addition, they explain that taken individually, each model has its strengths and flaws. In their opinion, only a synthesis of all three models would undergird a theology of mission for the third Christian millennium, which Bevans and Schroeder define as "prophetic dialogue" (2004, 348; cf. discussion on 348–95).

In a subsequent essay, Bevans discusses the need for contemporary mission to be multidirectional, mutual, and relational (2013, 159), while mindful of the fact that mission is, first and foremost, a *missio Dei*, that is, God's work of creation, celebration, healing, reconciling, and outreach in the world (2013, 160). Within this discussion, he explains the relationship between mission and church as follows:

> Mission, then, *precedes* the church. Mission is not about the church, but about the Reign of God. . . . Mission is for creation, not for the church. It is the self-giving of God to the world. In solidarity with the world, it is the church *for* the world, but above all the church *with* others. Mission should therefore be understood not as "mission of the church, but '*the church from and in mission.*'" (2013, 160–61)

Bevans reminds us that mission is all about discovering "what God is doing in the world, rather than thinking of ourselves as bringing and managing something"; therefore, "since mission is *participation in God's missionary life and work, mission is done in imitation of God*" (2013, 181, emphasis added).

I suggest that Jesus' mission to bring about the Reign of God in the Jewish society of his day that was chafing under Roman occupation best exemplified his understanding and embodiment of the *missio Dei* as discussed above by Bosch, Phan, and Bevans. It is instructive that the Gospel of Luke (4:16–19) unveils the inauguration of Jesus' earthly mission in the synagogue at Nazareth on the Sabbath, focusing on his appropriation of the Isaianic vision of deliverance and a new order, as well as revealing his self-realization of his calling and participation in the *missio Dei*. Specifically, Jesus self-identified with the Isaianic prophecy when he proclaimed to his fellow worshipers in the synagogue, "The Spirit of the Lord is upon me, because he has anointed me to bring good news to the poor. He has sent me to proclaim release to the captives and recovery of sight to the blind, to let the oppressed go free, to proclaim the year of the Lord's favor" (Luke 4:18–19, citing Isa. 61:1–2). More important, the incredulous synagogue worshipers heard Jesus make the audacious claim that this passage was being fulfilled; that is, his presence and his missional calling pointed to the realization of the Reign of God in their midst.

The canonical gospels portray Jesus as witnessing to the *missio Dei* among the peoples of his day, sharing their joys and sorrows, as well as despair and hope, without discriminating or differentiating against those who were marginalized by the broader first-century Jewish society. His table fellowship with tax collectors (Luke 7:34; Matt. 11:19) was radical, even by today's standards. He interacted with lepers, beggars, prostitutes, indeed the ordinary folk of his day who were rendered invisible by their nonstatus in Jewish society, sharing the pathos of human living in solidarity and empathy with them. He was at home among peoples across all social levels, from rabbis, lawyers, and teachers of the Law to lepers, prostitutes, and tax collectors. Moreover, Jesus spoke of his mission of bringing about the Reign of God in terms of being the "salt of the earth" (Matt. 5:13), "light of the world," and "city built on a hill" (Matt. 5:14), as well as the yeast that leavens the flour from the inside (Luke 13:20–21; Matt. 13:33). Just as salt adds flavor and yeast leavens the flour *from within*, so too Jesus articulated the *missio Dei from within* the daily ordinary life experiences of those around him, such that the Reign of God comes into fruition at the grassroots and among the people within the ordinary rhythms of their daily lives. Moreover, the metaphors of "light of the world" and "a city built on a hill" point to a deeper realization within the Asian context that "truth does not impose itself, but rather *attracts* everyone and everything to itself by its beauty, splendour and fascination" (Wilfred 1988, 427, emphasis added).

Among the many accounts of Jesus' witness to the *missio Dei* in the canonical gospels, I would like to make the case that Jesus' encounter with the Samaritan woman in John 4:4–42 best illustrates how Jesus' embodiment of the *missio Dei* could undergird a contemporary theology of mission among the peoples in Asia. Indeed, Jesus' encounter with the Samaritan woman within the complexities of Jewish-Samaritan interactions could offer a valuable lesson for doing mission among the peoples in contemporary pluralistic Asia. Although the Jews of Jesus' day ostracized and stigmatized the Samaritans as outsiders, especially for their nonparticipation in worship at the Temple of Jerusalem, Jesus was clearly comfortable with interacting with the Samaritan woman and did not view her as sinful, unclean, or any way inferior to Jews.

Nonetheless, for the longest time Christians have read the account of Jesus and the Samaritan woman in John 4 as an account of Jesus who liberated an adulterous woman from sin. In *The Misunderstood Jew: The Church and the Scandal of the Jewish Jesus*, the Jewish New Testament scholar Amy-Jill Levine criticizes such a stereotypical Christian reading that sees the Samaritan woman as culturally deviant, ritually unclean, sinful, shameless, marginalized, and needing to be saved by Jesus (Levine 2006, 135, citing the pivotal findings of Neyrey 2003, 124; cf. Levine 2006, 138). Levine seeks to make the case that there "is much to be celebrated in the story of the Samaritan woman, not the least of which is the depiction of a successful female evangelist" (Levine 2006, 138). She reminds us that in "the context of John 4, it is Jesus, the Jew in the Samaritan area, who is the 'outsider,' who behaves in a shameless way, and who is marginal to the community" (Levine 2006, 135; cf. 138). By contrast, the Samaritan woman is "so fully integrated into and accepted by her Samaritan village" that the townsfolk accepted her testimony of Jesus (Levine 2006, 135). She rightly notes that the Samaritan townspeople "are not likely to believe the testimony of a marginalized, shameless sinner" (Levine 2006, 135).

The story in John 4 opens with a weary Jesus, tired and exhausted from traveling, who sat by Jacob's Well near the town of Sychar at the sixth hour. He requested a drink of water from a Samaritan woman who came to draw water from the well (John 4:5–7). Jesus, a traveler sojourning through Samaria, was worn out by a long journey, much like anyone who is weary of one's lifelong arduous journey. Here we find a powerful image of a Jesus in touch with the pathos and struggles of humanity, experiencing the same weariness and exhaustion of daily living. Two implications can be drawn from the fact that Jesus did not merely pass through Samaria as quickly as he could, but lingered and stayed, even though he was clearly an outsider, a minority in majority Samaritan territory.

First, notwithstanding the general suspicion that Jews and Samaritans might harbor against each other, Jesus saw no insurmountable problem in pausing his sojourn at Jacob's Well in Sychar and expecting a Samaritan to offer him an act of hospitality, even though he was an outsider in the Samaritan milieu. His disciples as Jews were likely echoing Jewish stereotypes about Samaritans when they viewed the Samaritan woman with a mixture of disdain and suspicion, but Jesus was more than willing and happy to ask her for a drink of water, thereby initiating a mutual interaction between a Jew and a Samaritan. At a deeper level, this would suggest that God would have no problem immersing and interacting with practitioners of the great religious traditions of Asia. By extension, Asian Christians should not hesitate to immerse themselves deeply in the pluralistic Asian milieu and interact with their fellow Asians across religious boundaries.

Second, and on a deeper level, a tired and thirsty Jesus was present at the well before the arrival of the Samaritan woman. He longed for water to quench his thirst but lacked a bucket to get water from the well. As a human person, he knew what it was like to be tired and thirsty. In turn, this image of a tired and thirsty Jesus in Samaritan territory points to an image of a God who is in touch with the overarching pathos of humanity beyond the boundaries that define and demarcate institutional religions. It is also a reminder to us that God is already present in the world ahead of humanity, waiting patiently for humanity's arrival and meeting humanity not as a triumphant and powerful God descending to earth, but a God who, from the beginning is fully immersed in the pathos of humanity's daily travails.

On the one hand, Jesus' asking the Samaritan woman for a drink of water enabled him to open a dialogue with her across cultural and religious boundaries. In turn, this paved the way for Jesus and the Samaritan woman to go beyond their respective positions and enter into each other's horizons, thereby experiencing a mutual bond that connected them. Here, we see not a triumphant Jesus out to debate with the Samaritan woman, but rather a human Jesus looking to engage with the Samaritan woman on her home turf, giving us a foretaste of God engaging with humanity in the *missio Dei* and modeling how Asian Christians could engage and interact with their fellow Asian neighbors today.

On the other hand, in seeing Jesus ask the Samaritan woman for a drink of water, we see a Jesus who could beg for water without denying his ability to give water. Indeed, when Jesus interacted with the Samaritan woman, he did so not from a position of triumph and strength, but from a shared commonality— two persons both thirsting and looking for water at the same time. It is noteworthy that Jesus, the missioner of the *missio Dei*, demonstrated that mission is not a one-way street where missioners offer the gospel to the people around them. Jesus and the Samaritan woman were both receivers and givers, thereby demonstrating the necessity for mutuality in mission. On a deeper level, the mutuality between them exemplifies the mutuality of the *missio Dei*, where God not only gives but also receives what humanity is able to offer within the rich diversity of cultures and pluralism of religions.

Thus no one is exclusively a giver or a receiver. Both have something to give and something to receive, even the Samaritan woman. Likewise, Asian Christians and their fellow Asians are both givers and recipients in the context of their mission among the peoples in Asia. Just as Jesus could receive water from the Samaritan woman without denying his capacity to offer her living water, so too Asian Christians could receive from their fellow Asians who practice other religious traditions without denying their capacity to witness their Christian faith to them. This is a far cry from the triumphant foreign missionaries of the colonial past who came to Asia looking to give the Christian gospel to Asians and expecting that Asian religions have nothing to offer to Christianity. Thus, mission among the peoples is about mutual giving and receiving, not triumphalistic conquest and displacement.

A conversation that began with a simple request for a drink of water developed into a deeper spiritual conversation about the living water that gives eternal life (John 4:10–15), followed by Jesus inviting the Samaritan woman to bring her husband to join in their conversation (John 4:16–18). Following the interpretation that is proposed by Amy-Jill Levine, who challenges the traditional Christian interpretation of the Samaritan woman as a sinner (2006, 135, 138), I would like to suggest that Jesus was neither scolding the Samaritan woman nor berating her lack of morals. Reading the pericope at face value, what we see here is the Samaritan woman being profoundly struck by Jesus' deep empathy and solidarity with the pathos of her life situation with six different men. Instead of condemning her, Jesus reached out to her in the painful anguish of her pathos. In turn, the Samaritan woman recognized that Jesus was not the average Jewish man who ostracized Samaritans as outsiders, but rather a prophet who sought to touch her life, empathizing with the pathos of her pain and struggles, and offering her living water to heal her pain.

In response to the Samaritan woman's question of whether true worship took place at the Temple of Jerusalem or on Mount Gerizim, Jesus spoke of worshiping God "neither on this mountain nor in Jerusalem," but rather worshiping God "in spirit and truth" because "God is spirit" (John 4:21–24). Taken at face value, Jesus' response was revolutionary because he was proclaiming the coming of a new order where there is no distinction between Jew and Samaritan but everyone worships God "in spirit and truth" (John 4:23, 24).

What follows next is most remarkable. On the strength of her encounter with Jesus and having been quenched by the mutual sharing of water, the Samaritan woman became a missioner in her own right to witness the gospel to her fellow Samaritan townsfolk. In abandoning her water jar and going into town to share the Good News of Jesus among the townsfolk who were her family, neighbors, and friends, she demonstrated that her deep thirst and yearning was quenched by Jesus. In doing so, she embodied the call to do mission among the peoples par excellence. Indeed, it was neither Jesus nor his disciples who preached to the Samaritans, but the Samaritan woman who witnessed to Jesus' offer of new life among the Samaritans of her village. In turn, the Samaritans invited Jesus to stay with them on the strength of her testimony (John 4:40).

More significant, the Samaritan woman was able to bring the Good News to her fellow Samaritans by virtue of a shared heritage. Instead of an outsider preaching to strangers, we see in this case the Samaritan woman who was in a missional quest to witness the gospel as an insider among her peoples. In this sense, her witness to her fellow Samaritans reminds us of the power of the historical mission among the peoples of the Korean Confucian *yangban* who introduced the gospel among their fellow Koreans or indigenous Chinese evangelists and preachers who spread the gospel and established communities of faith throughout China without foreign missionary assistance, as discussed in chapter 1. In the context of contemporary pluralistic Asia, a mission among the peoples that draws inspiration from Jesus' encounter with the Samaritan woman would be able to serve as a catalyst for a new way of being church in pluralistic Asia and an impetus for new opportunities to do Christian mission in Asia.

Moving from Jesus' undertaking of the *missio Dei* in his day to the challenges of doing mission in present-day Asia, we would need to discern the *missio Dei* in pluralistic Asia, that is, discovering what God is doing in mission with the diverse religious traditions in Asia and their wealth of soteriological insights about living in this world and beyond. In our discussion of the variety of theological responses to the challenges of plurireligious Asia in chapters 2 and 3, we note that the religious pluralism of Asia is not something that has to be confronted and overcome, but rather accepted by Asian Christians as a constitutive dimension of the Asian milieu. If Asian Christians are called to imitate the example of Jesus' missional outreach to the Samaritan woman at the well, this means that they would have to search for nonconfrontational ways of witnessing the message of the Christian gospel in a world scarred by wars, violence, and massive socio-economic displacements. Just as Jesus transcended the sectarian divide between Samaritans and Jews to reach out and touch the life of the Samaritan woman, so too Asian Christians as mission-ers would seek to transcend the boundaries that separate them from their fellow Asian neighbors of other religions.

Proposition 3

Mission among the peoples is inspired by an orthopathos *that illumines divine empathy and solidarity with the pathos of the suffering and bro-kenness in the daily life experiences of the Asian peoples.*

From the foregoing discussion in Proposition 2, we see that the call to mission among the peoples invites Asian Christians to step into the shoes of those around them in their daily life experiences in the manner that Jesus entered into the life of the Samaritan woman in John 4. In order for Asian Christians to be credible missioners in the context of the immense challenges of postcolonial Asia, it is not enough for them to speak about pov-erty and marginalization in objective and abstract terms. Asian Christians are challenged to move away from merely reflecting on the suffering and marginalization of others from the safety and comfort of an objective and detached position, or spiritual-izing the suffering and marginalization that are experienced by many Asians. It goes without saying that contemporary missioners are called to cultivate and embody a deep spirit of empathy and solidarity with Asian peoples in the manner of Jesus' empathy and solidarity with the people around him. The missiologist Donal Dorr reminds us that the notion of solidarity best articulates the heart of Jesus' mission, as well as the church's mission (2000, 191). As Dorr explains, Jesus' own mission was shaped by his sharing life with ordinary people and experiencing their daily struggles. He then unpacks the implications of this insight as follows:

> Since solidarity was at the heart of the mission of Jesus, it must also be central to the mission of the church and

of any Christian who engages in missionary work of any kind. Like Jesus, we are called to share the life of the people among whom we feel called—and have chosen—to work. For each of us, mission cannot really begin until we are able, with some authenticity, to experience the people we live and work with as "my people." For us, as for Jesus, sharing in the life of a community is not just a preliminary to mission but is the very core of mission. For it is our solidarity with others which is the basis both for our openness to *receive* what they have to offer and for our willingness and eagerness to *share* with them the gift of faith in Jesus and the other gifts we have been given. (2000, 191–92, emphasis added)

Moreover, Dorr contends that those who do mission *without* solidarity with the people that they encounter are not genuine missioners, but rather "exploiters and colonizers" (2000, 191).

Within the notion of mission among the peoples, the call to solidarity, interdependence, and collaboration between Asian Christians and other Asian peoples is grounded in the *orthopathos* that enables them to understand and share in the divine solidarity with the *pathos* of humanity in general, as well as the minoritized and marginalized people in Asia in particular. The theological paradigm of *orthopathos* has been articulated by the Puerto Rican theologian Samuel Solivan in his book *The Spirit, Pathos, and Liberation: Toward an Hispanic Pentecostal Theology* (1998). Solivan seeks to present the case for *orthopathos* as the theological template that integrates *empathy* and *solidarity* for the suffering into the very act of theologizing (1998, 60). He notes that the *pathos* of the suffering of the minoritized and marginalized is often experienced as poverty, exile, homelessness, and voicelessness, as well as desolation and despair.[1] He reminds us that no one suffers for suffering's sake. On the contrary, people suffer because of "oppressive, classist, racist and sexist systems of society," as well

---

[1] For the discussion of *pathos* experienced as poverty, see Solivan 1998, 97; for exile and homelessness, 24, 137; for voicelessness, 33; for desolation and despair, 26, 71.

as "their inability to overcome the structures that oppress them" (1998, 61). In particular, Solivan highlights the importance and necessity of *orthopathos* as follows:

> Pathos points to and highlights the importance that should be given to a people's suffering, dehumaniza-tion, pain and marginalization. *Orthopathos* seeks to show how correct doctrine uninformed by a people's suffering often tends to be stoic, apathetic and distant. Orthodox approaches to suffering and pain are often allegorized or dealt with in the context of either the result of sin or slothfulness or a means by which one is tempered spiri-tually. These responses represent an aspect of the truth, but fall short of a holistic response that is present in the Scriptures. (1998, 12)

Solivan further explains that *orthopathos* places Christians in the midst of any community that is struggling with suffering and marginalization, affording them a direct involvement with, and firsthand existential participation in, the experience of pathos in the lives of those who are living on the margins of society. As far as he is concerned, *orthopathos* promotes human empathy, which leads to human solidarity, and ultimately, human praxis or actions to liberate and transform the world. He also points out that "*orthopathos* as an interlocutor seeks to or links us in com-munity with those who suffer" (1998, 37).

From the biblical perspective, Solivan undergirds his under-standing of *orthopathos* within the divine-human covenantal rela-tionship in the Hebrew Bible. Here, he focuses on a God who is not aloof or indifferent to the human condition, but rather a God who is touched by human suffering and sympathetic to the human condition, and who "engages the situation of the Israelites' pathos by responding concretely to their needs" (1998, 76). Within the framework of the New Testament, he draws attention to God's "kenotic empathy" with humanity, as exem-plified in the incarnation, as well as a God who moves beyond merely identifying with human suffering to transforming human suffering, thereby rendering human weakness and suffering as occasions for God to manifest divine strength (1998, 77–89). Moreover, he insists that divine empathy is unconditional for everyone who suffers, including the poor but not merely limited to the poor (1998, 149). He further asserts that *orthopathos* not only "empowers sufferers for the long-term struggle with their present, and often long-term, conditions" (1998, 65), but is also a liberative pathos that serves as the force and catalyst from suffering to liberation.

Solivan views *orthopathos* as "the power of the Holy Spirit in one's life that transforms pathos, suffering and despair into hope and wholeness" (1998, 27). In his opinion, the "*ortho* aspect of *orthopathos* is rooted in the distinction between suffering which results in self-alienation, and suffering that can somehow be a source for liberation and social transformation" (1998, 61). As he explains:

> Much has been said about pathos, suffering, oppression and alienation, all of which point to passivity, victimization, acquiescence, self-alienation and surrender. . . . *Orthopathos* addresses death, and offers a word of life and hope. *Orthopathos* is the empowering of the disempowered, the raising up of the down-trodden. . . . *Orthopathos* is the holistic empowerment of the Holy Spirit in one's life that leads to the transformation of pathos, suffering, and alienation. (1998, 146)

Finally, Solivan also makes it clear that the "concept of *orthopathos* addresses the need for a bridge between the truth claims made by orthodoxy and the liberating engagement sought by orthopraxis. It takes seriously the 'who' and 'what' that lie between the claim of rightness and the doing of right" (1998, 68; cf. 11). Thus, Solivan broadens the ambit of theology beyond *orthodoxy* and *orthopraxis* to include *orthopathos* as an attempt to integrate *orthodoxy* and *orthopraxis* within an all-encompassing and transformative power of divine empathy and solidarity with human pathos. This theological shift has significant missiological implications that go to the very heart of the task of doing mission among the peoples in Asia.

I would like to suggest that the template of *orthopathos* could provide the link to promote empathy and solidarity between Asian Christians as missioners and other Asian peoples with the pathos of suffering and marginalization that emerge from their daily life experiences. From the vantage point of *orthopathos*, Asian Christians as missioners are called to empathize with, as well as enter into, the suffering of others as Jesus did with the Samaritan woman at the well and as God did with Israel and continues to do so throughout human history with the marginalized and voiceless, bringing about a prophetic and liberative transformation. For the Christian gospel to overcome the negative and life-destroying aspects human pathos, Asian Christians seek to immerse themselves in the daily lives of their fellow Asian neighbors, sharing their daily struggles and imaging Christ to them. In a spirit of mutuality, *orthopathos* provides the epistemological framework for Asian Christians as missioners to be in solidarity with, and share the liberative praxis of the Christian gospel with, the people they encounter.

Hence, when Asian Christians as missioners are able to enter fully into the pathos of the human condition as experienced by their fellow Asian neighbors whom they encounter in daily life, they would be able to lay the groundwork for their Asian neighbors to experience, receive, and integrate the redemptive message of the Christian gospel in their daily lives. By being fully immersed among the Asian peoples and sharing their lives, Asian Christians are well placed to sow the seeds among the peoples that would enable their openness to, as well as reception of, the redemptive power of the Christian gospel. Thus, *orthopathos* becomes the bridge that integrates the *orthodoxy* of the gospel message and the *orthopraxis* of human action. In this regard, the spirit of *orthopathos* is also able to authenticate and highlight the relational and empathetic dimensions of the mission among the peoples in Asia that would enable Asian Christians to witness and express the healing and salvific dimensions of the Christian gospel among their Asian neighbors. In the absence of *orthopathos*, missioners would run the risk of preaching a cold, creedal, and cerebral gospel that downplays the pathos of the suffering and marginalized.

Proposition 4

Mission among the peoples is empowered by an orthopraxis *that enables the Christian Gospel to engage with the religious pluralism of Asia in a spirit of interreligious hospitality.*

In chapter 2, we read how Asian Christians realize that their life experiences are defined by the fact that for over two thousand years Christianity has at best been a minority religion in Asia, a world that is dominated by many of the world's ancient great religions. For them, it is not about re-evangelizing a continent that was previously Christian, rebuilding Christendom in a continent that has now been lost to postreligious secularism and relativism, but rather learning to live and prosper in a pluri-religious milieu that has always been defined by the other great religions of the world. More specifically, Asian Christians, as a religious minority in many parts of Asia, have no choice but to explore new ways of overcoming the antagonism and chauvinism of the religious majority around them. As a religious minority, Asian Christians complain about the majority scapegoating them for social ills and pressuring them to lose their distinctive racial-ethnic or religious features and become fully assimilated in the mainstream of society. They find themselves on the losing end of an "us-versus-them" rhetoric and political manipulations of religious differences by the religious majority that often go down the dangerous path of a power game that politicizes religion and plays off majority and minority communities in the interest of political expediency.

In view of the foregoing, the paradigm of mission among the peoples recognizes the fact and reality that religious pluralism is here to stay in Asia. Therefore, Asian Christians are called to explore new ways of doing Christian mission that would take into account the complex and tense relational dynamics between Asian Christians as a religious minority vis-à-vis their religious majority neighbors in the pluralistic Asian milieu. In this regard, I argue that this model of mission affords an opportunity for Asian Christians to promote positive encounters that are grounded in mutual hospitality and mutual relations beyond toleration simpliciter. There is a necessity for majority-minority relations to go beyond mere toleration because toleration per se only accentuates the domination of the majority group over other minority groups. In other words, the majority group continues to maintain its hegemony over other minority groups by either extending or withholding toleration without any recourse by the minority groups.

Amos Yong has used the Parable of the Good Samaritan to illustrate his point that religious diversity and plurality is part of God's universal plan of salvation. After pointing out that "Jewish attitudes toward Samaritans in the first century parallel in many ways conservative Christian and Pentecostal attitudes toward those in other faiths," he observes that this parable challenges conventional assumptions by presenting Jews as having to learn how to embody God's love for the neighbor from the Samaritans, who are the "religious others." He suggests that not only can Christians learn from the "religious others" but also that God might choose to be revealed through other religions in unexpected ways (2007, 60). In particular, Yong wonders aloud:

> Do Jews need to love their neighbors in order to inherit eternal life, even if such neighbors were despised as their enemies? Put in our context, do Christians not need to love their neighbors of other faiths in order to be saved? If so, don't Christians need those in other faiths for our own salvation as much as if not more than those in other faiths need Christians to bear witness to the gospel for their salvation? (2007, 61)

Moving on, Yong constructs what he calls a pneumatological theology of interreligious hospitality (2007, 65) that is rooted in mutuality and reciprocity between Christianity and other religions. He explains that although Christians cannot be responsible for the actions of others, they can and should take responsibility for their own attitudes and actions in a world where religious believers are becoming more hostile and antagonistic toward those who are different from them. In his own words:

Pentecostals and all Christians can and should bear witness to Jesus the Christ in word and in deed, while listening to, observing, and receiving from the hospitality shown them by those in other faiths. The result may be either mutual transformation of an unexpected kind, perhaps akin to the transformation experienced by Peter as a result of his encounter with Cornelius, or perhaps even our very salvation, such as described in the parable of one whose life was received as a gift through the hand of the good Samaritan. (2007, 66)

As far as Yong is concerned, the "religious others" are more than simply the objects of conversion by Asian Christians. Rather, these "religious others" are the guests, friends, and neighbors of Asian Christians, with both sides extending mutual friendship and reciprocal hospitality. Yong further insists that his pneumato-logical theology of interreligious encounter

not only allows but also obliges us to cultivate different dispositions toward those in other faiths than those tradi-tionally promoted; not only allows but also requires that we look for dialogical situations and opportunities involv-ing religious others; not only allows but also necessitates our establishing friendships and opening our homes for table fellowship with those of other faiths. (2007, 66)

Thus, Yong's vision of a pneumatological theology of inter-religious hospitality that welcomes believers of other religions in a spirit of friendship and neighborliness exemplifies the ideals of a mission-among-the-peoples model, Asian Christians living and working together with their Asian neighbors of other religions in a shared spirit of hospitality and solidarity for the betterment of their communities. He also reminds us of the importance of the quintessential Asian trait of dialogue, which has the potential to bring about opportunities for two or more parties, with their different worldviews, to enter into each other's horizons, thereby creating deeper levels of understanding and friendship.

Indeed, the call to witness the gospel in plurireligious Asia goes beyond merely proclaiming abstract doctrines or rational arguments to rooting the gospel in the Asian milieu within a framework of hospitality that would enable the Good News to be experienced and appropriated by the Asian peoples in a spirit of mutuality and relationality. This is because a theology of mission among the peoples that is rooted and empowered by a spirit of hospitality has the potential to foster thoughtful conversation, attentive listening, mutual dialogue, and finally, witness and conversion. Moreover, with the onslaught of migration that is causing great upheavals among different social, ethnic, and religious groups throughout Asia, a theology of hospitality is all the more relevant and necessary as an antidote to violence and turbulence, affording opportunities for hosts and guests to interact and engage with each other. At the same time, one should also acknowledge the reality that encouraging the majority to move away from reluctant tolerance to mutual trust of, and hospitality toward, diverse minority communities is often easier said than done. Hence, this model of mission has to contend with the vexing dilemma of whether it is feasible and realistic in view of the enormous challenges posed by religious fundamentalists and exclusivists in many parts of Asia.

The explosive situation in India that was explored in chapter 2 exemplifies the challenges facing the task of Christian mission in general and mission among the peoples in particular. Within the volatile dynamics of a dominant Hindu majority vis-à-vis an assertive Christian minority, it is legitimate to ask whether the mission-among-the-peoples approach smacks of naïveté in the face of vitriol, hate, and exclusivism that are being spewed by right-wing Hindutva militant groups against the Indian Christian minority. In response, this model highlights the fact that triumphalistic and aggressive proselytism merely begets more tension and conflict between majority and minority groups. In contrast, a template of mission among the peoples focuses on relationality and mutuality, seeking to build friendships, deepen relationships, listening and learning from, as well as sharing the wisdom of the Christian gospel, among family members, neighbors, friends, and strangers. In the process of doing so, the mission among the peoples is also participating in the broader *missio Dei*, God's own engagement and outreach to the world since the beginning of creation.

In this vein, Robert Schreiter makes the case for mission to embrace the more difficult task of facilitating and working for reconciliation at all levels of society as an integral part of the Christian witness (1992, 1998). Likewise, the Statement of the Executive Body of the Catholic Bishops' Conference of India (CBCI) in response to the Orissa violence against Indian Christians is unequivocal that a tit-for-tat response will only worsen things. According to the Indian Catholic bishops, one cannot fight religious exclusivism with religious exclusivism. One can disarm religious exclusivism only with Christian love. As the CBCI puts it, "No matter how great the threat that may confront us, we cannot renounce the heritage of love and justice that Jesus left us." This is because "when Jesus went about healing the sick, associating with outcasts and assisting the poor, those works were not allurements but the concrete realization of God's plan for humankind: to build a society founded on love, justice and social harmony" (CBCI 2008, 816).

On a similar note, the Catholic archbishop of Delhi, Vincent Concessao, points out that inflammatory Christian tracts that disparage and denigrate Hinduism are counterproductive because "they give fanatics a battering ram to crush Indian Christianity at large" (cited in Gonsalves 2008, 806). Likewise, the Indian theologian Sebastian Madathummuriyil puts forward the case for the Indian church to "re-examine the Church's imperialistic objectives of mission that reflects exclusivist and totalitarian tendencies," as well as to rediscover its identity, "paying heed to the challenges posed by religious, cultural, ideological, and linguistic pluralism" (cited in Boodoo 2010, 118). In particular, Madathummuriyil thinks that as a minority community in India, the Indian church is well positioned to be a prophetic voice for peace and harmony among Hindus, Muslims, and Christians in India against the backdrop of the Hindutva ideology of homogeneity of religion, culture, and language. In his own words:

To be a prophetic Church in the Indian context, then, would imply, on the one hand, forfeiting traditional strategies of mission and, on the other hand, enhancing measures for regaining trust and confidence of both Hindus and Muslims through dialogue in an age of widespread anti-Christian sentiments. (Cited in Boodoo 2010, 118)

Without a doubt, dialogue as a source of reconciliation can arise from only genuine relations of mutuality and solidarity between majority and minority communities at the grassroots level. In turn, dialogue could pave the way for conversion, forgiveness, and healing. The common good is promoted at all levels when barriers are broken down, the fires of hatred are quenched, bridges are built between majority and minority communities, and goodwill is promoted at grassroots levels to foster reconciliation and harmony, thereby breaking the vicious cycle of hate, fear, mistrust, and violence.

In any articulation of a theology of hospitality that undergirds a theology of mission among the peoples, the foundation for any intercultural and interreligious interaction, as well as mutual dialogue between different ethnic and religious communities, is typically built on a shared vision of life that all communities can identify with and call their own. For example, within the Malaysian sociocultural context, the concept of *muhibbah* (goodwill) is able to capture the spirit of hospitality and goodwill between the many ethnic and religious communities of Malaysia (Munusamy 2012; Thu 1995; Batumalai 1990, 11–20; Batumalai 1991, 403–30). Etymologically, the term *muhibbah* is a relational concept that is derived from the Arabic *muhabbat,* which means a bond of love and affection among friends. Traditionally, *muhibbah* captures the relationship of communal solidarity and empathy that underlies the spirit of neighborliness (*semangat kejiranan*), thereby promoting harmony for the well-being of everyone in the broader community (*masyarakat*). The fruits of *muhibbah* are manifested in a communal spirit of goodwill, hospitality, harmony, acceptance, generosity, courtesy, consensus, compromise, and peace.

For example, the spirit of *muhibbah* is manifested when different ethnic communities come together to celebrate each other's

festivals in a spirit of harmony and goodwill. A quintessentially
Malaysian communal way of celebrating cultural and religious
festivals is the traditional open house (*rumah terbuka*), whereby
families would invite friends and neighbors across ethnic and
religious communities to come together and celebrate the festival with them. Therefore, it is typical to find families, neighbors,
and friends across ethnic and religious groups celebrating Lunar
New Year in a Malaysian Chinese family's open house or enjoy-
ing the food and company at a Malaysian Muslim family's open
house for *Hari Raya Aidil Fitri* or *Eid al-Fitr,* marking the end of
the fasting month of *Ramadan.* In a similar vein, Malaysian Hindus would throw open houses for the Hindu Festival of Light
(*Deepavali* or *Diwali*), while Malaysian Christians do the same for
a uniquely Malaysian way of celebrating Christmas.

In addition, the spirit of *muhibbah* is put into action in the
communal practice of *gotong royong*, which is a collaborative project or mutual aid activity that seeks to benefit a family, neighbor, or the community (*masyarakat*) as a whole. Besides Malaysia,
the spirit of *gotong royong* is also practiced in Indonesia (Geertz
1983; Bintarto 1980; Jay 1969; Koentjaraningrat 1961). Within
the Indonesian Javanese context, the anthropologist Clifford
Geertz defined *gotong royong* as "joint bearing of burdens" (Geertz
1983, 211). Geertz further pointed out that together with "*rukun*
(mutual adjustment) and *tolong-menolong* (reciprocal assistance),"
gotong royong is part of "an enormous inventory of highly specific
and often quite intricate institutions for effecting the cooperation
in work, politics, and personal relations alike" that "governs social
interaction with a force as sovereign as it is subdued" (1983, 211).

In this regard, the spirit of *gotong royong* permeates both rural
and urban communities in Malaysia and Indonesia. In the traditional Malaysian village setting, if a family, neighbor, or the
community needs help, the whole community will pitch in to
organize a *gotong royong* to render the necessary assistance. For
example, in rural communities throughout Malaysia, the entire
community works in *gotong royong* at the planting and harvesting
season. In urban settings throughout Malaysia, ethnic communities in cities organize *gotong royong* activities, for example, clean-
ing up the local neighborhood, fundraising for local projects, and

other cooperative projects to strengthen the bond of solidarity within their own communities around shared ideals or goals.

The underlying thread in the concept of *muhibbah* in both rural and urban contexts, as well as its tangible manifestation in the spirit of *gotong royong,* is unity (*perpaduan*) that emerges when *muhibbah* is able to frame the context for meaningful dialogue and collaboration between different groups and communities within the Malaysian society. Thus, *muhibbah* is able to function as the glue that holds together the social fabric of the multiethnic, multilingual, multireligious, and pluricultural Malaysian society, thereby promoting peace and harmony between the different ethnic communities. In this respect, one could therefore say that the paradigm of *gotong royong* is able to undergird intracommunity as well as intercommunity solidarity across all levels of the Malaysian society.

On the basis of the foregoing, the Malaysian Chinese theologian Thu En Yu has proposed a theology of racial reconciliation and harmony in Malaysia in the aftermath of the violent racial riots of May 13, 1969, which is contextualized within the paradigm of *muhibbah* (Thu 1995). The Malaysian Indian theologian and retired assistant Anglican bishop of West Malaysia, Sadayandy Batumalai has constructed a Malaysian theology of *muhibbah* that would enable Malaysian Christians to engage in prophetic witness of the gospel in dialogue and collaboration with other Malaysians (Batumalai 1990, 11–20; 1991, 403–30). Batumalai's missional theology of *muhibbah* follows his earlier work that utilizes the Japanese theologian Kosuke Koyama's theological paradigm of "neighborology" (Koyama 1999, 64–67) to construct a Malaysian contextual theology of "neighborology" that would enable Malaysian Christians to live out the gospel values in witness to their fellow Malaysians of other religious faiths in a nonconfrontational manner (Batumalai 1986). What unites both Yu's and Batumalai's theological endeavors is their understanding that the paradigm of *muhibbah* is able to challenge the various ethnic and religious communities in Malaysia to look beyond rivalry in a spirit of harmony and goodwill to heal hurts and divisions that emerged in the aftermath of the racial riots of May 13, 1969.

I would like to suggest that the Malaysian spirit of *muhibbah* is also echoed in the Final Statement of the FABC's Fifth Faith Encounters in Social Action (FEISA V), titled the *Pastoral Care of Migrants and Refugees: A New Way of Being Church*. Specifically, FEISA V calls on Asian Catholics to take the initiative at parish level to provide pastoral care to migrants, receiving and assisting them in their moment of greatest need, taking the initiative to reach out and visit them because, as non-Catholics, they "may not have the courage to visit Catholic churches" (Eilers 2007, 119). Among other things, local parishes could offer space and hospitality to the migrants who "need a place where they can gather together for prayers or to have their religious celebrations or just for a friendly gathering among themselves" (Eilers 2007, 120).

Mission among the Peoples in Multicultural and Plurireligious Malaysia

How would a model of mission among the peoples work in practice? To answer this question, let us take Malaysia as a case study. Contemporary Malaysia is a multiethnic, multilingual, multireligious, and multicultural society comprising Malays (50.4 percent), Chinese (23.7 percent), aboriginals/indigenous (11 percent), and Indian (7.1 percent). About 60 percent of the population of Malaysia is Muslim. Christians are exclusively non-Malays and constitute around 9.0 percent of the population, followed by Hindus (6.5 percent), and followers of Chinese religions (2.5 percent). At the same time, Malaysia is also a socially and politically volatile society divided by an explosive mix of ethnicity and religion. Although Islam is the official religion of Malaysia and the majority of Malaysians are Muslims, freedom of religion in Malaysia is guaranteed under article 11(1) of the Malaysian Federal Constitution, which states, "Every person has the right to profess and practise his religion and, subject to Clause (4), to propagate it." However, article 11(4) of the Malaysian Federal Constitution also empowers the federal and state governments to pass laws against the propagation of non-Muslim religions among the Muslims: "State law and in respect of the Federal Territories of Kuala Lumpur and Labuan, federal law may control or restrict the propagation of any religious doctrine or belief among persons professing the religion of Islam." The simmering discontent between the Malays and Chinese, the two dominant ethnic groups in Malaysia, came to an explosive clash in the series of violent racial riots, stoked by extremist Malay nationalists against the Chinese community, beginning on May 13, 1969 (Goh 1971; Comber 1983).

In the aftermath of these riots, the Malaysian government embarked on a policy of national reconciliation to rebuild a shattered society. In an ironic twist, the cornerstone of the Malaysian government's policy of national reconciliation is the New Economy Policy (NEP), which institutionalized communalism, Malay dominance in nation building, and Malay sovereignty (*Ketuanan Melayu*) over the other minority communities in all matters— political, social, and economic. In reality, the NEP resulted in widespread economic inefficiency, corruption scandals, cronyism, and nepotism as a small Malay elite controlled the political and economic levers of powers to the exclusion of ordinary Malays and other races. As the tangible economic benefits of the NEP failed to trickle down to the ordinary Malays in rural communities, the Islamic Parti Islam Se-Malaysia (PAS) emerged to champion Islamization as the alternative to the cronyism and corruption of the NEP. In response to the popularity of PAS's Islamization platform, the ruling political elite adopted a similar policy of Islamization to blunt PAS's tactics (Kahn and Loh 1992).

To say that the Malaysian government's heavy-handed program of Islamization has resulted in increased religious tensions between the majority Muslim and other religious minority communities in Malaysia is an understatement. As members of a religious minority, Malaysian Christians have found themselves in the direct line of legislation and programs aimed at giving Islam a privileged position over the other religious faiths in Malaysia. For example, federal legislation was passed in 1981 to ban possession of Indonesian translations of the Bible. In response to vociferous protests by Malaysian Christians, a concession was made in 1982 to allow them to use the Indonesian translation for personal devotions and public worship. However, current law prohibits the dissemination and circulation of any Indonesian or

Malay translation of the Bible among Muslims in Malaysia. In 1991, the Malaysian Parliament passed legislation to prohibit the use in non-Islamic literature of, among other things, the term "Allah" for God. Malaysian Christians were outraged against this prohibition of the use of "Allah" for God, because it impinged on their right to use the term "Allah" in Malay language translations of the Bible, as well as in public worship and prayer meetings (Walters 2002).

Non-Muslims in Malaysia are also rankled by legislation that criminalizes apostasy (*takfir*) by Muslims and the actions of non-Muslims who proselytize their faith to Muslims. The law against apostasy drew international headlines and condemnation in the case of Lina Joy, who filed a suit before the Malaysian Federal Court to compel the Malaysian National Registration Department to record her change of religion from Islam to Christianity on her identity card after her baptism as a Roman Catholic. On May 30, 2007, her appeal was dismissed by a 2–1 majority, and she and her Christian fiancé were forced to leave Malaysia under threats of violence from Malaysian Muslim activists. In addition, the Malaysian Federal Court ruling further inflamed interreligious tensions as non-Muslim minorities perceive this to be yet another nail in the coffin for the erosion of religious freedom in Malaysia (Walters 2007).

In response to the relentless pressure from the Malay Muslim majority, the Christian Federation of Malaysia (CFM) was established in 1986 as an umbrella organization for Malaysian Christians by the Roman Catholic Church, the Council of Churches of Malaysia (CCM) representing the mainline Protestant Churches, and the National Evangelical Christian Fellowship (NECF) representing the Evangelical, Brethren, and Pentecostal churches. The CFM comprises about five thousand member churches and encompasses around 90 percent of the total Christian population of Malaysia. It seeks to present a united Christian front to negotiate with the Malaysian government on religious issues. The CFM is also an active member of the Malaysian Consultative Council of Buddhism, Christianity, Hinduism and Sikhism (MCCBCHS). The MCCBCHS was established in 1983 to promote understanding, mutual respect, and cooperation among the different religions in Malaysia, resolve interreligious issues, and make representations to the Malaysian government on religious matters (Tan and Ee 1984, 13). In practice, the MCCBCHS has become an organized channel for dialogue between the non-Muslims and the Malaysian government on issues of religious freedom and the impact of encroaching Islamization on the rights of the non-Muslim religious minorities to practice their faith without interference or fear.

Hwa Yung's essay "Islam in South East Asia and Christian Mission" (2003) seeks to respond to the challenges of the Malaysian socioreligious context as outlined above. Although Hwa Yung does not use the term "mission among the peoples" in this essay, nonetheless he provides tantalizing insights into how such a model would work in practice in an environment marked by fear and distrust between the two communities of faith. According to him, Christian-Muslim relations are marked by two overarching issues. First, in view of the "more than a thousand years of problematic Christian-Muslim relations, together with the recent events of September 11 and the American responses in Afghanistan and Iraq, Christians need to revisit the question of how they wish to resolve tensions with Muslims and live in peace with them." Second, Christians have to find a way to live out their missional calling to bring the love and salvation of Christ to all peoples in general, and Muslims in particular, notwithstanding their hostility toward Christians. In response, Hwa Yung begins by saying that Asian Christians have to address both issues together, taking seriously "the respective integrity of each faith, both of which are overtly missionary" (2003, 220).

He then proposes a way forward as follows:

> The call to live at peace with all is inherent in the gospel (Romans 12:18). It is therefore our Christian duty to do all that is possible to work towards peace, harmony and true mutuality in our relations with Muslims. Dialogue, mutual understanding and bridges of friendships must therefore be pursued, both at the personal level and at the communal and international levels. (2003, 221)

Although Hwa Yung insists that Christians have to remain faithful to their missional calling, he is also aware that debates and intellectual arguments will never resolve the conflicting truth claims between both faiths. Hence, he thinks that the way forward is "the way of the heart." As he explains:

> This does not mean that we merely forget about all differences in truth claims and just let hearts connect. Rather, it would mean that the Muslim heart must be touched by the heart of God through Christian love, humble service, suffering, and if necessary, martyrdom. (2003, 222)

Clearly, what Hwa Yung advocates here reinforces what the mission-among-the-peoples approach is all about. Mission is not simply a unidirectional proclamation of the truth claims of the Christian gospel against the truth claims of other religions. As Hwa Yung rightly points out, this traditional approach to mission would inevitably lead to violence and bloodshed among the followers of both religious communities. Rather, mission entails that Asian Christians practice a holistic life witness to the gospel that seeks to break down barriers of hostility and division among Muslims and Christians, as well as build mutual trust and friendship in a spirit of hospitality. Indeed, the "way of the heart" that Hwa Yung speaks of, which entails "Christian love, humble service, suffering, and if necessary, martyrdom," summarizes succinctly the vision and ideals of a notion of mission among the peoples.

Asian Christians recognize that all of the great religions of the world today, including Christianity, trace their beginnings to Asia. They are also aware that despite over two millennia of indigenous presence in Asia, Christians continue to make up only a small proportion of the total population of Asia. They further know that Christian mission has to rethink how it handles the issue of religious pluralism and find ways of working together with the other great religions of Asia toward the *missio Dei*, which inspires and empowers the missional witness of Asian Christians.

This chapter proposed a new way of looking at mission that responds to the challenges of the task of doing Christian mission in Asia amid the complexities of cultural diversity, religious pluralism, political upheavals, and socioeconomic disintegration, as well as migration and dislocations. It examined the significance and implications of the paradigm of mission among the peoples for rethinking the task of doing Christian mission in Asia and discussed why this paradigm best exemplifies the future of Christian mission in Asia in a manner that transcends denominational boundaries and theological loyalties. By reiterating the importance of complementary and relational perspectives of Christian mission—from, among, and with the peoples—this template of mission among the peoples highlights the *missio Dei* that is enfleshed in the missional witness of Jesus.

As missioner par excellence, Jesus' solidarity and empathy with the people around him in general, and the Samaritan woman at the well in particular, pointed to the success of his missional outreach and interaction across all segments of the Jewish society of his day. It is no longer the case of doing something *to* others, but rather working *among* and *with* others in a spirit of empathy and solidarity. In this regard, the paradigm of mission among the peoples is inspired and empowered by the mutual hospitality between Jesus and the Samaritan woman at the well. Just as Jesus was both the recipient and giver of water, so too Asian Christians are called to be both recipients and givers to their fellow Asians.

Mission *among* and *with* the Asian peoples would be at home with the challenges of cultural diversity, religious pluralism, and the immense poverty and marginalization of the Asian peoples. Within the internal framework of Christianity and church, this model highlights the limitations of the old sending-receiving model of mission toward a World Christianity model of intra-ecclesial mutuality and collaboration within the contemporary world that is shaped by the forces of globalization and transnationalism. In other words, the paradigm of mission among the peoples transcends borders and boundaries. In doing so, it reveals the deeper multidirectional, interrelational, and transnational dimensions of doing Christian mission in today's "flat" world. As the well-known *New York Times* columnist Thomas Friedman notes, in the "flat" world that is being shaped by the forces of globalization and transnationalism, historical institutional structures, geographical boundaries, and other forms of division are increasingly becoming irrelevant (Friedman 2007).

From a theological perspective, this concept of mission among the peoples is rooted in a trinitarian framework of *orthodoxy* that is directed toward God and the *missio Dei*, *orthopraxis* that imitates the missional outreach of Jesus, and *orthopathos* that is empowered by the Spirit working across boundaries and divisions to gather all peoples together in a new Pentecost for today. The paradigm of mission among the peoples recognizes God's presence and reign in the world, as well as God's outreach within and outside the Christian community. Indeed, the *orthodoxy* of the mission among the peoples situates the contemporary missional witness of the Christian gospel within the universality of God's reign, and in so doing makes the *missio Dei* its calling and priority. The *orthopraxis* of the mission among the peoples seeks to enable the gospel message to engage with the religious pluralism of the Asian peoples in a spirit of interreligious hospitality that is inspired by Jesus' own engagement with the Samaritan woman at the well. The *orthopathos* of the mission among the peoples is inspired by the depth of divine empathy and solidarity with the pathos of human suffering and brokenness.

Within the framework of mission among the peoples in Asia, the Asian experience of *orthopathos* is a significant contribution to the broader framework of Christian mission. Many Asian Christians find it logical to take *orthopathos* as the starting point of this model. For them, the *orthopathos* that inspired and empowered by the Spirit leads to the *orthopraxis* of Jesus' missional witness of the *orthodoxy* of the *missio Dei* and God's reign, enabling the Christian gospel to engage with religious pluralism in the spirit of interreligious hospitality. At the same time, *orthopathos* is able to undergird *orthodoxy*'s emphasis on proclaiming the gospel and complements *orthopraxis*'s emphasis on liberative action by emphasizing the need for empathy and solidarity with the pathos of suffering and brokenness of the Asian peoples today as an important theological resource. Missioners cannot enter into the world of the Asian peoples if they are unable to empathize and be in solidarity with the pathos of the suffering and marginalization that are experienced daily by the Asian peoples.

In particular, taking *orthopathos* rather than *orthopraxis* as the starting point of the mission among the peoples in Asia points to the deeper understanding that before Asian Christians embark on missional witness, they have to reflect on the worldviews, assumptions, attitudes, and dispositions that they bring to their praxis of missional witness. One could make the case that in the absence of *orthopathos*, they would not be able to build bridges to the adherents of other religions, thereby remaining alien and inaccessible to others. Clearly, the notion of mission among the peoples emphasizes the paramount importance of relationality and mutuality in missional engagements. No longer is the missional quest seen as a unilateral or one-way street of bringing something *to* the religious others. Rather, attention is focused on the fact that the missional quest in Asia has to be nonconfrontational, welcoming, inviting, with an emphasis on mutuality and relationality.

In other words, *orthopathos* not only reminds Asian Christians of their common humanity with their fellow Asians, and indeed with all women and men around the world, it also challenges Christians to be open to receive the gifts of the religious others, as well as share their gifts with them too. In addition, *orthopathos* takes *orthopraxis* a step further by transforming suffering and marginalization into resources for liberation. Through *orthopathos*, Asian Christians are called to walk barefoot together with those who suffer, seeing and experiencing from the vantage point of the suffering. Moreover, *orthopathos* also broadens the ambit of missional endeavors by pointing out that the necessity for *orthopathos*'s critical introspective focuses on daily living. Although *orthopraxis* is an essential epistemological component of the task of mission, enabling missioners to identify the social, cultural, political, economic, and other factors that significantly affect the daily lives of peoples they encounter, nevertheless by itself *orthopraxis* is insufficient for a well-rounded mission theology. The *orthopraxis* of Asian mission theologies would run the risk of a distortive emphasis on the materialist aspects of salvation, and the *orthodoxy* of Asian mission theologies would run the risk of being divorced from the daily existential realities of Asians, if both theological dimensions are not complemented by the critical introspective dimension of *orthopathos*. Without *orthopathos*, the cognitive dimensions of theology are separated from the affective, thereby dehumanizing the task of mission.

By focusing on compassion and introspection, *orthopathos* paves the way for a more holistic vision and understanding of theology that unites mind (*orthodoxy*), body (*orthopraxis*), and spirit (*orthopathos*). Thus, *orthopathos* seeks to complement *orthopraxis*'s active struggle against oppression, exploitation, and discrimination with *orthopathos*'s introspective and innate spirit of compassion and interiority, as well as *orthopraxis*'s goal of satisfying unmet human needs with *orthopathos*'s intuitive and interior mystical aspects of prayer, contemplation, and compassion. Unless *orthopraxis* emerges out of, and is nourished by *orthopathos*, it cannot be truly liberative and transformative in the daily lives of Asians. Critical introspective *orthopathos* also reminds us that society is interdependent. Without *orthopathos*, the Christian gospel would always be deemed as alien and foreign, and therefore unable to take root in the Asian soil.

Finally, Asian Christians also realize that before they can transform other Asians, they have to transform themselves first, which can be done only through relationships of love and reconciliation with other Asians in the fullness of their interrelated webs of religions, cultures, ethnicities, and other identity markers. Through a missional outreach that is carried out among the Asian peoples, Asian Christians seek to be a listening and welcoming community of faith. Asian Christians are both hosts and guests with their fellow Asians. In other words, while witnessing to the gospel is an important dimension of mission, in practice this witnessing is exemplified in the values of friendship and trust, relationality and relationship-building, dialogue and consensus, as well as solidarity and empathy, as constitutive elements of doing mission among the peoples in Asia. Unless their fellow Asians put their trust and feel secure in the communities of faith of the Asian Christians, the Christian gospel would remain superficial, marginal, and foreign, unable to take root in Asia.

Chapter 5

The Challenges of
Contemporary Migrations
in Diasporas and Cyberspace

To say that we are currently living in an age of migration in Asia is an understatement. Without a doubt, migration is a contemporary global phenomenon that is deeply embedded in the lives of millions of Asians, as well as shaping and transforming those lives. According to the International Organization for Migration's *World Migration Report 2011*, about one billion people (or one in seven of the world's population) are migrants (2011, 49). The World Migration Report 2011 also notes that five of the top ten emigration countries are located in Asia, namely India (second), China (fourth), Bangladesh (sixth), Pakistan (seventh), and the Philippines (ninth) (IOM 2011, 68, citing World Bank 2011, 3). As people move, they bring with them their cultures, religious traditions, and ways of living. Beyond the geographical boundaries of homelands and diasporas, the large-scale migration of Asian youth and the Generation Y or millennials of Asia across virtual boundaries into the realm of cyberspace in today's digital age is also transforming generational, communal, societal, and socioreligious ties beyond the familiarity of past precedents. The implications of such virtual migrations are profound and await further in-depth discussion by missiologists and missioners.

In recent decades, a close nexus has been drawn between migration as a contemporary phenomenon and its important interdisciplinary implications (Brettell and Hollifield 2008; Castles and Miller 2009; Rytter and Olwig 2011). In turn, this has generated the interest of religion scholars and theologians in exploring the religious and theological implications of migra-tion. This has resulted in excellent critical discussions on migra-tion and its theological implications (Campese and Ciallella 2003; Groody and Campese 2008; Groody 2009; Padilla and Phan 2013), biblical perspectives on migration (Ruiz 2011), migration and gender (Cruz 2010; Parreñas 2001; Bonifacio and Angeles 2009), and the theological implications of migration in Asia (Baggio and Brazal 2008). Moreover, the increasing waves of migrations by Asians have profound implications for Christian theology and identity construction in general, and the theology of Christian mission in particular (Burns, Skerrett, and White 2000; Ebaugh and Chafetz 2000). In his pioneering study of ethnic migrants and the emergence of American religion, the US historian Timothy Smith notes that migration is "often a theologizing experience" (1978, 1174).

Within Roman Catholic circles, both Pope John Paul II and the Pontifical Council for the Pastoral Care of Migrants and Itinerant Peoples' 2004 Instruction, *Erga migrantes caritas Christi,* speak of the need for outreach to migrants as part of the task of doing Christian mission, especially the pastoral care of Christian migrants in diasporic communities globally. Peter Phan observes that no matter how much migrants endeavor to make a new life for themselves in their newly adopted lands, they often remain marginal in their new worlds. As he explains, "Being immigrant means being at the margin, or being in-between or being betwixt and between" two worlds, the native homeland and the adopted country (Phan 1999b, 162–63). On the other side of the coin, Jehu Hanciles is emphatic that "every Christian migrant is a potential missionary" (Hanciles 2008, 6).

Likewise, Stephen Bevans writes that Christian mission "done in the light of migration is a radical commitment to the margin-alized" (2013, 171). In particular, Bevans speaks highly of migrant Christians witnessing "by their lives of faith and by their vital and vibrant church communities," as well as by their indigenous churches, social justice efforts, peacemaking initiatives, and out-reach efforts to their hosts (2013, 168). Bevans also outlines the important roles that migrant Christians can play as agents of rec-onciliation:

Migrant Christians can engage in interreligious dialogue at every level, especially with members of their own cultural and ethnic groups, and they are perhaps the best church agents in the ministry of reconciliation among their own congregations. In addition, they can be bridges between their own migrant communities and the host communities, as various personal, cultural, political, and ecclesial actions of reconciliation are needed. (2013, 168)

In this chapter, I consider how the concept of mission among the peoples in Asia could respond to the challenges and implications of Asians on the move to geographical diasporas and into cyberspace, and reflect on the theological and missiological implications of such engagements. In the case of the former, I explore how the Federation of Asian Bishops' Conferences' (FABC's) theology of migration is able to address the daily challenges faced by migrants in Asia. Although the FABC does not use the term "mission among the peoples," I endeavor to show that the FABC's theology of migration exemplifies the task of doing Christian mission among the Asian migrants. In the case of the latter, I discuss how an emphasis on mission among the peoples could provide a framework for reaching out to the youth and the millennials who congregate, network, and construct new lives in cyberspace. I would venture that the large-scale migration of Asian youth and the millennials into the frontier of cyberspace is as momentous as, if not more significant than, migration across geographical frontiers. Indeed, the future of Christian mission in Asia hinges on how Asian Christians seek new ways of missional witness among the migrants across geographical and virtual frontiers.

Mission among the Asian Migrants

Migration in Asia: An Overview

The phenomenon of migration in Asia has a long, varied, and complex history stretching back thousands of years. Beginning with the nomadic tribes that wandered the vast expanse of the Asian continent in search of water and grazing lands, the trade caravans that traveled on the famed Silk Routes across vast stretches of Asia, and the invading armies that displaced peoples and communities from their ancestral lands, migration has always defined the Asian continent in every age. In addition, the history of the world Christian movement reveals that migration and Christian mission are closely intertwined. In the early decades of the World Christian movement, we read about the migration of Jewish and Gentile Christians across the Mediterranean world, such as in Acts 8:1 on the scattering of Greek-speaking Christians following the martyrdom of Stephen, and in Acts 18:1–3 on Prisca and Aquila fleeing Rome for Corinth, where they established a new house church. The author of the *Epistle to Diognetus* spoke of second-century Christians, whose view was that "any foreign country is a motherland, and any motherland is a foreign country" (cited in Hanciles 2008, 1). In addition to the westward migration of Christians from Jerusalem, we must not overlook the migratory journeys of Assyrian missionaries and merchants along the Silk Road, who brought the Christian gospel and Assyrian Christianity to India and China, as discussed in the first chapter of this book.

Although nomadic tribes and trade caravans have come and gone, large-scale migration continues unabated in Asia. The principal difference between the past and the present is the fact that the pace of migration was much slower three thousand years ago, when the first caravans ventured far beyond familiar territory in search of new trading opportunities. The beginning of the twentieth century saw the massive rise in migration that was facilitated by the great steamships, propeller airplanes, and transcontinental railways. At the start of the twenty-first century, the world is witnessing the growth of large-scale internal and external displacements that are made possible by affordable international travel, advanced telecommunications, and broadband Internet. Today's migration patterns in Asia include internal migration from rural to urban centers (Chinese youth leaving the countryside for work in the coastal regions of China), external migration from economically depressed countries to economically booming countries (e.g., Filipinos working in oil-rich Arab nations), and refugees fleeing violence and persecution (e.g., Tamils fleeing Sri

Lanka and Rohingya leaving Myanmar). Migration can be voluntary (economic migrants in search of jobs) or forced (refugees, asylum seekers, and internally displaced persons who are fleeing persecution in their homelands).

At the same time, immigrants, whether they were voluntary or involuntary immigrants, are welcomed by some and resented by others. On the one hand, the abundant array of ethnic restaurants, galleries, and festivals is often welcomed because they add spice and zesty variety to otherwise staid lives. On the other hand, complaints of cultural "assault," cultural relativization, and cultural "pollution" are growing increasingly frequent and strident. Indeed, migration becomes the bogeyman that embodies the fear, uncertainty, and insecurity about a community's self-identity vis-à-vis others, leading to the absolutization of its ethnic and cultural identity against what it perceives as the threat of encroachment by others. In extreme cases, it can stir up feelings of xenophobia, ethnocentrism, racism, and nationalism.

Moreover, one also has to acknowledge the reality that today's large-scale globalized migration patterns are fueled and abetted by immense poverty, extreme socioeconomic imbalances, and violent ethnic and religious strife, as well as the insatiable demand for cheap labor and cheap products. The magnitude of this problem is especially dire in Asia. Many Asians are migrants, whether willingly or unwillingly. Voluntary migrations are often exemplified by the many Filipinos, Indonesians, Indians, Bangladeshis, Chinese, and others who seek better opportunities outside their homelands as construction workers, domestic helpers, and factory workers. Involuntary migrants include not just refugees who are fleeing wars, social strife, economic upheavals, political instability, religious tensions and persecution, but also the many economic migrants, especially vulnerable women and children, who are exploited and trafficked by underworld gangs, smuggling networks, and secret societies for cheap labor and sex trafficking. The sheer violence and abject dehumanization that many of these women and children experience reveal the dark underbelly of migration; this situation calls for a concerted response on the part of everyone to redress these problems.

In the context of Asia, the movement of peoples also brings about the movement of cultures and religions, resulting in increasing cultural diversity and religious pluralism across Asia, as the majority community in host countries are often faced with the challenges of welcoming and integrating incoming migrant communities. The US historian, Peter Stearns aptly characterizes migrations as "cultures in motion" (2001). The challenges of migration for interfaith relations between the native majority community and migrant minority communities in the host country can no longer be ignored.

Mission and the Challenges of Migration

Migration, whether voluntary or involuntary, documented or undocumented, is more than transnational or global population mobility simpliciter. Migration often leads to the commodification and exploitation of the human person, resulting in the abuse and dehumanizing of the human person. As the late Indian theologian S. Arokiasamy explained, migration "reveals the vulnerability of people's lives, their insecurity, exploitation, joblessness, uprootedness, political uncertainty and humiliating treatment as outsiders or foreigners" (1995, 9). Writing from both personal experience and academic research, Peter Phan draws attention to the "existential condition of a transnational immigrant and refugee," which includes "violent uprootedness, economic poverty, anxiety about the future, and the loss of national identity, political freedom, and personal dignity" (2003, 8). As Phan explains in an earlier autobiographical essay, "Being immigrant means being at the margin, or being in-between or being betwixt and between" two worlds, that is, the native homeland and the adopted country (Phan 1999b, 162–63). Drawing from his own experience as a refugee, Phan writes that the migrants' quest for self-identity is affected by their marginal status:

> To be betwixt and between is to be neither here nor there,
> to be neither this thing nor that. Spatially, it is to dwell
> at the periphery or at the boundaries. . . . Socially, to be

betwixt and between is to be part of a minority, a member of a marginal(ized) group. Culturally, it means not being fully integrated into and accepted by either cultural system, being a *mestizo*, a person of mixed race. . . . Psychologically and spiritually, the person does not possess a well-defined and secure self-identity and is often marked with excessive impressionableness, rootlessness, and an inordinate desire for belonging. (Phan 1999a, 113)

What goes without saying, but what is often overlooked by many is the reality that the movement of peoples invariably brings about the movement of religions. The Maryknoll missioner and missiologist William LaRousse expresses it succinctly when he points out that migration not only "brings Christians into contact with other believers but it also brings other believers into contact with Christians" (LaRousse 2008, 155). James H. Kroeger, also a Maryknoll missioner, points out the reality that migrants are often "not only culturally alienated, but also religiously marginalized; frequently, they are relegated to the status of belonging to a minority, 'foreign' religion" in situations where they "follow a religious tradition different from their host country" (Kroeger 2008, 225–26).

In practical terms, as Muslims from Mindanao move into predominantly Christian Sabah, and Christian Filipinos work in the Muslim nations of West Asia, the implications of migration for ecumenical and interfaith relations can no longer be ignored. Indeed, migration leads to an increasing cultural diversity and religious pluralism in different parts of Asia. At the same time, many communities are confronted with the complex reality of cultural diversity and religious pluralism that is brought about by a relentless onslaught of people constantly on the move for social, political, or economic reasons. Not surprisingly, both the migrants and their host communities are often ill prepared to handle the inevitable cultural shock that arises when different social, cultural, ethical, and religious dimensions are brought together in an explosive mix. The Jesuit theologian Thomas Michel describes it as follows:

There is often the culture shock of moving from a simultaneously supportive and restrictive village society, where ethical and religious values are handed on and enforced by the community, to the secularized, individualistic, highly mobile world of industrialized societies. There are hence, the difficulties of social integration, often compounded by feelings of being unwanted or unaccepted by the host societies. (1985, 182)

According to Michel, many migrants come from countries where "their religions were not merely faith commitments, but also determined familial and social relationships and shaped the rhythm and structure of daily life, as well as the moral and value systems which they had known and live by." As these migrants move to more pluralistic and secular environments, they "have difficulty finding mosques, temples, or other places of prayer, centers for gathering during their free time, and the lack of facilities for following the dietary prescriptions of their faith" (1985, 182). Hence, any discussion of the ecumenical, intercultural, and interreligious implications of migration in Asia would have to address the difficult questions of the pastoral care of Christian migrants and refugees in predominantly non-Christian regions of Asia, on the one hand, as well as non-Christian migrants and refugees in predominantly Christian communities, on the other hand.

Migration in the Documents of the FABC

Although the FABC has not used the phrase "mission among the peoples" to describe its missional outreach to migrants, asylum seekers, and refugees, as well as the multitude of internally displaced persons (IDPs) in Asia, I suggest that the paradigm of mission among the peoples best exemplifies what the FABC hopes to achieve. Indeed, a survey of their documents reveals that in practice, the FABC has consistently sought to carry out a mission among the peoples in Asia who are on the move, whether voluntarily or involuntarily.

It is true that the early documents of the FABC did not deal directly with the issue of migration and its challenges. A survey of the FABC documents in the 1970s and 1980s reveals only minor references to migrants in the *Syllabus of "Mission Concerns"* of BIMA (Bishops' Institutes on Missionary Apostolate) III (1982) and the Final Statement of BIMA IV (1988). Specifically, article 11 of BIMA III's *Syllabus of "Missionary Concerns"* states that the "pastoral care for the great number of Asians who have emigrated from their homelands for economic reasons demands the serious missionary concern of the churches" (Rosales and Arévalo 1992, 108). In a similar vein, BIMA IV encourages the bishops to use "the mobility and migration of the faithful as an opportunity to spread the Gospel of Christ" and "inspire, educate, and organize . . . migrants to be witnesses of Christ wherever they may go" (Rosales and Arévalo 1992, 294). In the absence of any formal statement from the FABC during this period, individual episcopal conferences in Asia released their own statements on migration, for example, the Philippines in 1988, Taiwan in 1989, and Japan in 1993 (Battistella 1995).

FABC V:
Journeying Together toward the Third Millennium (1990)

The major turning point came with the Fifth FABC Plenary Assembly, which was held in Bandung, Indonesia, in 1990 with the theme, "Journeying Together toward the Third Millennium." In its Final Statement, the FABC Plenary Assembly acknowledged the injustice of both voluntary and involuntary migration in the Asian milieu:

We are deeply conscious, therefore, that within our context of change there is the unchanging reality of injustice. There remains in Asia massive poverty. . . . Poverty likewise drives both men and women to become migrant workers, often destroying family life in the process. Political conflict and economic desperation have driven millions to become refugees, to living for years in camps that are sometimes in

effect crowded prisons. (FABC V, art. 2.2.1, in Rosales and
Arévalo 1992, 276–77)

In response, FABC V asserts that Asian Christians "must live
in *companionship*, as true *partners* with all Asians as they pray, work,
struggle and suffer for a better human life, and as they search
for the meaning of human life and progress" (FABC V, art. 6.2,
in Rosales and Arévalo 1992, 283). The Asian bishops insist that
Asian Christians must walk in solidarity with the "exploited
women and workers, unwelcome refugees, victims of violations
of human rights," seeking to "denounce, in deeds, if it is not
possible to do so in words, the injustices, oppressions, exploita-
tions, and inequalities resulting in so much of the suffering that is
evident in the Asian situation" (FABC V, art. 6.4, in Rosales and
Arévalo 1992, 283–84).

FABC-OHD:
Journeying Together in Faith with the
Filipino Migrant Workers in Asia (1993)

Following in the footsteps of FABC V, which had included
migration as one of the many issues facing the Asian church as
it journeys toward the third Christian millennium, the FABC
Office of Human Development (FABC-OHD) continued the
discussion by organizing a symposium on Filipino migrant
workers in Asia. This symposium was held in Hong Kong in
1993 and was attended by delegates of the episcopal conferences and diocesan commissions of Hong Kong, Macau, Malaysia, Japan, the Philippines, Singapore, South Korea, Taiwan, and
Thailand. The Final Statement of this symposium, titled "Journeying Together in Faith with the Filipino Migrant Workers in
Asia," began by acknowledging the contributions of millions
of migrant workers from the Philippines to the growing global
economy (Eilers 1997, 47). Although it observes that migration has "both positive and negative effects on the country of
origin as well as the receiving country" (1997, 48–49), it points
out that those Filipino migrant workers, male and female alike,

often experience serious human rights abuses. For example, Filipino women, who are often employed in the domestic and entertainment sectors, are "frequently submitted to humiliation, harassment and sexual abuse" (1997, 50). Filipino men, who constitute the single largest national group in the seafarers and fish workers sector, not only "face physical and verbal abuse," but also experience difficulties in claiming compensation for disabilities (1997, 50).

Moreover, the symposium participants also recognized the consequences of migration for the disintegration of the family unit with deleterious effects on children and their parents (Eilers 1997, 50). The symposium delegates concluded:

> There is a very urgent need to take seriously the implications of migration on marriage and family life. The social, spiritual and moral implications need urgent assessment by all. Husbands separated from wives, and children from parents are a direct consequence of contract labor migration, showing signs of breakdown of both marriages and families. (Eilers 1997, 55)

On the theological aspects of migration, the symposium delegates viewed migration as a reality that not only points to the birth of a new world order based on the growing interdependence among nations, but also confirms the fundamental right of every person to migrate freely because "the world belongs to everyone" (Eilers 1997, 51). They also reiterated that the Asian church has to

> accompany the Migrant as a Human Person, following the example of Christ himself. This journeying of the Church together with the Migrant Worker, is the sign of solidarity within the universal Church and a sharing in the common evangelizing mission entrusted to all the followers of Christ. Growing in faith as a local Church, made up of people of different nationalities is a new sign of unity. (Eilers 1997, 53)

On the one hand, the symposium delegates affirmed that migration should not be forced and insisted that migrants' human rights must be respected, and they should not be subject to inhumane working and living conditions (Eilers 1997, 52). On the other hand, they also urged both the originating and receiving churches to address the root causes of migration and its negative impact on migrants. Specifically, they emphasized that churches that are receiving migrants ought to welcome and assist them to "relate, participate and integrate themselves to the local Church in the various activities, and at the same time be able to share their faith and cultural heritage with the local Church and people" (Eilers 1997, 53). This is because local receiving churches have the responsibility to protect the rights and promote the dignity of these migrant workers, working "closely with the local Government to make available services to the migrants who are a very important part of the labor force and contribute to the economy and society" (Eilers 1997, 54).

FABC VI:
Christian Discipleship in Asia Today:
Service to Life (1995)

The next plenary assembly, FABC VI, which was held in Manila in 1995, briefly highlighted "the insecurity and vulnerability of migrants, refugees, the displaced ethnic and indigenous peoples, and the pain and agonies of exploited workers, especially the child laborers in our countries" (FABC VI, art. 7, in Eilers 1997, 4). At this plenary assembly, the Asian bishops characterized the plight of migrants as follows:

> Special attention is given to the displaced in our societies: political and ecological refugees and migrant workers. They are marginalized and exploited by the system, denied their place in society and must go elsewhere to seek a dignified life. In welcoming them we expose the causes of their displacement, work toward conditions for a more human living in community, experience the uni-

versal dimension of the Kingdom (Gal. 3:28) and appreciate new opportunities for evangelization and intercultural dialogue. (FABC VI, art. 15.5, in Eilers 1997, 11)

FABC's
Colloquium on Church
in Asia in the 21st Century (1997)

Two years later, the topic of migration came up for discussion at the FABC's Colloquium on Church in Asia in the 21st Century (Pattaya City, Thailand, 1997), which was organized by the FABC-OHD and focused on the theme "Towards a Communion and Solidarity in the Context of Globalization." On the issue of migrants and their challenges, the colloquium participants suggested that dioceses intervene more actively to "take up the cause of migrant workers through the legal process of the host country by providing financial support and lawyers to fight for their rights" (Eilers 2002, 40). The Final Statement of this colloquium also outlines four practical steps that the Asian bishops could implement to address the challenges and needs of migrants and their families. First, it recommends that the migrant commissions of episcopal conferences initiate bilateral meetings. Second, it suggests that formation programs be organized for the training of pastoral workers for migrants. Third, it proposes that diocesan pastoral programs also cater to the pastoral care of the families of migrants. Fourth, it highlights the need to link the issue of migration with the broader issue of human labor (Eilers 2002, 40).

FABC VII:
A Renewed Church in Asia on a
Mission of Love and Service (2000)

At the beginning of the third Christian millennium, the issue of migration was discussed at the Seventh Plenary Assembly (Samphran, Thailand, 2000) of the FABC. At this plenary assembly, the Asian bishops focused, among other things, on the ever-growing migration and refugee movements and called for an urgent and adequate pastoral response to address their dehumanizing plight:

> In the light of the teaching of the Church, we affirm that migration and refugee movements, which result in depersonalization, loss of human dignity and the break up of families, are moral issues confronting the conscience of the Church and that of our Asian nations. As for the Church in Asia, these pose urgent pastoral challenges to evolve life-giving, service-oriented programs of action within the pastoral mission of the Church. The Church should join hands with all who are concerned with the rights of the migrants and their situation, keeping in mind that the migrants themselves are to be the primary agents of change. (FABC VII, art. 5, in Eilers 2002, 11)

FABC VIII:
The Asian Family:
Toward a Culture of Integral Life (2004)

The Asian bishops further developed their theology of migration at their Eighth Plenary Assembly (Daejeon, South Korea, 2004), which focused on Asian families and the challenges they face in their daily life struggles. In their final statement, they identified the twin forces of globalization and urbanization as accounting for the bulk of contemporary migration patterns in Asia (Eilers 2007, 6). The Asian bishops drew attention to the deleterious impact of migration on Asian families:

> It is true that salaries [migrants] earn abroad are significantly much more than they can earn in their home countries, but at the price of the stability of their families, the proper education and maturation of their children, who are deprived of the presence, the guidance, and love of both parents at their most formative and impressionable age. (FABC VIII, art. 15, in Eilers 2007, 6)

Moreover, the Asian bishops also warned of the cultural dislocations and breakdown in family and communal ties between these migrants and their families and communities back home (FABC VIII, art. 16, in Eilers 2007, 7). According to them, "Migrant workers and their families urgently need great pastoral care from the churches of sending and receiving countries" (FABC VIII, art. 17, in Eilers 2007, 7).

FEISA V:
Pastoral Care of Migrants and Refugees:
A New Way of Being Church (2002)

Organized by the FABC-OHD, the Faith Encounters in Social Action (FEISA) seeks to promote interreligious dialogue through social involvement, emphasizing that the Asian church needs to ground its mission and outreach in a threefold dialogue with the Asian peoples in the fullness of their cultures, religious traditions, and their poverty (Eilers 2007, 89). Specifically FEISA V, entitled "'From Distrust to Respect . . . Reject to Welcome': Study Days on Undocumented Migrants and Refugees," which met in Kota Kinabalu, Malaysia, in 2002, has sought to make explicit the connection between migration, mission, and engagement with the plurireligious Asian milieu. Its final statement, which is titled "Pastoral Care of Migrants and Refugees: A New Way of Being Church," is a thorough discussion on the challenges faced by undocumented migrants and refugees and what the Asian church could do to respond to these challenges.

FEISA V takes as its starting point Pope John Paul II's insistence in his 1996 World Migration Day Message on Undocumented Migrants that "a migrant's irregular legal status cannot allow him/her to lose his/her dignity, since he/she is endowed with inalienable rights, which can neither be violated nor ignored" (Eilers 2007, 111; see also John Paul II 1996). John Paul II was adamant that the church should defend the rights of the undocumented migrants:

> In the Church no one is a stranger, and the Church is not foreign to anyone, anywhere. As a sacrament of unity and

thus a sign and a binding force for the whole human race, the Church is the place where illegal immigrants should be recognized and accepted as brothers and sisters. . . . Solidarity means taking responsibility for those in trouble. For Christians, the migrant is not merely an individual to be respected in accordance with the norms established by law, but a person whose presence challenges them and whose needs become an obligation for their responsibility. "What have you done to your brother?" (cf. Gen. 4:9). The answer should not be limited to what is imposed by law, but should be made in the manner of solidarity. (1996)

Taking its cue from John Paul II, the document goes on to articulate the premise that both undocumented migrants and asylum seekers "remain children of God" and "deserve Christian love and protection" to maintain their human dignity, notwithstanding that they often "have no legal right to remain in a given national territory" (Eilers 2007, 111). FEISA V reiterates the "inalienable dignity and rights of people on the move" and "acknowledges the right of sovereign nation-states to regulate the movement of people across their borders," but it is equally adamant that "this right must be exercised at the service of the universal common good" (Eilers 2007, 117). As it explains:

People on the move must not be reduced to instruments of economic or political strategies. All of their human rights must be respected. The freedom of people to move should be preserved and restrictions imposed only where this is necessary in order to protect the common good. People have a right to move in order to seek safety, freedom and a decent level of material welfare. (Eilers 2007, 117)

Hence, it insists that the Asian church should treat all migrants alike in its pastoral outreach regardless of their status and what their motivations may be for leaving their homelands:

Whatever the reason is, the Church that embodies the mission of Christ cannot remain indifferent to issues relat-

ing [to or] affecting people on the move. The Church
that is universal both in outlook and in its essence is duty
bound to learn from the migrants and at the same time,
respond to their needs. (Eilers 2007, 114)

It maintains that Asian Christians should begin by listening "to
people in an irregular situation or in search of asylum, in order
to know exactly what their situation is, and also provide them
with their basic needs" because "asylum-seekers and migrants in
an illegal situation have the right to be provided with the necessary means of subsistence" (Eilers 2007, 115). As the document
explains:

Christian solidarity simply sees the need to take care of
human beings, especially young people, minors and children who are incapable of defending themselves because
they lack protection under the law and often do not know
the language of the country in which they have been
obliged to seek refuge due to natural catastrophes, wars,
violence, persecution, even genocide in their own country
or due to existing economic conditions such as to endan-
ger their physical integrity or life itself. (Eilers 2007, 115)

FEISA V further contends that the Asian Church "seeks to
defend the dignity and rights of people on the move regardless
of their race, religion and legal status," and in particular, "paying
attention not only to the practical and physical needs, but also to
their social, psychological and spiritual needs" (Eilers 2007, 118).
Pope Benedict XVI made a similar point when he called on
Christians "to open their arms and hearts to every person, from
whatever nation they come" in his address to the 2006 assembly of the Pontifical Council for the Pastoral Care of Migrants
and Itinerant Peoples on the theme of "Migration and Itinerancy
from and towards Islamic Majority Countries" (2006).

On the issue of poverty and migration, the document
acknowledges the reality of poverty as the force behind much
of the mass migrations in Asia, whether internal or external, voluntary or involuntary and recommends that the Asian church

should stand in solidarity with the poor and marginalized (Eilers 2007, 128–29). On the one hand, it recognizes that the problems of migration are legion and arise "because of the terrible situation surrounding the migration phenomenon: of injustice, discrimination, violence, violation of rights, inhuman living and working conditions, and fear especially for those who are undocumented, etc." (Eilers 2007, 113). On the other hand, the document asserts that it is also "an opportunity, because in our globalised world, it gives concrete chances for people of different nationalities, cultures and creeds to come together, know each other and share with one another," thereby removing or at least reducing prejudice and indifference (Eilers 2007, 113). FEISA explains the theological basis for this outreach to migrants of other religions as follows:

> Making the migrants/refugees the target of our pastoral care is our concrete way of witnessing to the people of Asia. Being a "little flock" in the midst of other ancient religions/beliefs, the Asian Church cannot remain "inward looking." The Good News is not only to be preached but it is to be lived/practised in concrete day-to-day circumstances of many faiths. Thus, efforts to provide pastoral care to migrants have to include inter-religious dimensions. The Church can and should take the initiative. By doing so, we are witnessing to the mission of Christ through our actions. (Eilers 2007, 122–23)

Thus, for FEISA V, interreligious dialogue is imperative and integral to the Asian church's theology and praxis of migration; that is, the Asian church "dialogues with all regardless of creed, nationality, race, political stance, or other discriminatory factors, especially the undocumented or documented status of migrant workers" (Eilers 2007, 125).

But the document goes one step further to insist that in addressing the needs of migrants, the Asian church "must work together with people of other faiths or none," joining with "all people of goodwill to respond to other sisters and brothers affirming their full humanity and the inalienable rights that arise from their humanity" (Eilers 2007, 118). Further, it points out that migration facilitates interreligious encounters. This applies to Asian Christians migrating to non-Christian countries in Asia, as well as non-Christian migrants interacting with them. In the first instance, FEISA V refers to Asian Christians who migrate to non-Christian countries in Asia, pointing out that they can be "living witnesses of Christ through Christian love of the members for one another and for the migrant, both Christian and non-Christian" (Eilers 2007, 113). In particular, the document encourages Asian Christian migrants "to invite their friends of other religions to the church where they may receive a warm reception" (Eilers 2007, 120). In a similar vein, the Pontifical Council for the Pastoral Care of Migrants and Itinerant Peoples' 2004 Instruction, *Erga migrantes caritas Christi,* calls on local churches to welcome, provide help and hospitality to, and seek to integrate migrants within their local communities regardless of their religions (2004, no. 42). It speaks of the Catholic Church's mission to non-Christian migrants as first and foremost "the witness of Christian charity, which itself has an evangelizing value that may open hearts for the explicit proclamation of the gospel when this is done with due Christian prudence and full respect for the freedom of the other" (2004, no. 59).

In the second instance, FEISA V states that the Asian church "can and should take the initiative of providing pastoral care to migrants with inter-religious dimensions" (Eilers 2007, 129). It explains that the Asian church should not only "see and understand the dignity of other faiths" but also receive and assist these migrants in their moment of greatest need, taking the initiative to reach out and visit them because as non-Catholics, they "may not have the courage to visit Catholic churches" (Eilers 2007, 119). In this regard, FEISA V suggests that local parishes could offer space and hospitality to these migrants who "need a place where they can gather together for prayers or to have their religious celebrations or just for a friendly gathering among themselves" (Eilers 2007, 120, cf. 130). This suggestion echoes what Pope John Paul II had said in his Message for the 88th World Day of Migration entitled "Migration and Inter-Religious Dialogue" (2002):

The parish represents the space in which a true peda-
gogy of meeting with people of various religious convictions and cultures can be realized. . . . the parish community
can become a training ground of hospitality, a place where
an exchange of experiences and gifts takes place. This cannot
but foster a tranquil life together, preventing the risk of tension with immigrants who bring other religious beliefs with
themselves. . . . Every day, in many parts of the world, migrants,
refugees and displaced people turn to Catholic organizations
and parishes in search of support, and they are welcome irre-
spective of cultural or religious affiliation (arts. 3, 5).

Moreover, the document emphasizes the need to give special
attention to refugees and IDPs as an outgrowth of the church's
ministry to the poor, oppressed, and marginalized (Eilers 2007,
114). Specifically, it insists that the Asian church needs to include
ecumenism and interreligious dialogue in its outreach work with
refugees because the church

is most critical in this region where we belong to the
minority and we work in the midst of rich, diverse, and
important religious and cultural traditions. The spirit of
ecumenism and interreligious dialogue should thus permeate our programming processes. While our faith spurs us to
serve the refugees, it does not become the criteria for refugees to avail themselves of our services. (Eilers 2007, 117)

Finally, in recognition of the fact that highly skilled pastoral
workers are needed to engage with migrants in the fullness of
their cultures, religions, and poverty, FEISA V makes the following recommendation:

To fully understand the needs of the migrants, the
Church must equip herself with the knowledge and skills
required for this minority. These include knowledge of
the languages of migrants, the provision of possibilities for
migrants to express their faith with their language and
culture, if necessary, of missionaries capable to be with

migrants or mediators of faith and cultural dialogue. (Eilers 2007, 130)

This point is also echoed by *Erga migrantes caritas Christi*, which suggests that

> the ordinary Catholic faithful and pastoral workers in local Churches should receive solid formation and information on other religions so as to overcome prejudices, prevail over religious relativism and avoid unjustified suspicions and fears that hamper dialogue and erect barriers, even provoking violence or misunderstanding (2004, no. 69).

Clearly, FEISA V sees the phenomenon of ongoing migration in Asia within the broader framework of migration as "part and parcel of human civilization" (Eilers 2007, 112) and "a natural phenomenon" that arises from "the inherent right of people to move" (Eilers 2007, 114). At the same time, the document also acknowledges that not all migrations are freely and voluntarily undertaken. It contends that the Asian church has to respond to the dilemma of Asians who migrate in a quest to ensure their survival because of physical or economic threats (Eilers 2007, 114). As far as the FABC is concerned, migration cannot be separated from the complex interplay of social, economic, class, religious, and political factors that interact to displace people from their homelands. Whether voluntary or forced, migration reveals the vulnerability, insecurity, uncertainty, and humiliation of millions of Asians who find themselves on the move, either internally or beyond their national borders, as they deal with survival, uprootedness, and exploitation in their quest for a better life for themselves and their families.

An Emerging FABC Theology of Mission among the Migrants

From the outset, the FABC's theology of mission among the migrants in Asia is rooted in a "commitment and service to life" that has been the foundation and the hallmark of the FABC's theology of mission, as discussed in chapter 3 of this book. For the FABC, its commitment and service to life also extend to migrants who often face discrimination, exploitation, persecution, or human rights abuses. As far as the FABC is concerned, migrants are not objects for proselytization, but rather persons for Asian Christians to reach out to and walk together with in solidarity.

The call for a "commitment and service to life" of the Asian migrants demonstrates the deep *orthopathic underpinnings* of FABC's theology of mission among the migrants. In practice, this "commitment and service to life" of the Asian migrants is demonstrated in walking together and accompanying the migrants in empathy and solidarity with the pathos that they experience in their daily lives. In this context, FEISA V summarizes it well when it states that migration "offers the Church all over the world an opportunity to reach out to the ones most discriminated [against] by society today. Being in solidarity with them offers us the opportunity to offer the Good News of the Gospel to them as individuals and as a community" (Eilers 2007, 128). In the same vein, FABC VI states:

> Our solidarity requires a resolve *to work with our Asian sisters and brothers in liberating our societies from whatever oppresses and degrades human life and creation, most especially from sin.* . . . Serving life demands communion with every woman and man seeking and struggling for life in the way of Jesus' solidarity with humanity. With our Asian sisters and brothers, we will strive to foster communion among Asian peoples who are threatened by glaring economic, social, and political imbalances. With them we will explore ways of utilizing the gifts of our diverse religions, cultures, and languages to achieve a richer and deeper Asian unity. We build bridges of solidarity and reconciliation with peoples of other faiths and will join hands with everyone in Asia in forming a true community of creation. (FABC VI, art. 14.2, in Eilers 1997, 8, emphasis added)

In practical terms, the *orthopraxic* facet of the FABC's theology of mission among the migrants is evident in the attention that is paid to the issues that give rise to the ever-growing number of migrants in Asia. These issues include poverty, economic marginalization, the overreliance on the remittances of economic migrants, environmental degradation, as well as racial, political, and religious tensions (see FABC VI, art. 15.5, in Eilers 1997, 11; FEISA V in Eilers 2007, 93). In particular, FEISA V is adamant in its theology of migration that the Asian church should advocate for the human dignity and rights of migrants regardless of race, religion, or legal status as part of its wider stance of advocating for the rights and aspirations of the poor and marginalized (Eilers 2007, 128–29).

The *orthodoxic* aspect of the FABC's theology of mission among the migrants of Asia is manifested when the FABC seeks to carry the *missio Dei* by bearing witness to the arrival of the Reign of God in Asia. Within the plurireligious context of Asia, the FABC seeks to integrate the intercultural and interreligious dimensions in its mission among the migrants of Asia. In this respect, the FABC has sought to undergird its theology of mission among the migrants of Asia within its broader theological threefold dialogue with the quintessentially Asian realities of diverse cultures, religions, and immense poverty. On this point, FEISA V insists that the "Good News is not only to be preached but it is to be lived and practised in concrete day-to-day circumstances among people of many faiths" (Eilers 2007, 130). Moreover, FEISA V's call for pastoral workers to learn the languages, cultures, and traditions of these non-Christian migrants so as to be able to interact with the migrants and assist them in retaining and expressing their own languages, cultures, and religious faiths is a clear and unequivocal repudiation of the temptation to proselytize among non-Christian migrants in their most vulnerable state.

Mission among the Digital Natives of Asia: New Frontiers of Mission

The Rise of the Digital Natives

Today's young adults, known as Generation Y or the millennials, are very different from their predecessors, known colloquially as the baby boomers and Generation X, in their familiarity with technology. Don Tapscott labels them the "Net Generation" and notes that they are well known for being technologically adept, having grown up in a world that is marked by rapid digital and online growth (Tapscott 2009). Living in cyberspace within the world of social media, they are able to multitask with ease, texting, instant messaging, or chatting away online, all while trying to read or pay attention in class. Not surprisingly, many of their parents, teachers, and employers, who are typically baby boomers or part of Generation X, often find such behavior either amusing or annoying at best, or disconcerting at worst.

In an important paper titled "Digital Natives, Digital Immigrants," Marc Prensky writes that today's young adults "have not just changed incrementally from those of the past, nor simply changed their slang, clothes, body adornments, or styles, as has happened between generations previously" (Prensky 2001a, 1). He argues that a "really big *discontinuity* has taken place" in the form of a "singularity" that "changes things so fundamentally that there is absolutely no going back" (2001a, 1, emphasis added). He identifies this singularity as "the arrival and rapid dissemination of digital technology in the last decades of the twentieth century" (2001a, 1). In a subsequent paper that draws on the latest research in neurobiology, social psychology, and studies done about children using games for learning, Prensky (2001b) concludes that the brains of young adults have physically changed as the result of growing up in a world of constant exposure to digital media.

Prensky draws a distinction between "digital immigrants" and "digital natives." He explains that "digital natives" are "native speakers of technology, fluent in the digital language of computers, video games, and the Internet," whereas "digital immigrants" are those "who were not born into the digital world" but have at some later point in their lives "become fascinated by and adopted many or most aspects of the new technology" (Prensky, 2001a, 1, 3). In particular, he argues that digital immigrants and digital natives often talk past one another because they are using different modes of communicating and relating. Shaped and socialized by the predigital world, digital immigrants often find themselves playing catch-up to digital natives as they struggle to adapt to new developments in digital technology. By contrast, having grown up immersed in the digital world, digital natives have a completely different mind-set compared to digital immigrants. Likewise, Don Tapscott points out that these millennials, who have grown up as the "Net Generation" in the digital world of cyberspace, often prefer to interact and relate to each other on social media using smartphones and tablets as their usual means of communication (Tapscott 2009).

Prensky's and Tapscott's insights are supported by two important studies conducted by the Pew Internet and American Life Project's *Teens and Technology* (2005) and *Teens and Social Media* (2007). The first of these two studies concluded that US teens are enveloped by communication technologies, with the Internet and smartphones playing a central role in defining and shaping their lives. Among other things, it noted that 87 percent of teens ages twelve to seventeen are online and observed a significant growth in the number of teens who do most of their daily routine (playing games, keeping in touch with friends and the news, shopping) online. Going a step further, *Teens and Social Media* observed that 64 percent of online teens are engaged in online content creation (blogging, posting photos and videos online). The 2007 study found that girls dominate in the area of content creation (35 percent of all teen girls blog compared to 20 percent of boys), while boys dominate in the area of posting video content online (19 percent of boys versus 10 percent of girls). In addition, it also revealed that teens often go beyond merely creating and sharing online content to participating in conversations fueled by such creating and sharing. For example, 89 percent of teens who post photos say that people post comments on their photos.

Cyberspace and the Rise of Social Media

These findings are noteworthy for their revelation of the centrality of cyberspace and the social networking communities, as well as social media platforms and apps, in the lives of digital natives. Indeed, cyberspace has emerged as today's cutting-edge frontier for creative content creation, sharing, and communication as part of the so-called Web 2.0 revolution (Tapscott and Williams

2008, 2010). The term "Web 2.0" was first introduced by Darcy DiNucci to define an emerging understanding of cyberspace that is "understood not as screenfuls of text and graphics but as a transport mechanism, the *ether through which interactivity happens*" (DiNucci 1999, 32, emphasis added). DiNucci contrasts Web 2.0 with Web 1.0, where the latter "loads into a browser window in essentially static screenfuls" (DiNucci 1999, 32). More important, DiNucci's definition of Web 2.0 highlights its fundamental defining characteristic,that is, the dynamic user-generated content in cyberspace that is both interactive and social in orientation. The Web 1.0 of the 1990s, with its centralized, static, and "read-only" websites, was noteworthy for its unidirectional and noninteractive orientation, whereas the Web 2.0 of the 2000s and beyond is characterized by the dynamic participation and interactivity in cyberspace in general, on social media in particular through blogging and microblogging, video and photo blogging, video and photo messaging, as well as podcasting, wikis, and other forms of crowdsourcing for creative content creation and sharing. In the case of wikis, of which Wikipedia is the most prominent example, visitors are able to collaborate in creating and editing a site's contents, resulting in a site with dynamic user-generated and moderated contents (Tapscott and Williams 2008).

The original poster child for the dynamic and interactive aspect of Web 2.0 is Myspace. Although the Myspace of today is but a pale shadow of its past, it deserves a place in the history of cyberspace as a trailblazing social media platform where users were able to post personal profiles, music clips, videos, photos, blogs, and wall posts, as well as invite comments and feedback from friends and visitors. From its inception in 2003 until it was surpassed by its principal competitor Facebook in 2009, Myspace was especially popular with teenagers and musicians who often used it as a social media platform to promote their bands and new releases.

The social media platform du jour, Facebook, was created by Mark Zuckerberg with his friends Dustin Moskovitz and Chris Hughes while they were undergraduates at Harvard. It has since evolved into a global social media platform that enables users to join social networks that are organized by school, workplace, city, organization, or social group. Users can add friends, invite others to accept them as friends, interact with their friends through wall posts, status updates, profile updates, photo and video sharing, and so forth.

Beyond Facebook and its ilk, one finds an explosion of personal blogs that are often hosted on Tumblr, Wordpress, or Blogger. Unlike the static personal webpages of Web 1.0 that were typically hosted on Geocities, Tripod, or Angelfire, the interactive nature of the blogs of Web 2.0 allow visitors to leave comments and engage in interactive conversation with the owners of and other visitors to those blogs. In turn, the Web 2.0 blogging phenomenon has spawned the microblogging phenomenon, of which Twitter is the best-known example, thanks to the preeminent role it played together with Facebook in mobilizing the masses for protests and demonstrations in the Arab Spring of 2010–11 (Cambié 2012, 28, 30–31). The runaway success of Twitter arises from its ability to allow users to send short text-based posts called "tweets" to their followers via mobile devices, who could, in turn, retweet these short messages or reply by posting their own short thoughts and comments. The limitations of Twitter's text-based platform has led to the creation of new dynamic and interactive photo and video messaging and sharing platforms such as Instagram, Snapchat, Vine, and Keek, which complement older photo- and video-sharing platforms such as Flickr, Photobucket, Youtube, and Vimeo.

As digital natives, the youth and millennials are part of this social movement that is rapidly transforming the social media landscape of Asia. From East to West Asia, South to Southeast Asia, one finds an increasing number of youth and millennials in the urban centers of these regions who have migrated to cyberspace and are using social media apps on mobile devices to interact with their friends and acquaintances in social networking communities. Indeed, these Asian digital natives often congregate and interact in cyberspace using both global social media apps such as Facebook, Twitter, or Instagram, as well as thriving indigenous Asian competitors such as Weibo, QQ, Renren, and WeChat in China, Cyworld in South Korea, and Mixi in Japan. In view of the foregoing, Asian church leaders and missioners will find themselves increasingly marginalized and having little to no impact and influence on the lives of Asian digital natives if they continue to avoid encountering these digital natives who have migrated to and are now deeply ensconced in cyberspace.

Engaging the Youth and Millennials of Asia in Cyberspace

On the one hand, many Asian church leaders and missioners are often hesitant to interact virtually with Asian digital natives in cyberspace because they perceive such online interactions via social media to be antithetical to the essence of traditional missional witness that emphasizes the personal dimension of human relationships. In some cases, their reluctance to do so comes about because of their unfamiliarity with the constantly changing world of cyberspace and social media apps. In other cases, it could also be traced to their fear of being unable to control the messy, complicated, and often antinomian atmosphere that pervades many social media communities in cyberspace. This is not surprising, in view of the fact that Asian church leaders and missioners have been trained to serve in a world that they grew up in through face-to-face contact, whether formally or informally, rather than in the social media world of the Asian digital natives. Nevertheless, although face-to-face encounters are important, they constitute only a small proportion of the lives of young digital natives in contemporary Asia. Once digital natives leave those face-to-face interactions in church-based services, meetings, and gatherings, Asian church leaders and missioners are no longer privy to the ups and downs, successes and struggles, achievements and challenges that Asian digital natives experience in their daily lives.

On the other hand, one could make the case that the "impersonal" aspect of online interactions could ironically be its very strength, affording digital natives the opportunity to share their deepest secrets, struggles, hopes, and dreams. In this vein, social media often become the vehicle for Asian digital natives to be who they really are or want to be without the fear of humiliation, shame, anxiety, or embarrassment that could arise from face-to-face interactions. Moreover, Asian youth and millennials often reveal firsthand both the pathos and joys of their daily lives through their thoughts, quotes, photos, videos, music clips, and so on that they post online or comment on. In other words, Asian church leaders and missioners would discover that in the "flat" world of cyberspace and social media communities, Asian youth and millennials are often able to let their guard down and be themselves, without the masks that they wear in face-to-face interactions with their family and church elders.

In reality, it is often easier for Asian church leaders and missioners to enter into cyberspace and *friend* the Asian digital natives on social media, rather than persuade the digital natives to leave their social media world. Moreover, by being among Asian digital natives in social media communities, Asian church leaders and missioners are also able to respond in an *orthopathic* spirit of solidarity, empathy, and encouragement to the pathos of the often messy, complicated, and chaotic daily life struggles of Asian digital natives up close. This is because digital natives often share deeply on social media about their struggles with the pathos of family problems, depression, bullying, substance abuse, addictions, struggles with sexual orientation, and so forth. Frequently, they are not ready for in-person outreach, especially if they perceive their elders to be scolding or berating them for their nonconformity to sociocultural norms and expectations. Not surprisingly, they are usually more comfortable relating online, free from the pressure to conform to the expectations of their family or church elders.

It goes without saying that Asian church leaders and missioners should not be afraid to take advantage of the new technologies of their time. There is precedent in this, as evidenced by the examples of the apostle Paul and the Protestant reformer Martin Luther. In the New Testament, we see how Paul kept in touch with the communities he founded through circular letters, which were subsequently reproduced, passed on, and shared in viral fashion among other nascent communities as sources of teaching and spiritual inspiration. Martin Luther was able to capitalize on printing, which was the new technology of his day, to spread his views across a broad audience, who in turn circulated and shared his tracts among their friends and neighbors in a manner akin to retweeting tweets on Twitter or liking and sharing posts on

Facebook. In a similar vein, Asian church leaders and missioners would do well to follow the footsteps of Paul and Luther to
make full use of today's digital technology and networking tools
in social media.

One could also look at the other side of the coin and consider that Asian youth and millennials are drawn to social media
communities because these communities are often egalitarian
in orientation without rigidly defined structures of leadership
and authority. This spirit of egalitarianism appeals to many Asian
digital natives who find this environment to be empowering and
nourishing. As a result, many Asian youth and millennials are able
to be creative, voice their thoughts, as well as figure out who they
are, what they want to be, and how they relate to others without the critical and judgmental comments of their elders. Moreover, this egalitarian orientation of social media often encourages
grassroots activities, empowering even the most lowly and weak
to voice their thoughts, participate, and even take the lead in
organizing various activities, as exemplified by the use of social
media to galvanize and mobilize young adults and millennials
against dictatorship in the Arab Spring movement (Cambié 2012,
28, 30–31). In the United States, the highly successful grassroots
activism for Barack Obama's campaign for the US presidency
was built on, and nourished by its presence and activism in major
social media communities such as Facebook, Twitter, Youtube,
and Reddit, as well as its own highly successful social media platform, mybarackobama.com (Hendricks and Denton 2010; Harfoush 2009; Plouffe 2009). Hence, the successes of the Obama
presidential campaign in the United States and the Arab Spring
in West Asia both highlight the potential of social media to challenge and change the status quo in society.

At the same time, one should also acknowledge that this egalitarianism often frightens church leaders and missioners who fear
that they will be unable to control the discourse that goes on in
social media communities. Indeed, digital natives can often bypass
the centralized church bureaucracy, where everything requires the
prior approval of the pastor or youth minister, by going online to
create a Facebook or Tumblr group on their own, inviting their
friends to join and post content, and having an active group up

and running within twenty-four hours. Nonetheless, what is so threatening to church leaders and missioners—the lack of control over direction and activities—is paradoxically social media communities' greatest strength and asset, giving digital natives a sense of identity, belonging, achievement, and self-worth.

As a result, an all-encompassing missional witness of Asian Christians ought to include a missional quest within social media communities in cyberspace. Otherwise, Asian church leaders and missioners would find themselves increasingly marginalized in the lives of Asian digital natives. Without a doubt, church leaders and missioners have to go where the Asian digital natives are, be willing to walk in solidarity and empathy with them in their social media worlds, just as Jesus traveled through Samaria, stopped by Jacob's Well, and waited for the Samaritan woman in her world. By interacting with digital natives and journeying in solidarity and empathy with them in their social media communities, Asian church leaders and missioners demonstrate their openness to life's ambiguities, accepting not just the beautiful and good, but also the ugliness and chaotic messiness that are revealed in social media sharings.

It is certainly true that the virtual world of social media cannot replace personal face-to-face relationships. There will be occasions when church leaders and missioners have to be able to look at people in the eye, offer them a hug, and listen to them in a genuine one-to-one conversation. However, one has to acknowledge that one could use social media tools to extend and enhance missional witness and outreach, especially among those people who prefer the safe distance of virtual communication rather than face-to-face meetings. There will always be people who would avoid making appointments with church leaders and missioners, but who would bare their struggles, pains, and hurts online. Sometimes, online meetings could lead to face-to-face meetings in real life. Sometimes the online interactions are sufficient for healing and transformation. Whatever the case may be, online interactions enable church leaders and missioners to reach out to those who may otherwise avoid them in person, thereby allowing them to expand their missional outreach and witness.

At the same time, church leaders and missioners in Asia have to consider carefully their own calling, gifts, and talents, as well as discover the extent to which they could make the best use of their gifts and talents within social media communities. On the one hand, the quest to carry out missional witness in social media communities may not always be the right strategy for those church leaders and missioners who lack the requisite personality or temperament to be successful in the virtual confines of cyberspace. On the other hand, church leaders and missioners in Asia would find social media to be an invaluable missional outreach tool to interact and engage with digital natives in new ways. In this respect, the missional quest to build and deepen relational bonds in social media communities is an antidote to an otherwise uncritical and fearful mentality that merely sees cyberspace as a world of sin and depravity.

Mission among the Youth and Millennials of Asia in Cyberspace

From a theological perspective, Asian church leaders and missioners are called to reflect critically on their missional quest among the youth and millennials of Asia. Accepting the reality that the social media landscape is not a challenge to be confronted and overcome, but rather the *grundnorm* of the digital natives' world, Asian church leaders and missioners are challenged to seek new ways of relating to the complexities that underline the social media landscape, with an emphasis on empathy, mutuality, and solidarity with Asian digital natives. More specifically, Asian church leaders and missioners cannot fulfill their missional witness until they are able to engage fully in a mission among the Asian digital natives within their social media communities, just as Jesus engaged in a mission among the poor, dispossessed, and marginalized within their social worlds.

If Asian church leaders and missioners want to influence the lives of youth and millennials today, they need to immerse themselves in the world of cyberspace and social media in the manner that Jesus immersed himself in the world of Samaria of the Samaritan woman at Jacob's Well. To put it differently, if Jesus were present in today's world of Asian youth and millennials, the contemporary equivalent of him going to Samaria and hanging out at Jacob's Well could be him in cyberspace and using social media to interact with these digital natives. Just as Jesus would not have been able to interact with the Samaritan woman had he avoided Jacob's Well, likewise, Asian church leaders and missioners would be out of the loop with digital natives if they avoid social media interactions in cyberspace.

In addition, rather than forcing digital natives to conform to the mind-set and worldviews of the predigital world of their elders, Asian church leaders and missioners also have a responsibility to reach out in a mission *among* the Asian digital natives within their world and on their terms. Indeed, Jesus did the same with the Samaritan woman at Jacob's Well in her world of Samaria and on her terms. Jesus did not invite the Samaritan woman to leave Samaria and her family, village, and community for the Jewish world. Likewise, if by Jesus being present at Jacob's Well enabled the Samaritan woman to open up to him in a safe and nonthreatening environment, so too, social media could open up new vistas of interaction between Asian church leaders and digital natives, allowing digital natives to chat or seek help and guidance in an environment that is neutral and nonjudgmental. By engaging in empathy, solidarity, and sharing, church leaders and missioners are able to listen to what digital natives are sharing and receive what they have to offer before responding efficaciously to their needs, just as Jesus received water from the Samaritan woman before offering her the water of life.

In practical terms, the task of mission among the youth and millennials of Asia begins not from on high, but from below. It takes as its starting point the daily experiences of digital natives as they struggle with the pathos and challenges of life's curveballs. Hence, there is a need for church leaders and missioners in Asia to immerse themselves in the contemporary realities of the digital natives in their social media communities, engaging and interacting dialogically with them on their hopes, anxieties, and fears of daily living. In addition, Asian church leaders and missioners have to realize that their missional outreach and witness to youth and millennials is not a one-way or unidirectional outreach from missioner to the recipients of missional outreach. Instead, they have to discern the presence of God in social media communities and be sensitive to the workings of the Spirit in these communities.

In other words, Asian church leaders and missioners must be able to transcend an uncritical paternalism that gives rise to the presumption that they are in charge and have full knowledge of the Truth, while digital natives are merely passive recipients of that knowledge. Instead of hierarchy, control, and dependence, church leaders and missioners are called to recognize and foster mutuality, interdependence, empathy, solidarity, and collaboration between missioners and digital natives, eschewing the dichotomy between missioners as givers and digital natives as the "objects" or recipients of missional witness. In today's global and intercon-nected world that is rooted in interdependence and solidarity, church leaders and digital natives in Asia are both simultaneously missioners and recipients of missional witness, just as Jesus and the Samaritan woman at Jacob's Well were mutually receivers and givers of water, as explored in chapter 4.

As Asian Christians continue their missional witness of the *missio Dei* and the presence of the Reign of God in Asia to their fellow Asians in today's realities, they realize that they are not apart from, but rather a part of, the larger diverse and pluralis-tic family of Asian peoples across the continent. Together with the Asian peoples and indeed all of humanity, Asian Christians also acknowledge that as part of the worldwide human family, they are not merely sojourning in this world together, but also co-pilgrims journeying toward God. The call to respond to and embed the *missio Dei* within the framework of the task of doing mission among the peoples in Asia means that Asian Christians are called to seek out everyone in the manner that Jesus did in his time. If Jesus interacted with everyone across social, religious, class, and other boundaries, so too Asian Christians seek to inter-act with everyone across geographical, cultural, religious, and social boundaries. In the context of twenty-first-century Asia, this would include migrants across geographical frontiers and the virtual frontier of cyberspace. If Jesus could be found at Jacob's

Well in Samaria, Asian Christians are called to be missioners and witnesses in today's wells in emerging geographical diasporas and cyberspace.

More fundamentally, the missional call of Asian Christians to solidarity, empathy, sharing, and mutual collaboration with migrants across geographical and virtual frontiers is grounded in Jesus' own empathy and solidarity with all of humanity. Jesus came to this world to share in the life of ordinary people, experience the pathos of their daily life struggles, and engage fully in the ambiguities and complexities of daily living. Following in the footsteps of Jesus, Asian Christians are called to put into practice the same kind of empathy, solidarity, engagement, and collaboration with migrants in geographical and virtual diasporas. By immersing themselves in the geographical diasporas and social media communities in cyberspace, Asian Christians are able to share in and serve life in empathy and solidarity with Asian migrants of all stripes, just as Jesus did in his earthly life in his mission among the peoples of his day.

Epilogue:
Imagining New Possibilities

When we look back at the history of Christian mission in Asia, we can take stock of how far Christianity has come across vast expanses of land and multitudes of peoples over two millennia. We began in chapter 1 with a bird's-eye view of the history of Christian mission in Asia; although not exhaustive, it highlighted key milestones in Asian mission history, beginning with the Assyrian missionaries moving eastward to China and southward to India, and ending with the beginning of the twentieth century, when many missionaries were optimistic that the Christianization of Asia was within reach. We read about the problems that arose in an unholy alliance between Christian mission and European imperialism and empire building. One need not be reminded about the shortcomings of the Portuguese and Spanish imperial patronage of the Christian missions, or military protection of the Christian missions by the English and French colonial authorities against hostile natives. Not surprisingly, the unfair stereotype of Christianity as the white man's religion continues to persist in many parts of postcolonial Asia, resulting in Christians being harassed in countries such as India, Pakistan, Malaysia, China, and elsewhere.

Chapter 1 also presented success stories of Christian mission in Asia, including the remarkable birth of Korean Christianity, testifying to the power of a mission *by* Koreans and *among* Koreans in the beginning without the outside assistance of foreign missionaries. We also saw how the Jesuit missionaries Matteo Ricci and Roberto de Nobili were able to achieve success when they accepted the necessity of abandoning their European

Christian Mission among the Peoples of Asia

identities and becoming Chinese and Indian respectively. What is important to note here is that Ricci and Nobili succeeded because they assumed the identity of their adopted communities, such that it became a mission *by* and *among* the locals. Recall Ricci's testimony to his former schoolmate, "I have become a Chinaman. In our clothing, in our books, in our manners, and in everything external we have made ourselves Chinese" (Jensen 1997, 43).

Chapter 1 also highlighted success stories concerning the rise and significant growth of indigenous church movements in China in the early twentieth century, such as the True Jesus Church, Jesus Family, and the Little Flock or Local Church, as well as itinerant revivalist preachers proclaiming an indigenous Chinese Christianity that was independent of foreign control. These church movements and evangelists laid the foundation for the tenacious survival of Chinese Christianity through World War II and the early decades of communist rule, resulting in the subsequent growth of Chinese Christianity from the 1970s onward.

Chapter 2 began with a critical look at two momentous events for Christian mission in the twentieth century: the Edinburgh World Missionary Conference of 1910 for Protestant Christians and the Second Vatican Council (1962–1965) for Roman Catholics, followed by an evaluation of their implications for doing Christian mission in Asia. This chapter also explored the challenges of postcolonialism, nationalism, fundamentalism, and exclusivism in the culturally diverse and religious plural Asian landscape on the task of doing Christian mission in Asia. We unpacked the implications of Asian Christians as a minority community or "little flock" (*pusillus grex*) in the sea of majority communities comprising the practitioners of the great Asian religions. We also evaluated the theological perspectives of several European and Asian theologians and the Asian Catholic bishops at the 1998 Synod for Asia on the vexing issue of religious pluralism and its implications for Asian Christianity. Finally, this chapter reminded us of the Vietnamese American Catholic theologian Peter C. Phan's advice to Asian Christians that they should take their Asianness seriously as the context of being Christian in Asia. The Malaysian-born Chinese American Pentecostal theologian

Amos Yong proposes a biblical paradigm for understanding Asian religious pluralism through the Pentecost event in Luke-Acts, and the Malaysian Chinese Methodist missiologist Hwa Yung puts forward the symbol of a mango (yellow on inside and outside) instead of a banana (yellow outside, white inside) as emblematic for Asian Christianity.

Chapter 3 presented the mission theology of the Federation of Asian Bishops' Conferences (FABC). It analyzed the FABC's mission theology through a fivefold framework of mission embracing the pluralism of Asia, being rooted in a commitment and service to life in pluralistic Asia, promoting harmony in response to hatred and violence, engaging in a threefold dialogue with Asian cultures, religions, and the poor, and seeking to usher in the Reign of God in Asia. We read of the FABC's acceptance of Christianity's minority status in the sea of Asian religions, as well as its quest for doing mission among Asians not as outsiders but as insiders, in empathy and solidarity with fellow Asians on a common pilgrimage of life. In particular, the quest for doing Christian mission among fellow Asians is accentuated by the FABC's firmly rooting its missional outreach within the cultural, religious, and socioeconomic complexities arising from the daily life experiences of fellow Asians. The FABC also seeks to connect their missional outreach in Asia with the *missio Dei* through its desire to bring about the Reign of God in Asia.

Chapter 4 proposed a mission among the peoples in Asia that recognizes God's presence and reign in the world, as well as God's outreach within and outside the Christian community. It outlined a trinitarian foundation of mission that embodies *orthodoxy*, *orthopathos*, and *orthopraxis*. Indeed, the *orthodoxy* of mission among the peoples situates the contemporary missional witness of the Christian gospel within the universality of God's reign, and in so doing makes the *missio Dei* its calling and priority. The *orthopathos* of the mission among the peoples is inspired by the depth of divine empathy and solidarity with the pathos of human suffering and brokenness. Building on *orthodoxy* and *orthopathos*, the *orthopraxis* of the mission among the peoples seeks to enable the gospel message to engage with the religious pluralism of the Asian peoples in a spirit of interreligious hospitality that is inspired by Jesus' own engagement with the Samaritan woman at the well.

A careful reexamination of Jesus' missional witness to the Samaritan woman at the well drew out important lessons to undergird a new way of doing mission among the peoples in Asia that emphasizes solidarity and empathy with the marginalized and minoritized peoples of Asia. Here, mission among the peoples in Asia is no longer a one-way street of the colonial missions of the past that brought missionaries from Europe and North America to Asia. In the context of postcolonial Asia, Asian Christians are called to be both recipients of and givers of the "water of life" to their fellow Asians, just as Jesus was both the recipient and giver of life-giving water to the Samaritan woman. Moreover, Jesus' encounter with the Samaritan woman also reminds us that Asian Christians, as missioners, have to enter into and immerse themselves fully in the world of the Asian peoples. The spirit of *orthopathos* reminds Asian Christians of their common humanity with their fellow Asians and all of humanity, just as Jesus' empathy with the Samaritan woman transcended the Samaritan-Jew divide and brought Jesus into her world. Chapter 4 also made the point that *orthodoxy*, *orthopathos*, and *orthopraxis* are complementary dimensions of a holistic approach to doing Christian mission among the peoples throughout Asia, uniting mind (*orthodoxy*), body (*orthopraxis*), and spirit (*orthopathos*).

Chapter 5 unpacked the implications of chapter 4 by exploring how the "mission among the peoples" in Asia would be able to respond to the challenges of Asians moving across geographical borders and virtual frontiers. What unites chapters 4 and 5 is the underlying realization that models and strategies proposed to address the challenges of evangelization in highly secularized environments may not be relevant and appropriate to Asia, the birthplace of the great religious traditions of the world that continue to draw and inspire Asian adherents. Unlike Europe, Asia has not had the experience of a dominant Christendom where an institutionalized Christianity shaped leadership and politics, society and culture, identity and peoplehood, public religion and popular devotions. Missional strategies that seek to confront the forces of secularism and relativism, so as to rebuild Christianity's prominence in the public arena and shape the public discourses that are being articulated in Europe and the Americas often fall short in the Asian contexts where Christians have always constituted the religious minority, with the exception of the Philippines. At the same time, chapter 5 also highlighted the importance of missional outreach in virtual frontiers, where the youth of Asia are increasingly gathering. Just as printing transformed the medieval world, ushering in the Reformation and new ways of doing Christian mission, so too, the rise and adoption of social media and the rapid growth of cyberspace in Asia are raising new challenges for doing Christian mission among the youth and young adults in Asia.

To conclude, today's Asian Christians realize that the historical legacy of Western colonialism and imperialism in Asia means that they have to chart a different course for articulating the *missio Dei*. The call to do mission *among* and *with* the peoples in Asia points to a new way of transcending the limitations of the old sending-receiving model of mission. It highlights the possibility and potential of an intra-ecclesial and mutual collaborative of mission by and for Asians. In turn, this mutual approach to mission is undergirded by a threefold framework of *orthodoxy* that is rooted in the *missio Dei*, *orthopathos* that is empowered by the Holy Spirit, and *orthopraxis* that is inspired by Jesus' missional outreach, thereby transcending boundaries and frontiers to gather the peoples of Asia together in an Asian Pentecost. Simply put, mission among the peoples in Asia is missional outreach that is able to reach out in empathy and solidarity with the pathos of widespread human suffering in Asia.

In the final analysis, Asian Christians hold in the palm of their hands the future of Christian mission in Asia. Moving beyond past precedents, they are called to rethink and reenvision new ways of missional witness among Asians who are migrating into new geographical and virtual diasporas. Ultimately, the quest for doing Christian mission among the contemporary migrants of Asia across geographical diasporas and cyberspace is limited only by the imagination of Asian Christians. As missioners for the greater glory of God, Asian Christians should trust that the Spirit would lead them to do great wonders for God's people across all worlds and frontiers, in faithfulness to the *missio Dei* and witnessing to the fruits of God's reign in Asia.

Works Cited

Aagaard, Anne Marie. 1974. "Missio Dei in katholischer Sicht." *Evangelische Theologie* 34:420–33.

Abbott, Walter M., ed. 1966. *The Documents of Vatican II: All Sixteen Official Texts Promulgated by the Ecumenical Council 1963–1965. Translated from the Latin.* New York: America Press.

Aikman, David. 2003. *Jesus in Beijing: How Christianity Is Transforming China and Changing the Global Balance of Power.* Washington, DC: Regnery Publishing.

Amaladoss, Michael. 1988. "Foreign Missions Today." *East Asian Pastoral Review* 25:104–18.

———. 1991. "The Challenges of Mission Today." In *Trends in Mission: Toward the Third Millennium*, edited by William Jenkinson and Helene O'Sullivan, 359–97. Maryknoll, NY: Orbis Books.

———. 2000. "Missionary Challenges in Asia." *Jeevadhara* 30:339–50.

———. 2001. "Pluralism of Religions and the Proclamation of Jesus Christ in the Context of Asia." *Proceedings of the Catholic Theological Society of America* 56:1–14.

Anderson, Gerald H. 1974. "A Moratorium on Missionaries?" *Christian Century* 91 (2): 43–45.

Ariyaratne, A. T. 1999. "Sarvodaya Shramadana's Approach to Peacebuilding." In *Buddhist Peacework: Creating Cultures of Peace*, edited by David W. Chappell, 69–80. Somerville, MA: Wisdom Publications.

Arokiasamy, Soosai. 1986. *Dharma, Hindu and Christian according to Roberto de Nobili: Analysis of Its Meaning and Its Use in*

Hinduism and Christianity. Roma: Pontificia Università Gregoriana.

———. 1995. *Asia: The Struggle for Life in the Midst of Death and Destruction.* FABC Papers No. 70. Hong Kong: Federation of Asian Bishops' Conferences.

Arun, C. Joe. 2007. *Interculturation of Religion: Critical Perspectives on Robert de Nobili's Mission in India.* Bangalore: Asian Trading Corporation.

Ashiwa, Yoshiko, and David L. Wank. 2009. *Making Religion, Making the State: The Politics of Religion in Modern China.* Stanford, CA: Stanford University Press.

Baggio, Fabio, and Agnes M. Brazal, eds. 2008. *Faith on the Move: Toward a Theology of Migration in Asia.* Manila: Ateneo de Manila University Press.

Barth, Karl. 1956. *Church Dogmatics I/2: The Doctrine of the Word of God.* Translated by H. Knight and G. T. Thomson. Edited by G. W. Bromiley and T. F. Torrance. Edinburgh: T&T Clark.

Bartholomeusz, Tessa J. 2002. *In Defense of Dharma: Just-War Ideology in Buddhist Sri Lanka.* London: Routledge.

Battistella, Graziano. 1995. "For a More Abundant Life: Migrant Workers in Asia." In *Sixth Plenary Assembly Background Paper: Journeying Together in Faith with Migrant Workers in Asia.* FABC Papers No. 73, 1–16. Hong Kong: Federation of Asian Bishops' Conferences.

Batumalai, Sadayandy. 1986. *A Prophetic Christology for Neighbourology: A Theology for a Prophetic Living.* Kuala Lumpur, Malaysia: Seminary Theoloji Malaysia.

———. 1990. *A Malaysian Theology of Muhibbah: A Theology of a Christian Witnessing in Malaysia.* Kuala Lumpur, Malaysia: Seminari Theoloji Malaysia.

———. 1991. *An Introduction to Asian Theology: An Asian Story from a Malaysian Eye for Asian Neighbourology.* Delhi: ISPCK.

Bayly, Susan. 1989. *Saints, Goddesses, and Kings: Muslims and Christians in South Indian Society, 1700–1900.* Cambridge: Cambridge University Press.

Bays, Daniel H. 1996. "The Growth of Independent Christianity in China, 1900–1937." In *Christianity in China: From
the Eighteenth Century to the Present*, ed. Daniel H. Bays,
307–16. Stanford, CA: Stanford University Press.

———. 2012. *A New History of Christianity in China*. Malden,
MA: Wiley-Blackwell.

Benedict XVI. 2006. "Address of May 15, 2006, to the Plenary
Assembly of the Pontifical Council for Migrants and Trav-
elers." *L'Osservatore Romano,* May 24, p. 9.

Bevans, Stephen. 1996. "Inculturation of Theology in Asia (The
Federation of Asian Bishops' Conferences, 1970–1995)."
Studia Missionalia 45:1–23.

———. 2013. "Migration and Mission: Pastoral Challenges,
Theological Insights." In *Contemporary Issues of Migration
and Theology*, edited by Elaine Padilla and Peter C. Phan,
157–77. New York: Palgrave Macmillan.

Bevans, Stephen, and Roger Schroeder. 2004. *Constants in Context: A Theology of Mission for Today*. Maryknoll, NY: Orbis
Books.

Bhatt, Chetan. 2001. *Hindu Nationalism: Origins, Ideologies, and
Modern Myths*. New York: Berg.

Bintarto, R. 1980. *Gotong-royong: Suatu Karakteristik Bangsa Indonesia*. Surabaya, Indonesia: Bina Ilmu.

Bonifacio, Glenda Tibe, and Vivienne S. M. Angeles, eds. 2009.
Gender, Religion, and Migration: Pathways of Integration. Lanham, MD: Lexington Books.

Boodoo, Gerald M. 2010. "Catholicity and Mission." *Proceedings of
the Catholic Theological Society of America* 65:117–18.

Bosch, David. 1991. *Transforming Mission: Paradigm Shifts in Theology of Mission*. Maryknoll, NY: Orbis Books.

Boxer, Charles R. 1951. *The Christian Century in Japan, 1549–
1650*. Berkeley: University of California Press.

———. 1969. *The Portuguese Seaborne Empire: 1415–1825*. New
York: Knopf.

Brenda, Harry Jindrich, and John A. Larkin, compilers. 1967. *The
World of Southeast Asia: Selected Historical Readings*. New
York: Harper & Row.

Brettell, Caroline B., and James F. Hollifield, eds. 2008. *Migration Theory: Talking across Disciplines.* 2nd ed. New York: Routledge.

Broomhall, Marshall, ed. 1901. *Martyred Missionaries of the China Inland Mission.* New York: Fleming H. Revell.

Burns, Jeffrey M., Ellen Skerrett, and Joseph M. White, eds. 2000. *Keeping Faith: European and Asian Catholic Immigrants.* Maryknoll, NY: Orbis Books.

Burrows, William R. 2001. "A Response to Michael Amaladoss." *Proceedings of the Catholic Theological Society of America* 56:15–20.

————. 2013. *Jacques Dupuis Faces the Inquisition: Two Essays by Jacques Dupuis on Dominus Iesus and the Roman Investigation of His Work.* Eugene, OR: Pickwick Publications.

Cambié, Silvia. 2012. "Lessons from the Front Line: The Arab Spring Demonstrated the Power of People—and Social Media." *Communication World* (January-February): 28–32.

Campese, Gioacchino, and Pietro Ciallella, eds. 2003. *Migration, Religious Experience, and Globalization.* New York: Center for Migration Studies.

Castles, Stephen, and Mark J. Miller. 2009. *The Age of Migration: International Population Movements in the Modern World.* 4th ed., rev, New York: Guilford Press.

Catholic Bishops' Conference of India (CBCI). 1998. "Responses to the *Lineamenta.*" *East Asian Pastoral Review* 35:112–29.

————. 2008. "Violence against Christians: Statement of the Executive Body of the Catholic Bishops' Conference of India." *Vidyajyoti Journal of Theological Reflection* 72:814–17.

Chandler, Stuart. 2004. *Establishing a Pure Land on Earth: The Foguang Buddhist Perspective on Modernization and Globalization.* Honolulu: University of Hawai'i Press.

Chia, Edmund. 2003. *Thirty Years of FABC: History, Foundation, Context and Theology.* FABC Papers No. 106. Hong Kong: Federation of Asian Bishops' Conferences.

Ching, Julia. 1993. *Chinese Religions.* Maryknoll, NY: Orbis Books.

Ching, Yu-ing. 1995. *Master of Love and Mercy: Cheng Yen.* Nevada City, CA: Blue Dolphin Publishing.

Chung, David. 2001. *Syncretism: The Religious Context of Christian Beginnings in Korea.* Albany: State University of New York Press.

Colombo, Domenico, ed. 1997. *Enchiridion Documenti della Chiesa in Asia: Federazione delle Conferenze Episcopali Asiatiche, 1970–1995.* Bologna: Editrice Missionaria Italiana.

Comber, Leon. 1983. *13 May 1969: A Historical Survey of Sino-Malay Relations.* Kuala Lumpur: Heinemann Asia.

Costa, Cosme Jose. 1997. *A Missiological Conflict between Padroado and Propaganda in the East.* Pilar, Goa: Pilar Publications.

Cruz, Gemma Tulud. 2010. *An Intercultural Theology of Migration: Pilgrims in the Wilderness.* Leiden: Brill.

Deegalle, Mahinda, ed. 2006. *Buddhism, Conflict and Violence in Modern Sri Lanka.* New York: Routledge.

DiNucci, Darcy. 1999. "Fragmented Future." *Print* 53 (4): 32, 221–22.

Dorr, Donal. 2000. *Mission in Today's World.* Maryknoll, NY: Orbis Books.

Drummond, Richard H. 1971. *A History of Christianity in Japan.* Grand Rapids, MI: William B. Eerdmans.

Dupuis, Jacques. 1997. *Toward a Christian Theology of Religious Pluralism.* Maryknoll, NY: Orbis Books.

———. 1999. "'The Truth Will Set You Free': The Theology of Religious Pluralism Revisited." *Louvain Studies* 24:211–63.

Ebaugh, Helen Rose, and Janet Saltzman Chafetz, eds. 2000. *Religion and the New Immigrants: Continuities and Adaptations in Immigrant Congregations.* Walnut Creek, CA: AltaMira Press.

Edinburgh 2010. "Common Call." http://www.edinburgh2010.org/fileadmin/Edinburgh_2010_Common_Call_with_explanation.pdf

Eilers, Franz-Josef, 1997. *For All the Peoples of Asia.* vol. 2: *Federation of Asian Bishops' Conferences Documents from 1992 to 1996.* Quezon City: Claretian Publications.

———. 2002. *For All the Peoples of Asia,* vol. 3: *Federation of Asian Bishops' Conferences Documents from 1997 to 2001.* Quezon City: Claretian Publications.

————. 2007. *For All the Peoples of Asia,* vol. 4: *Federation of Asian Bishops' Conferences Documents from 2002 to 2006.* Quezon City: Claretian Publications.

Elison, George. 1973. *Deus Destroyed: The Image of Christianity in Early Modern Japan.* Cambridge, MA: Harvard University Press.

Esteves, Sarto. 2005. "Violence against the Cross." In *Religion, Power and Violence: Expression of Politics in Contemporary Times,* edited by Ram Puniyani, 277–89. Thousand Oaks, CA: Sage.

Federation of Asian Bishops' Conferences. 1987. *Theses on Interreligious Dialogue: An Essay in Pastoral Theological Reflection.* FABC Papers No. 48. Hong Kong: Federation of Asian Bishops Conferences.

Fernandes, Angelo. 1991. "Dialogue in the Context of Asian Realities." *Vidyajyoti Journal of Theological Reflection* 55:545–60.

Fernando, Lorenzo. 2000. "CBCI and FABC on Religious Pluralism." *Vidyajyoti Journal of Theological Reflection* 64:857–69.

Flannery, Austin, ed. 1982a. *Vatican Council II: The Conciliar and Post Conciliar Documents.* Vol. 1: *The Conciliar and Postconciliar Documents.* Collegeville, MN: Liturgical Press.

————. 1982b. *Vatican Council II: The Conciliar and Post Conciliar Documents.* Vol. 2: *More Postconciliar Documents.* Collegeville, MN: Liturgical Press.

Fox, Thomas C. 2002. *Pentecost in Asia: A New Way of Being Church.* Maryknoll, NY: Orbis Books.

Friedman, Thomas L. 2007. *The World Is Flat: A Brief History of the Twenty-First Century.* Further updated and expanded. New York: Farrar, Straus and Giroux.

Geertz, Clifford. 1983. "Local Knowledge: Fact and Law in Comparative Perspective." In Clifford Geertz, *Local Knowledge: Further Essays in Interpretive Anthropology,* 167–234. New York: Basic Books.

Geffré, Claude. 1993. "La singularité du Christianisme à l'âge du pluralisme religieux." In *Penser la foi: Recherches en théologie aujourd'hui: Mélanges offerts à Joseph Moingt,* edited by J. Doré and and C. Theobald, 351–69. Paris: Cerf-Assas.

————. 1998. "Le pluralisme religieux comme question théologique." *La vie spirituelle* 3:580–86.

General Secretariat of the Synod of Bishops. 1997. "'Lineamenta' for the Special Assembly of the Synod of Bishops for Asia." *Origins* 26 (31): 502–20.

Ghosh, Palash. 2013. "Virgin Mary in a Sari: Hindus Outraged by Christian Statue Depicting Blessed Mother and Jesus in Indian Tribal Dress." *International Business Times,* July 10, 2013. http://www.ibtimes.com/virgin-mary-sari-hindus-outraged-christian-statue-depicting-blessed-mother-jesus-indian-tribal-dress

Goh, Cheng Teik. 1971. *The May Thirteenth Incident and Democracy in Malaysia.* Kuala Lumpur: Oxford University Press.

Gómez, Felipe. 1986. "The Missionary Activity Twenty Years after Vatican II." *East Asian Pastoral Review* 23:26–57.

Gonsalves, Francis. 2008. "Carrying in Our Bodies the Marks of His Passion." *Vidyajyoti Journal of Theological Reflection* 72:801–7.

Grant, Patrick. 2009. *Buddhism and Ethnic Conflict in Sri Lanka.* Albany: State University of New York Press.

Groody, Daniel G. 2009. "Crossing the Divide: Foundations of a Theology of Migration and Refugees." *Theological Studies* 70:638–67.

Groody, Daniel G., and Gioacchino Campese, eds. 2008. *A Promised Land, a Perilous Journey: Theological Perspectives on Migration.* Notre Dame, IN: University of Notre Dame Press.

Hanciles, Jehu J. 2008. *Beyond Christendom: Globalization, African Migration, and the Transformation of the West.* Maryknoll, NY: Orbis Books.

Harfoush, Rahaf. 2009. *Yes We Did: An Inside Look at How Social Media Built the Obama Brand.* Berkeley, CA: New Riders.

Harrington, Ann M. 1993. *Japan's Hidden Christians.* Chicago: Loyola University Press.

Hayward, Susan. 2011. "The Spoiler and the Reconciler: Buddhism and the Peace Process in Sri Lanka." In *Between Terror and Tolerance: Religious Leaders, Conflict, and Peacemaking,* edited by Timothy D. Sisk, 183–200. Washington, DC: Georgetown University Press.

Hendricks, John Allen, and Robert E. Denton Jr., eds. 2010. *Communicator-in-Chief: How Barack Obama Used New Media Technology to Win the White House*. Lanham, MD: Lexington Books.

Hogg, W. Richey. 1980. "Edinburgh 1910—Perspective 1980." *Occasional Bulletin of Missionary Research* 4 (4): 146–53.

Hopkins, Howard C. 1979. *John R. Mott, 1865–1955: A Biography*. Grand Rapids, MI: William B. Eerdmans.

Hwa Yung. 1997. *Mangoes or Bananas: The Quest for an Authentic Asian Christian Theology*. Oxford: Regnum International.

———. 2003. "Islam in South East Asia and Christian Mission." *Transformation* 20 (4): 220–22.

Indian Catholic Bishops. 1998. "Responses to the *Lineamenta*." *East Asian Pastoral Review* 35:112–29.

Indonesian Catholic Bishops. 1998. "Responses to the *Lineamenta*." *East Asian Pastoral Review* 35:54–85.

International Organization for Migration (IOM). 2011. *World Migration Report 2011*. Geneva: International Organization for Migration.

Japanese Catholic Bishops. 1998. "Responses to the *Lineamenta*." *East Asian Pastoral Review* 35:86–111.

Jay, Robert R. 1969. *Javanese Villagers: Social Relations in Rural Modjokuto*. Cambridge, MA: MIT Press

Jenkins, Philip. 2006. *The New Faces of Christianity: Believing the Bible in the Global South*. New York: Oxford University Press.

———. 2007. *The Next Christendom: The Coming of Global Christianity*. Rev. ed. New York: Oxford University Press.

Jensen, Lionel M. 1997. *Manufacturing Confucianism: Chinese Traditions and Universal Civilization*. Durham, NC: Duke University Press.

John, T. K. 1987. "The Pope's 'Pastoral Visit' to India: A Further Reflection." *Vidyajyoti Journal of Theological Reflection* 51:58–66.

John Paul II. 1994. *Tertio millennio adveniente*. *Origins* 24:401–16.

———. 1996. Message for World Migration Day on Undocumented Migrants. http://www.vatican.va.

———. 1999. *Ecclesia in Asia*. *Origins* 29:357–84.

————. 2002. "Migration and Inter-Religious Dialogue." Message of the Holy Father for the 88th World Day of Migration. www.vatican.va.

Jones, Owen Bennett. 2009. *Pakistan: Eye of the Storm*. 3rd ed. New Haven, CT: Yale University Press.

Kahn, Joel S., and Francis Loh Kok Wah, eds. 1992. *Fragmented Vision: Culture and Politics in Contemporary Malaysia*. Honolulu: University of Hawai'i Press.

Keith, Charles, 2012. *Catholic Vietnam: A Church from Empire to Nation*. Berkeley: University of California Press.

Koentjaraningrat, Raden Mas, 1961. *Some Social-Anthropological Observations on "Gotong Rojong" Practices in Two Villages of Central Java*. Ithaca, NY: South East Asia Program, Department of Far Eastern Studies, Cornell University.

Koyama, Kosuke. 1999. *Water Buffalo Theology*. 25th anniversary ed. Maryknoll, NY: Orbis Books.

Kroeger, James H. 2008. "Living Faith in a Strange Land: Migration and Interreligious Dialogue." In *Faith on the Move: Toward a Theology of Migration in Asia*, edited by Fabio Baggio and Agnes M. Brazal, 219–51. Manila: Ateneo de Manila University Press.

LaRousse, William. 2008. "'Go . . . and make disciples of all nations': Migration and Mission." In *Faith on the Move: Toward a Theology of Migration in Asia*, edited by Fabio Baggio and Agnes M. Brazal, 155–76. Manila: Ateneo de Manila University Press.

Latourette, Kenneth Scott. 1929. *A History of Christian Missions in China*. New York: Macmillan.

Lee, Ki-baik. 1984. *A New History of Korea*. Cambridge, MA: Harvard University Press.

Levine, Amy-Jill. 2006. *The Misunderstood Jew: The Church and the Scandal of the Jewish Jesus*. San Francisco: HarperSanFrancisco.

Lian Xi. 2010. *Redeemed by Fire: The Rise of Popular Christianity in Modern China*. New Haven, CT: Yale University Press.

Madsen, Richard. 1998. *China Catholics: Tragedy and Hope in an Emerging Civil Society*. Berkeley: University of California Press.

————. 2001. "Beyond Orthodoxy: Catholicism as Chinese Folk Religion." In *China and Christianity: Burdened Past, Hopeful Future*, edited by Stephen Uhalley and Xiaoxin Wu, 233–50. Armonk, NY: M. E. Sharpe.

Mbiti, John S. 1976. "Theological Impotence and Universality in the Church." In *Mission Trends*, no. 3: *Third World Theologies*, edited by Gerald H. Anderson and Thomas T. Stransky, 6–18. New York: Paulist Press; Grand Rapids, MI: William B. Eerdmans.

Meibohm, Margaret. 2002. "Past Selves and Present Others: The Ritual Construction of Identity at a Catholic Festival in India." In *Popular Christianity in India: Riting between the Lines*, edited by Selva J. Raj and Corinne G. Dempsey, 61–84. Albany: State University of New York Press.

Michel, Thomas. 1985. "The Church and Migrants of Other Faiths." *Seminarium* 37 (4): 175–88.

Micklethwait, John, and Adrian Wooldridge. 2009. *God Is Back: How the Global Revival of Faith Is Changing the World*. New York: Penguin Press.

Minamiki, George. 1985. *The Chinese Rites Controversy from Its Beginning to Modern Times*. Chicago: Loyola University Press.

Moffett, Samuel Hugh. 1998. *A History of Christianity in Asia*, vol. 1: *Beginnings to 1500*. 2nd rev. ed. Maryknoll, NY: Orbis Books.

————. 2005. *A History of Christianity in Asia*, vol. 2: *1500 to 1900*. Maryknoll, NY: Orbis Books.

Moltmann, Jürgen. 1977. *The Church in the Power of the Spirit: A Contribution to Messianic Ecclesiology*. London: SCM Press.

Mukherjee, Rila. 2004. "Contested Authenticities." *Rethinking History* 8:459–63.

Munusamy, Viyajan P. 2012. "Ethnic Relations in Malaysia: The Need for 'Constant Repair' in the Spirit of Muhibbah." In *Handbook of Ethnic Conflict: International Perspectives*, edited by Dan Landis and Rosita D. Albert, 119–36. New York: Springer.

Mveng, Engelbert. 1985. *L'Afrique dans l'Église: Paroles d'un Croyant*. Paris: Editions L'Harmattan.

Nacpil, Emerito P. 1971. "Mission but Not Missionaries." *International Review of Mission* 60:356–62.

Nedungatt, George. 2001. *The Synod of Diamper Revisited.* Rome: Pontifico Instituto Orientale.

Neill, Stephen. 1984. *A History of Christianity in India: The Beginnings to AD 1707.* Cambridge: Cambridge University Press.

———. 1990. *A History of Christian Missions.* 2nd ed. Revised by Owen Chadwick. Harmondsworth, Eng.: Penguin.

Neyrey, Jerome H. 2003. "What's Wrong with This Picture? John 4, Cultural Stereotypes of Women, and Public and Private Space." In *A Feminist Companion to John,* vol. 1, edited by Amy-Jill Levine, 98–125. Sheffield: Sheffield Academic Press.

Nguyen Ngoc Huy. 1998. "The Confucian Incursion into Vietnam." In *Confucianism and the Family*, edited by Walter A. Slote and George A. De Vos, 91–103. Albany: State University of New York Press.

Ohm, Thomas. 1962. *Machet zu Jüngern alle Völker: Theorie der Mission.* Freiburg: Erich Wevel Verlag.

Padilla, Elaine, and Peter C. Phan, eds. 2013. *Contemporary Issues of Migration and Theology.* New York: Palgrave Macmillan.

Palmer, Martin. 2001. *The Jesus Sutras: Rediscovering the Lost Scrolls of Taoist Christianity.* New York: Ballantine.

Panikkar, Raimon (Raimundo). 1974. "The Hindu Ecclesial Consciousness: Some Ecclesiological Reflections." *Jeevadhara* 4:199–205.

———. 1979. "The Myth of Pluralism: The Tower of Babel—A Meditation on Non-Violence." *Cross-Currents* 29 (2): 197–230.

———. 1984. "Religious Pluralism: The Metaphysical Challenge." In *Religious Pluralism*, edited by Leroy S. Rouner, 97–115. Notre Dame, IN: University of Notre Dame Press.

———. 1987. "The Jordan, the Tiber and the Ganges: Three Kairological Moments of Christic Self-Consciousness." In *The Myth of Christian Uniqueness*, edited by John Hick and Paul Knitter, 89–116. Maryknoll, NY: Orbis Books.

————. 1991. "Indic Christian Theology of Religious Pluralism
from the Perspective of Interculturation." In *Religious Pluralism: An Indian Christian Perspective*, ed. Kuncheria Pathil,
252–99. Delhi, India: ISPCK.

————. 1995. "Philosophical Pluralism and the Plurality of Religions." In *Religious Pluralism and Truth: Essays on Cross-Cultural Philosophy of Religion*, edited by Thomas Dean, 33–43.
Albany: State University of New York Press.

————. 1997. "Whose Uniqueness?" In *The Uniqueness of Jesus:
A Dialogue with Paul F. Knitter*, edited by Leonard Swidler
and Paul Mojzes, 111–15. Maryknoll, NY: Orbis Books.

————. 1999. *The Intrareligious Dialogue*. Rev. ed. New York: Paulist.

Parreñas, Rhacel Salazar. 2001. *Servants of Globalization: Women,
Migration, and Domestic Work*. Stanford, CA: Stanford University Press.

Pathil, Kuncheria. 2003. "India, Christianity in." In *New Catholic
Encyclopedia*, 2nd ed., vol. 7, edited by Berard L. Marthaler,
391–406. Detroit: Gale.

Pechilis, Karen, and Selva J. Raj, eds. 2013. *South Asian Religions:
Tradition and Today*. New York: Routledge

Pew Internet and American Life Project. 2005. *Teens and Technology*. Washington, DC. http://www.pewinternet.org/
Reports/2005/Teens-and-Technology.aspx.

————. 2007. *Teens and Social Media*. Washington, DC. http://
www.pewinternet.org/Reports/2007/Teens-and-Social-
Media.aspx.

Pew Forum on Religion and Public Life. 2011. *Global Christianity: A Report on the Size and Distribution of the World's Christian Population*. Washington, DC: Pew Research Center.

Phan, Peter C. 1998. *Mission and Catechesis: Alexandre de Rhodes
and Inculturation in Seventeenth-Century Vietnam*. Maryknoll,
NY: Orbis Books.

————. 1999a. "Betwixt and Between: Doing Theology with
Memory and Imagination." In *Journeys at the Margin:
Toward an Autobiographical Theology in American-Asian Theol-
ogy*, edited by Peter C. Phan and Jung Young Lee, 113–33.
Collegeville, MN: Liturgical Press.

————. 1999b. "Asian Catholics in the United States: Challenges and Opportunities for the Church." *Mission Studies* 16 (2): 151–74.

————. 2000. "*Ecclesia in Asia*: Challenges for Asian Christianity." *East Asian Pastoral Review* 37:215–32.

————. 2002. *The Asian Synod: Texts and Commentaries.* Maryknoll, NY: Orbis Books.

————. 2003. Review of *Introducing Theologies of Religion*, by Paul Knitter. *Horizons* 30:113–17.

————. 2003b. *Christianity with an Asian Face: Asian American Theology in the Making.* Maryknoll, NY: Orbis Books.

————. 2010. "An Interfaith Encounter at Jacob's Well: A Missiological Interpretation of John 4:4–42." *Mission Studies* 27:160–75.

————. 2011. "Vietnam, Cambodia, Laos, Thailand." In *Christianities in Asia*, edited by Peter C. Phan, 129–47. Malden, MA: Wiley-Blackwell.

Plouffe, David. 2009. *The Audacity to Win: The Inside Story and Lessons of Barack Obama's Historic Victory.* New York: Viking.

Pontifical Council for Interreligious Dialogue and the Congregation for the Evangelization of Peoples. 1991. *Dialogue and Proclamation: Reflections and Orientations on Interreligious Dialogue and the Proclamation of the Gospel of Jesus Christ. Origins* 21:121–35.

Pontifical Council for the Pastoral Care of Migrants and Itinerant Peoples. 2004. Instruction, *Erga migrantes caritas Christi.* http://www.vatican.va.

Prensky, Marc. 2001a. "Digital Natives, Digital Immigrants." *On the Horizon* 9 (5): 1–6.

————. 2001b. "Digital Natives, Digital Immigrants, Part II: Do They Really *Think* Differently?" *On the Horizon* 9 (6):1–6.

Prior, John Mansford. 1998. "A Tale of Two Synods: Observations on the Special Assembly for Asia." *Vidyajyoti Journal of Theological Reflection* 62:654–65.

Propaganda Fide, Sacra Congregatio de. 1907. *Collectanea Sacrae Congregationis de Propaganda Fide: Seu decreta, instructiones, rescripta pro Apostolicis Missionibus.* Vol. 1. Roma: Ex Typographia Polyglotta, Sacrae Congregationis de Propaganda Fide.

Quatra, Miguel Marcelo Quatra. 2000. *At the Side of the Multi-tudes: The Kingdom of God and the Mission of the Church in the FABC Documents (1970–1985)*. Quezon City: Clar-etian.

Raj, Selva J., and Corinne G. Dempsey, eds. 2002. *Popular Chris-tianity in India: Riting Between the Lines.* Albany: State Uni-versity of New York Press.

Rasiah, Jeyaraj. 2011. "Sri Lanka." In *Christianities in Asia*, edited by Peter C. Phan, 45–59. New York: Wiley-Blackwell.

Rosales, Gaudencio B., and C. G. Arévalo, eds. 1992. *For All the Peoples of Asia: Federation of Asian Bishops' Conferences Docu-ments from 1970 to 1991*. Maryknoll, NY: Orbis Books.

Ross, Andrew C. 1994. *A Vision Betrayed: The Jesuits in Japan and China: 1542–1742*. Maryknoll, NY: Orbis Books.

Rubinstein, Murray A. 1996. "Holy Spirit Taiwan: Pentecostal and Charismatic Christianity in the Republic of China." In *Christianity in China: From the Eighteenth Century to the Present*, edited by Daniel H. Bays, 353–66. Stanford, CA: Stanford University Press.

Ruiz, Jean-Pierre. 2011. *Readings from the Edges: The Bible and People on the Move*. Maryknoll, NY: Orbis Books.

Rytter, Mikkel, and Karen Fog Olwig, eds. 2011. *Mobile Bod-ies, Mobile Souls: Family, Religion and Migration in a Global World*. Aarhus: Aarhus University Press.

Samartha, Stanley J. 1980. "Unbound Christ: Towards Christol-ogy in India Today." In *Asian Christian Theology: Emerging Themes*, edited by Douglas J. Elwood, 145–60. Philadel-phia: Westminster.

———. 1991. *One Christ—Many Religions: Toward a Revised Christology*. Maryknoll, NY: Orbis Books.

———. 1993. "The Cross and the Rainbow: Christ in a Multi-religious Culture." In *Asian Faces of Jesus*, edited by R. S. Sugirtharajah, 104–23. Maryknoll, NY: Orbis Books.

Sanneh, Lamin. 2009. *Translating the Message: The Missionary Impact on Culture*. 2nd ed. Maryknoll, NY: Orbis Books.

Saulière, Augustine, and Savarimuthu Rajamanickam. 1995. *His Star in the East*. Madras: De Nobili Research Institute.

Schineller, Peter. 1990. *Handbook on Inculturation*. New York: Paulist Press.

Schreiter, Robert J. 1992. *Reconciliation: Mission and Ministry in a Changing Social Order*. Maryknoll, NY: Orbis Books.

———. 1998. *The Ministry of Reconciliation: Spirituality and Strategies*. Maryknoll, NY: Orbis Books.

Schrimpf, Monika. 2008. "The Pro- and Anti-Christian Writings of Fukan Fabian (1565–1621)." *Japanese Religions* 33:35–54.

Seager, Richard Hughes. 2006. *Encountering the Dharma: Daisaku Ikeda, Soka Gakkai, and the Globalization of Buddhist Humanism*. Berkeley: University of California Press.

Senanayake, Darini Rajasingham. 2009. *Buddhism and the Legitimation of Power: Democracy, Public Religion and Minorities in Sri Lanka*. Singapore: National University of Singapore Institute of South Asian Studies.

Seth, Michael J. 2006. *A Concise History of Korea: From the Neolithic Period through the Nineteenth Century*. Lanham, MD: Rowman & Littlefield.

Shorter, Aylward. 1994. *Evangelization and Culture*. London: Geoffrey Chapman.

Sisk, Timothy D., ed. 2011. *Between Terror and Tolerance: Religious Leaders, Conflict, and Peacemaking*. Washington, DC: Georgetown University Press.

Smith, Timothy L. 1978. "Religion and Ethnicity in America." *American Historical Review* 83:1155–85.

Solivan, Samuel. 1998. *The Spirit, Pathos, and Liberation: Toward an Hispanic Pentecostal Theology*. Sheffield, UK: Sheffield Academic.

Spence, Jonathan D. 1996. *God's Chinese Son: The Taiping Heavenly Kingdom of Hong Xiuquan*. New York: Norton.

Stanley, Brian. 2009. *The World Missionary Conference, Edinburgh 1910*. Grand Rapids, MI: William B. Eerdmans.

Stearns, Peter N. 2001. *Cultures in Motion: Mapping Key Contacts and Their Imprints in World History*. New Haven, CT: Yale University Press.

Tambiah, Stanley J. 1992. *Buddhism Betrayed? Religion, Politics and Violence in Sri Lanka*. Chicago: University of Chicago Press.

Tan, Jonathan Y. 2004a. "*Missio Inter Gentes*: Towards a New Paradigm in the Mission Theology of the Federation of Asian Bishops' Conferences." *Mission Studies* 21 (1): 65–95.

————. 2004b. "From 'Missio *ad* Gentes' to 'Missio *inter* Gentes': Shaping a New Paradigm for Doing Christian Mission in Asia. Part 1." *Vidyajyoti Journal of Theological Reflection* 68:670–86.

————. 2005a. "From 'Missio *ad* Gentes' to 'Missio *inter* Gentes': Shaping a New Paradigm for Doing Christian Mission in Asia. Part 2." *Vidyajyoti Journal of Theological Reflection* 69:27–41.

————. 2005b. "Missio inter Gentes: Vers uns nouveau paradigme de la theologie missionnaire." *Mission: Revue des sciences de la mission* 12 (1): 99–128.

————. 2005c. "Missio inter Gentes." *Spiritus: Hors Serie 2005: Ad Gentes 40 ans après*, 147–57.

————. 2006. *Menuju Suatu Paradigma Baru Dalam Teologi Misi*. Jakarta, Indonesia: Komisi Komunikasi Sosial Konferensi Waligereja Indonesia.

Tan, Paul Chee Ing, and Teresa Ee. 1984. "Introduction." In Tunku Abdul Rahman Putra, et al. *Contemporary Issues on Malaysian Religions*, 5–16. Petaling Jaya: Pelanduk Publications.

Tang, Li. 2002. *A Study of the History of Nestorian Christianity in China and Its Literature in Chinese: Together with a New English Translation of the Dunhuang Nestorian Documents*. Frankfurt am Main: Peter Lang.

Tapscott, Don. 2009. *Grown Up Digital: How the Net Generation Is Changing Your World*. New York: McGraw-Hill.

Tapscott, Don, and Anthony D. Williams. 2008. *Wikinomics: How Mass Collaboration Changes Everything*. Exp. ed. New York: Portfolio Penguin.

————. 2010. *Macrowikinomics: Rebooting Business and the World*. New York: Portfolio Penguin.

Taylor, Keith. 1983. *The Birth of Vietnam*. Berkeley: University of California Press.

Teixeira, Manuel. 1963. *The Portuguese Missions in Malacca and Singapore (1511–1958)*, vol. 3: *Singapore*. Lisbon: Agência-Geral do Ultramar.

Thaliath, Jonas. 1958. *The Synod of Diamper.* Rome: Pontificium Institutum Orientalium Studiorum.

Thangaraj, M. Thomas. 1999. *The Common Task: A Theology of Christian Mission.* Nashville, TN: Abingdon.

Thu, En Yu. 1995. "'Muhibbah': The Churches' Ministry of Reconciliation in the Pluralistic Society of Malaysia." D.Min. diss. San Francisco Theological Seminary.

Tinker, Tink. 2010. "The Romance and Tragedy of Christian Mission among American Indians." In *Remembering Jamestown: Hard Questions about Christian Mission,* edited by Amos Yong and Barbara Brown Zikmund, 13–27. Eugene, OR: Pickwick Publications.

Turnbull, Stephen. 1998. *The Kakure Kirishitan of Japan: A Study of Their Development, Beliefs and Rituals to the Present Day.* Richmond, Surrey: Curzon Press.

UCAN (Union of Catholic Asian News). 1998a. "Church Identity, Interreligious Dialogue, Justice among Synod Addresses." *UCAN Report AS9913.0973,* dated April 27, 1998. http://www.ucanews.com/story-archive/?post_name=/1998/04/27/church-identity-interreligious-dialogue-justice-among-synod-addresses&post_id=11302

————. 1998b. "Relations with Islam, Role of Family and Youth Will Impact Church, Synod Told." *UCAN Report AS9933.0973,* dated April 29, 1998. http://www.ucanews.com/story-archive/?post_name=/1998/04/29/relations-with-islam-role-of-family-and-youth-will-impact-church-synod-told&post_id=11330

————. 1998c. "Synod Asked to Affirm Asian Way of Evangelizing in a Decentralized Church." *UCAN Report IJ9977.0974,* dated May 7, 1998. http://www.ucanews.com/story-archive/?post_name=/1998/05/07/synod-asked-to-affirm-asian-way-of-evangelizing-in-a-decentralized-church&post_id=11364

Walbridge, Linda. 2002. *Christians of Pakistan: The Passion of Bishop John Joseph.* New York: Routledge.

Walls, Andrew F. 2002. *The Cross-Cultural Process in Christian History: Studies in the Transmission and Appropriation of Faith.* Maryknoll, NY: Orbis Books.

Walters, Albert Sundararaj. 2002. *We Believe in One God? Reflections on the Trinity in the Malaysian Context.* Delhi: ISPCK.
———. 2007. "Issues in Christian-Muslim Relations: A Malaysian Christian Perspective." *Islam and Christian-Muslim Relations* 18 (1): 67–83.
Wei, Yuan-Kwei. 1985. "Historical Analysis of Ancestor Worship in Ancient China." In *Christian Alternatives to Ancestor Practices*, edited by Bong Rin Ro, 119–33. Taichung, Taiwan: Asia Theological Association.
Wiest, Jean-Paul. 2007. "Chinese Youth and Religion Today." *Origins* 36 (33): 527–31.
Wilfred, Felix. 1988. "Inculturation as a Hermeneutical Question." *Vidyajyoti Journal of Theological Reflection* 52:422–36.
———. 1990. "Fifth Plenary Assembly of FABC: An Interpretation of Its Theological Orientation." *Vidyajyoti Journal of Theological Reflection* 54:583–92.
———. 1992. "The Federation of Asian Bishops' Conferences (FABC): Orientations, Challenges and Impact." In *For All the Peoples of Asia: Federation of Asian Bishops' Conferences Documents from 1970 to 1991*, edited by Gaudencio B. Rosales and C. G. Arévalo, xxiii–xxx. Maryknoll, NY: Orbis Books.
———. 1998. "What the Spirit Says to the Churches (Rev 2:7) A Vademecum on the Pastoral and Theological Orientations of the Federation of Asian Bishops' Conferences (FABC)." *Vidyajyoti Journal of Theological Reflection* 62:124–33.
Williams, Kenneth M. 1976. *The Church in West Malaysia and Singapore: A Study of the Catholic Church in West Malaysia and Singapore Regarding Her Situation as an Indigenous Church.* Johor, Malaysia: Melaka-Johor Diocesan Service.
Williams, Rowan. 2007. "Christianity in the Reinvention of China." *China Review* 40:1–3.
Wilson, Michael. 1974. "Synod of Bishops Fails to Agree." *Catholic Herald,* no. 4619, October 25, 1974, 1.
Wolf, Arthur P. 1974. "Gods, Ghosts and Ancestors." In *Religion and Ritual in Chinese Society*, edited by Arthur P. Wolf, 131–82. Stanford, CA: Stanford University Press

Woodside, Alexander Barton. 1971. *Vietnam and the Chinese Model: A Comparative Study of Vietnamese and Chinese Government in the First Half of the Nineteenth Century*. Cambridge, MA: Council on East Asian Studies, Harvard University.

World Bank. 2011. *Migration and Remittances Factbook, 2011*. Washington, DC: World Bank.

World Council of Churches. 2004. *Ecumenical Considerations for Dialogue and Relations with People of Other Religions*. Geneva: World Council of Churches.

Yates, Timothy. 1994. *Christian Mission in the Twentieth Century*. Cambridge: Cambridge University Press.

Yong, Amos. 2007. "The Spirit of Hospitality: Pentecostal Perspectives toward a Performative Theology of Interreligious Encounter." *Missiology* 35:55–73.

Younger, Paul. 1992. "Velankanni Calling: Hindu Patterns of Pilgrimage at a Christian Shrine." In *Sacred Journeys: The Anthropology of Pilgrimage*, edited by Alan Morinis, 89–99. Westport, CT: Greenwood Press.

Index

PREVIOUSLY PUBLISHED IN THE AMERICAN SOCIETY OF MISSIOLOGY SERIES

The American Society of Missiology Series, published in collaboration with Orbis Books, seeks to publish scholarly works of high merit and wide interest on numerous aspects of missiology—the study of Christian mission in its historical, social, and theological dimensions. Able presentations on new and creative approaches to the practice and understanding of mission will receive close attention from the ASM Series Committee.

1. Protestant Pioneers in Korea, Everett Nichols Hunt Jr.
2. Catholic Politics in China and Korea, Eric O. Hanson
3. From the Rising of the Sun, James M. Phillips
4. Meaning Across Cultures, Eugene A. Nida and William D. Reyburn
5. The Island Churches of the Pacific, Charles W. Forman
6. Henry Venn: Missionary Statesman, Wilbert R. Shenk
7. No Other Name? Paul F. Knitter
8. Toward a New Age in Christian Theology, Richard Henry Drummond
9. The Expectation of the Poor, Guillermo Cook
10. Eastern Orthodox Mission Theology Today, James J. Stamoolis
11. Confucius, the Buddha, and Christ, Ralph R. Covell
12. The Church and Cultures, Louis J. Luzbetak, SVD
13. Translating the Message: The Missionary Impact on Culture, Lamin Sanneh
14. An African Tree of Life, Thomas G. Christensen
15. Missions and Money (second edition), Jonathan J. Bonk
16. Transforming Mission, David J. Bosch
17. Bread for the Journey, Anthony J. Gittins, C.S.Sp.
18. New Face of the Church in Latin America, edited by Guillermo Cook
19. Mission Legacies, edited by Gerald H. Anderson, Robert T. Coote, Norman A. Horner, and James M. Phillips
20. Classic Texts in Mission and World Christianity, edited by Norman E. Thomas
21. Christian Mission: A Case Study Approach, Alan Neely
22. Understanding Spiritual Power, Marguerite G. Kraft
23. Missiological Education for the 21st Century: The Book, the Circle, and the Sandals, edited by J. Dudley Woodberry, Charles Van Engen, and Edgar J. Elliston

24. Dictionary of Mission: Theology, History, Perspectives, edited by Karl Müller, SVD, Theo Sundermeier, Stephen B. Bevans, SVD, and Richard H. Bliese
25. Earthen Vessels and Transcendent Power: American Presbyterians in China, 1837–1952, G. Thompson Brown
26. The Missionary Movement in American Catholic History, Angelyn Dries, OSF
27. Mission in the New Testament: An Evangelical Approach, edited by William J. Larkin Jr. and Joel W. Williams
28. Changing Frontiers of Mission, Wilbert R. Shenk
29. In the Light of the Word: Divine Word Missionaries of North America, Ernest Brandewie
30. Constants in Context: A Theology of Mission for Today, Stephen B. Bevans, SVD, and Roger P. Schroeder, SVD
31. Changing Tides: Latin America and World Mission Today, Samuel Escobar
32. Gospel Bearers, Gender Barriers: Missionary Women in the Twentieth Century, edited by Dana L. Robert
33. Church: Community for the Kingdom, John Fuellenbach, SVD
34. Mission in Acts: Ancient Narratives in Contemporary Context, edited by Robert L. Gallagher and Paul Hertig
35. A History of Christianity in Asia: Volume I, Beginnings to 1500, Samuel Hugh Moffett
36. A History of Christianity in Asia: Volume II, 1500–1900, Samuel Hugh Moffett
37. A Reader's Guide to Transforming Mission, Stan Nussbaum
38. The Evangelization of Slaves and Catholic Origins in Eastern Africa, Paul V. Kollman, CSC
39. Israel and the Nations: A Mission Theology of the Old Testament, James Chukwuma Okoye, C.S.Sp.
40. Women in Mission: From the New Testament to Today, Susan E. Smith
41. Reconstructing Christianity in China: K. H. Ting and the Chinese Church, Philip L. Wickeri
42. Translating the Message: The Missionary Impact on Culture (second edition), Lamin Sanneh
43. Landmark Essays in Mission and World Christianity, edited by Robert L. Gallagher and Paul Hertig
44. World Mission in the Wesleyan Spirit, Darrell L. Whiteman and Gerald H. Anderson (published by Province House, Franklin, TN)
45. Miracles, Missions, & American Pentecostalism, Gary B. McGee
46. The Gospel among the Nations: A Documentary History of Inculturation, Robert A. Hunt
47. Missions and Unity: Lessons from History, 1792–2010, Norman E. Thomas (published by Wipf and Stock, Eugene, OR)
48. Mission and Culture: The Louis J. Luzbetak Lectures, edited by Stephen B. Bevans
49. Comprehending Mission: The Questions, Methods, Themes, Problems, and Prospects of Missiology, Stanley H. Skreslet